OUTSTANDING
DISSERTATIONS IN
LINGUISTICS

Edited by
Laurence Horn
Yale University

A ROUTLEDGE SERIES

OUTSTANDING DISSERTATIONS IN LINGUISTICS
LAURENCE HORN, *General Editor*

SYNTACTIC FORM AND DISCOURSE FUNCTION IN NATURAL LANGUAGE GENERATION

Cassandre Creswell

Routledge
Taylor & Francis Group

NEW YORK AND LONDON

Published in 2004 by
Routledge
711 Third Avenue,
New York, NY 10017
2 Park Square, Milton Park,
Abingdon, Oxfordshire OX14 4RN

First issued in paperback 2016

Routledge is an imprint of the Taylor and Francis Group, an informa business

Copyright © 2004 by Taylor & Francis Group, a Division of T&F Informa.

Catalog record is available from the Library of Congress

ISBN 13: 978-1-138-99077-7 (pbk)
ISBN 13: 978-0-415-97104-1 (hbk)

For
Elna Creswell and Erma Leist

Acknowledgments

Many thanks to my dissertation advisors and committee: Ellen Prince, to whom I and this project owe an immeasurable intellectual debt; Aravind Joshi, whose subtle yet firm nudgings in the right direction make him an invaluable mentor; Robin Clark, for comments, skepticism, and high scientific standards; and Matthew Stone, for incredibly useful and prompt feedback and encouragement at all points during this project and for more than once lending an organization to my thoughts which was sorely needed.

Numerous others have been kind enough to discuss the many issues, problems, and questions I have run into during the course of this work. Their comments have enriched the content and scope of this dissertation. In particular, thanks go to Bonnie Webber, Ivana Kruijff-Korbayová, Lyn Walker, Dave Embick, Andy Schein, Zoubin Ghahramani, John Paolillo, Naomi Nagy, Chris Manning, Tom Morton, Maribel Romero, Sherry Ash, Doug Biber, Scott Schwenter, five anonymous reviewers for the 2nd International Natural Language Generation Conference, the entire DLTAG research group, and the Natural Language Processing Group at Microsoft Research.

Thanks to Larry DeWitt, the Social Security Administration Historian for permission to use and cite the SSA Online Oral History Archives.

The financial support I received as a doctoral student from the National Science Foundation, the Beinecke Brothers Foundation, the William Penn Fellowship Program, and the Department of Psychology at the University of Pennsylvania was without doubt a crucial component in making this work possible.

The Gatsby Computational Neuroscience Unit and the Department of Computer Science at the University of Toronto must be credited for the invaluable use of their resources when I was away from the University of Pennsylvania.

A special thanks is due Georgia Green, without whom I would have never known what pragmatics was or what it had to do with computer science.

Many linguists (and others) have provided the crucial components of camaraderie, humor, and a healthy dash of neuroticism without which my six years in Philadelphia would have been at best a long, dull journey and at worst a vale of tears in a web of terror. Among those due a very special shout out are Justin Mott, Na-Rae Han, Tom McFadden, Kieran Snyder, John Bell, Eon-Suk Ko, Xin Piao, Kira Merdiushev, Julie Alvarez, Sharon Sturtevant, Jon Colton, Atissa Banuazizi, Elsi Kaiser, Kimiko Nakanishi, Sophia Malamud, Jim Alexander, Amanda Seidl, Ron Kim, Stephanie Winters, Uri Horesh, Dan Johnson, Eva Banik, Alexander Williams, Mimi Lipson, Alexis Dimitriadis, Al Kim, Eleni Miltsakaki, Rashmi Prasad, Masato Kobayashi, Tsan-Kuang Lee, Tom Morton, and Andy Schein.

I thank my family, Mom, Dad, Annie, Cory, Tracey, Johnny, and John, who, despite being somewhat mystified about what I'm doing and why I'm doing it, have nonetheless been endlessly supportive and proud.

And finally, I thank my husband Matt Beal for his unfailing support and willingness to help. Without his knowledge of machine learning and Latex, this would be a very different book indeed.

Contents

List of figures

List of tables

SYNTACTIC FORM AND DISCOURSE FUNCTION IN NATURAL LANGUAGE GENERATION

OUTSTANDING DISSERTATIONS IN LINGUISTICS

CHAPTER 1

Introduction

1.1 The problem of syntactic choice

Users of natural languages, including English, have many ways to encode the same truth-conditional meaning. Besides a single "canonical" word order, as in (1), options include topicalizations, (2), left-dislocations, (3), it-clefts, (4), and wh-clefts, (5), among others.

(1) Ed grilled the steak.

(2) The steak, Ed grilled.

(3)   a. The steak, Ed grilled it.
     b. Ed, he grilled the steak.

(4)   a. It was Ed who grilled the steak.
     b. It was the steak that Ed grilled.

(5)   a. What Ed grilled was the steak.
     b. What Ed did was grill the steak.
     c. What happened was Ed grilled the steak.

Previous research on the use of these and other non-canonicals has shown that particular forms are appropriate only under particular discourse conditions (Prince, 1978, 1986, 1996, 1998, 1999; Green, 1980; Ward, 1988; Birner, 1994, 1996); among others. For example, forms like (3a) are only appropriate when the referent of the left-dislocated NP, in this case *the steak*, is a member of a partially-ordered set (poset) of entities, and its membership in this set is salient to the hearer.[1] Other conditions relevant to the use of these forms include the salience, familiarity, or inferability of particular predications or propositions within the discourse model. The discourse conditions posited in the literature that allow the felicitous use of these forms are necessary conditions. They are, however, not sufficient conditions for their use.

Vallduví (1990a) makes this point with respect to topicalization:

> "[T]here may be NPs that encode entities that are related via a poset to another entity in the discourse model which nevertheless appear in situ and not in a preposed slot. An example is (6) from Ward (1985:ex.109):
>
> (6) Colonel Bykov had delivered to Chambers in Washington six Bokhara rugs which he directed Chambers to present as gifts from him and the Soviet Government to the members of the ring who had been most co-operative. One of these rugs Chambers delivered to Harry Dexter White. Another he gave to...
>
> Here it is not only the preposed phrase *one of these rugs* which is in a poset relation with an entity in the previous discourse (set-subset), but also *Chambers* (identity), and *Harry Dexter White* (set-subset; HDW is a member of the ring)."(p.90)

As we will see in Section 1.3.1, similar examples can be found throughout natural language text. Given these types of examples, the discourse conditions on the use of these forms only indicate at most when speakers *can* acceptably use the forms. They are not, however, an adequate model of how, when, and why speakers in fact choose to do so. If we try to model the generation of these forms computationally based only on these conditions, it will result in overgeneration. The goal, then, of this dissertation is to identify additional factors that motivate speakers to choose these non-canonical forms. Identifying these factors will allow us (1) to construct a more accurate model of syntactic choice in human speakers and (2) to refine our computational model of syntactic choice for use in natural language generation systems.

1.2   Word order variation within the clause

A great variety of forms in English[2] encode in their form some indication of the speaker's assumptions about the status of the entities, properties, and events with respect to the hearer's mental model in general and model of the discourse in

---

[1]A fuller description of the discourse conditions on the use of the syntactic forms of interest here can be found in Section 1.2 below.

[2]In fact, perhaps all forms, depending on one's theory of lexical meaning; see (Nunberg, 1978).

particular.[3] For example, references to entities may appear as full noun phrases with indefinite, definite, or demonstrative determiners, as pronouns, or even be missing entirely, depending on whether the speaker regards them as new or old to the hearer, new or old to the discourse, and how closely the speaker expects the hearer to be attending to them at that point in the discourse (Gundel et al., 1993; Prince, 1992; Grosz and Sidner, 1986; Grosz et al., 1995).

Not only does the lexical form of a referential expression change, but its position or role within the clause may also vary depending on its assumed cognitive status. For instance, the alternation between double object and *to*-dative structures, locative inversion, *there*-insertion, and occurrence as a syntactic subject all appear to depend on a relative information-status distinction (Prince, 1981, 1992; Birner, 1994; Ward, 1998; Snyder, 2003). This holds for references to entities as well as references to propositions. For example, factive verb complements are readily able to appear in initial position within the clause, while their non-factive counterparts have a much more limited ability to do so, one which depends on their status with respect to speaker and hearer beliefs (Horn, 1986).

The forms that will be the subject of this study are those that are traditionally regarded as having something to do with *focus* and *contrast*, rather than those mentioned above whose discourse function appears to be encoding information status (hearer-old, discourse-new, etc. (Prince, 1992)). In particular, I will examine topicalization, left dislocation, it-clefts, and wh-clefts. These forms all appear to require a degree of hearer- or discourse-oldness, and additionally all relate to particular ways of structuring the discourse model.

1.2.1 Forms under consideration

This section explains which syntactic forms will be under consideration here, explicating the syntactic criteria used to demarcate the classes of forms under study. In addition, it will provide a brief sketch of the discourse functions these forms are used under in order to make the discussion of cases where the form-function mapping fails understandable. The full picture of the discourse functions of these forms as posited in previous literature is provided in Section 2.1, and readers unfamiliar with the literature on the discourse functions of syntactic forms may wish to begin there instead.

---

[3]By *encode in their form* I only mean that the use of such a form can be taken by the hearer to be an indication of the speaker's assumptions. I wish to make no claim here about how these forms' functions pair with them. Whether one wishes to claim that in a syntactic representation of the form this information is encoded in some inherent way, or whether the pairing is simply arbitrary is an interesting topic, but one which will not be explored here. See Prince (1996) and Snyder (2000) for discussion.

Constructions involving leftward movement

Topicalization and left-dislocation both involve an NP "displaced" to the left-periphery of the clause. In particular topicalizations have a non-vocative NP in initial, pre-clausal position and coreferential with a gap/trace somewhere in the clause. As shown in the corpus-based studies of Ward (1985) and Prince (1998), topicalizations are felicitous when two conditions hold: 1) the referent of the topicalized NP is a member of a salient partially-ordered set (poset), and 2) the open proposition expressed by the main clause, constructed by replacing the constituent receiving tonic stress by a variable, is salient to the hearer.[4] The corresponding conditions for the topicalization in (7a) are shown in (7b).

(7)   a. When mother was pregnant he said, "Nobody will believe it, but I hope it's a girl, **because a girl you can spoil**." (SSA, fbane)[5]

   b. Poset $P = \{$ BOYS, GIRLS$\}$; Open Proposition = YOU CAN DO X WITH y, SUCH THAT $y \in P$ AND $X = $ SPOIL

Left-dislocations differ syntactically from topicalizations in that the clause-initial NP is coreferential with a pronoun (or full NP) within the clause. They only require a single condition for felicitous usage. Here the clause-initial NP must stand in a salient poset relation with some previously evoked entity or entities in the discourse model, as illustrated in (8a).[6]

(8)   a. I can see obvious disabilities in some individuals, **others you can't see a thing wrong with them**. (SSA, tall)

   b. Poset $P = \{$INDIVIDUALS EXAMINED$\}$; OTHERS $\subset P$

---

[4]An identical syntactic form, referred to as *focus preposing*, which has different prosody, in particular a single tonic stress placed on a constituent displaced to clause-initial position, will be discussed in Chapter 2. This form differs from topicalization not only in its prosody but also in the very limited type of constituent that may be fronted, and in its corresponding discourse function. In general, focus preposings will not be included in the forms examined in this study.

[5]All citations in this format are references to oral history interviews from the Social Security Administration online oral history archives. The corpus is available online at http://www.ssa.gov/history/orallist.html. The filename of each source interview is the second part of the citation (e.g. for this citation *fbane*.)

[6]Left-dislocation can be used with another entirely separate function in English, in which it has a discourse processing effect, serving to remove discourse-new entities from certain syntactic positions, subjects and possessives, disfavored for such entities (Prince, 1998). For ease of explication, we will put aside this function for the remainder of this introductory discussion and return to it in Chapter 2.

Cleft constructions

Both wh-clefts and it-clefts have a two-part syntax with a focus and a presupposition (shown in SMALL CAPS and *italics*, respectively, in (9–10).) In wh-clefts, the *focus* constituent is post-copular; in it-clefts, it is post-copular, pre-*that* clause. The presupposition constituent is essentially an incomplete clause, one which is missing the constituent which appears instead in the focus. It is sentence-initial in wh-clefts and begins with a wh-word. In an it-cleft it is sentence-final and has either a *that* or a wh-word as a complementizer. The discourse function of these forms varies by type of cleft.

In a wh-cleft, the denotation of the presupposition constituent[7] must be material that (the speaker can assume) is in the hearer's consciousness at the time of utterance, either discourse-old or inferable from something else presented in the discourse (Prince, 1978). This is illustrated in (9) below, where the source of the salient open proposition is in the immediately preceding clause.

(9)   a. ...but they were vague in their minds then about what they meant by old age pensions. *Usually what they meant* was A PENSION PAID OUT OF GENERAL REVENUES WITH SOME KIND OF AN INCOME TEST. (SSA, ajaoral3)

       b. Open Proposition = THEY MEANT X, X = PENSION PAID OUT OF GENERAL REVENUES

In an it-cleft, in contrast, the existential closure of the open proposition denoted by the presupposition constituent should be a belief of the speaker (Dryer, 1996). However, the requirements on the information status of this proposition are less clear ; possibly it need not be as salient as for a wh-cleft (Prince, 1978; Ball, 1994; Dryer, 1996).[8] An example of an it-cleft's two components appears in (10).

(10)   a. You know that he never wanted to be President, **it was HIS WIFE *that wanted him to be President.*** (SSA, fbane)

       b. Open Proposition = X WANTED HIM TO BE PRESIDENT, X = HIS WIFE

---

[7]The semantics (and syntax) of wh-clefts remain the subject of debate. For discussion and detailed references, see Heycock and Kroch (1999). For the sake of discussion, I will assume that the wh-cleft denotes an open proposition with a variable in place of the missing constituent. However, I remain agnostic on the precise analysis here as it is not of direct relevance to the present project.

[8]In some cases the presupposition constituent can in fact be discourse- and hearer-new material, with the focus as discourse-old. This type of it-cleft, termed *informative-presupposition* it-clefts in (Prince, 1978) will be discussed in more detail in Chapter 2.

1.3   When condition-to-form mapping fails

In this section I present the pattern of distribution of these non-canonical forms relative to the discourse conditions on their use posited in the literature outlined in the previous section. The constraints on the use of these forms are presented as one-way conditionals in the literature.

(11)   If condition C does not hold, then the use of form f is infelicitous.

Unfortunately from the perspective of modeling the generation of these forms, such constraints are not useful. This is because the implication is only in one direction. The only time the use of a form f will be in violation of this implication is if condition C does not hold. When C does hold, f may or may not be used. Nothing about such a constraint actually constrains the choice of f, given C. In addition, in general the conditions given on the left-hand side of the above conditional often hold. Salient sets and open propositions abound in discourse. The non-canonical forms conditioned by the presence of these factors, however, are rare. These conditions then can only play the role of necessary conditions, not sufficient conditions, in licensing the use of these non-canonical forms.

Ideally then, what we want for a model of generation is a constraint of the following form:

(12)   If condition C holds, then the use of form f is required.

In fact, *required* may be an impossibly strong term to use when modeling the relationship between form and function in natural language. Nearly all form-function mappings are many-to-many and are likely to be in some way stochastic. Nonetheless, the goal of this project is to derive constraints closer to (12) than (11), with the term *required* replaced with *more probable*.

In the following sections we will look at three contexts that support the claim that rules of the type seen in (11) are inadequate as a model of when to choose the non-canonical forms of interest here. First, we will look at cases where the conditions hold, but either a non-canonical or a canonical form would be felicitous. Secondly, we will examine cases where the discourse conditions hold, but a non-canonical form is in fact infelicitous. Finally, we will examine cases where the discourse conditions hold and the use of a non-canonical form appears to be obligatory, in that the use of a canonical equivalent would not contribute the same meaning in an identical context. All of these cases present clues to how we can better model the generation of non-canonical forms. The model presented in Chapter 3 is intended to overcome the problems outlined here.

1.3.1 Non-canonical entirely optional

Because the conditions posited in the literature for constraining the use of the four non-canonical forms of interest here are so common in naturally-occurring discourse, it is easy to find cases where the conditions hold but the speaker[9] has chosen a canonical form, as in (6) above and here in (13).[10]

(13)   The AMA supported the fee schedule, opposed the expenditure targets and opposed the balanced billing limits, but their fervor seemed to be focused on the expenditure targets, not on the balanced billing. [...]The administration said they could live with the fee schedule if there were expenditure targets, **and they had no problems with balanced billing limits.** (SSA, ginsburg)

    a. and balanced billing limits they had no problems with.

In (13), the discourse conditions that permit topicalization hold. There is a salient open proposition, ADMINISTRATION FELT X ABOUT BALANCED BILLING LIMITS, and *balanced billing* is a member of a salient set, POLICIES THAT MIGHT BE ADOPTED. The topicalized version of the sentence appears acceptable in the context. However, the speaker chose not to use a topicalized sentence.

Equally problematic for determining the distribution of non-canonicals is the use of a non-canonical form when a canonical form in its place would not appear to significantly change the meaning. This is illustrated in (14), where the speaker uses a topicalized sentence even though the canonical order does not seem different in this context.

(14)   I think we were fortunate in the kind of leadership we had, generally. **Some of them, as you know, I'm not enthused about,** but generally speaking, the quality of our leadership was quite high. (SSA, davidkoral)

    a. I'm not enthused about some of them, as you know.

1.3.2 Non-canonical odd when conditions hold

As we might expect when given a constraint of the form in (11), instances where the antecedent is false, but the consequence is true are entirely possible. This is the case when even though necessary conditions hold, the use of non-canonical form in place of a canonical is infelicitous.

---

[9]Most examples in this and the following chapters are transcribed speech. A few, however, come from written genres. I will continue to use the term *speaker* however to refer to the agent who generated the tokens in question.

[10]The ubiquity of posets in the domain of discourse, no matter how they are defined, will be discussed below in 2.1.

For example, in (15), the writer is replying to a message about choosing a laptop on a newsgroup about laptops. The writer can assume the salience of the poset LAPTOPS and the open proposition WRITER WOULD DO X. However neither a topicalization nor a left-dislocation is felicitous here, as shown in (15a).[11]

(15) *(Subject: Re: Need Help Selecting a Laptop)*
      I would recommend a Toshiba. I just bought the 5105-S607 model and am quite pleased with it. (comp.sys.laptops, May 2, 2002)

    a. ?? A Toshiba I would recommend.

    b. ?? A Toshiba I would recommend it.

Example (16) is an excerpt from an oral history of a soldier's experience in WWII. The implicit question the text answers—*what did the speaker do then?*—can be assumed to always be salient. However, substituting a wh-cleft for a canonical sentence into any arbitrary point in the text is odd, as (16a) demonstrates.[12]

(16) And when I landed, they assigned me to a very, very bad transit camp on the other side of the river. And I couldn't stand it. It was muddy, difficult. I said, "I'm not going to stay here." I walked out. I was lucky, because I was wearing bars on my shoulders, so I could get away with it. And I asked around and found out that there were a number of officers and other people sleeping at the Grand Hotel, right opposite the race course, right in the center of Calcutta. So I went over there. **And I found a bed.** And that's where I stayed in Calcutta as long as I was there. (http://fas-history.rutgers.edu/oralhistory/addison.htm)

    a. ?? And what I did was find a bed.

1.3.3 Non-canonical form "obligatory"

The constraints of the form (11) only tells us when the use of a form f is not allowed. It does not tell us when the use of some form f is in some sense obligatory, i.e. when the use of a canonical form in the same context would have resulted in

---

[11]The unacceptability of the topicalization is not simply because the topicalized NP is an indefinite. As shown in Ward and Prince (1991), indefinite entities representing members of evoked sets are clearly preposable.

[12]The substitution of the similar, but more colloquial (1) seems more acceptable in this context. However, it would be improved if the speaker then followed it with some more supporting detail about finding the bed. This point will be further explored in Chapter 3.

(1) And what I did was I found a bed.

a different meaning or a less coherent discourse. In such cases, it seems that the non-canonical form is not only felicitous, but allows additional inferences that its canonical equivalent does not give rise to.

For example, in (17), without the it-cleft the hearer would conclude the speaker was uncertain about whether the president was at the conference. With the it-cleft, however, the uncertainty can only be about the cause of the president's absence because the remainder of the clause is marked as presupposed.

(17) The conference was to take place in November. [...] We managed to bring it off in November—just when the President had his gall bladder surgery. **I think it was his gall bladder surgery that kept him from being there,** but the thing came off OK. (SSA, lee)

    a. I think his gall bladder surgery kept him from being there.

In (18), the speaker is describing her four marriages. Without the left-dislocation in the second clause, the most natural interpretation of the second clause would be to infer that the event of meeting the second guy took place at the same time as the event in the preceding clause. With the left-dislocation, however, it is clear that the speaker is listing a separate marriage event.

(18) "The first time was 1968, just to get out of my dad's house," she says. **"Second guy, I just met him and didn't have anything else to do.** Didn't work out...Third and fourth times were business partners. We got married for business reasons." (*Philadelphia Inquirer, p. 4-J, 7/3/88*)

    a. I just met the second guy and didn't have anything else to do.

In the passage in (19), the speaker is discussing why he is dreading an upcoming cruise. In the final sentence, even with an intonational peak of prominence on *sharks* to mark the focus constituent as the subject, the canonical version is odd and difficult to understand compared with the it-cleft in the original.[13] In (20), the wh-cleft makes a perfectly clear introductory sentence for a new paragraph; the canonical sentence, however, results in a confusing, incoherent transition.

(19) Finally, I assume it's understood that I'm doomed to be seasick. [...] [P]erhaps pure anxiety will keep my stomach in knots. Because I've read Melville and seen Jaws a hundred times, it's not terrorists that worry me—**it's the threat of monstrous whales and sharks that has me spooked.** (*Philadelphia Weekly*, "The Shipping News", Quinn Eli, December 2001)

    a. ?? The threat of monstrous whales and sharks has me spooked.

---

[13]Note that the canonical version of (19) is just as odd when the preceding sentence is also replaced with a canonical to preserve parallelism, i.e. *Terrorists don't worry me.*

(20)   ...[T]he Bush administration has been unable—has scarcely tried—to articulate what this war is for.[...]More and more, this is our war alone, and the more the administration tries rhetorically to back out of the blind alley it's led us into, the less credible it sounds.
What this war ought to be for is democracy. (*Mother Jones*, Nov./Dec. 2002 p. 25)

    a.   ?? This war ought to be for democracy.

1.3.4   Summary: No One-to-One Mapping

The examples in the previous sections have demonstrated that the distribution of non-canonical forms does not correlate one-to-one with the presence of the necessary conditions posited in the literature. Instead of the obligatory co-presence of discourse conditions and form, we find (1) cases where the discourse conditions are present but the form is absent, and (2) cases where the discourse conditions are present, but the form is still infelicitous. Finally, we find cases where the discourse conditions hold, and the non-canonical is not merely acceptable, but in fact crucial to the meaning and coherence of the discourse in that particular context. All three of these cases are problematic for the adaptation of the constraints like (11) to the problem of selecting the form of a root-clause in natural language generation. This problem is explored in more detail in the following section.

1.4   Relevance for NLG

The purpose of a natural language generation system is to encode semantic or propositional content in a linguistic form easily understood by humans in order to communicate this content to the user of the system. Ideally, this content should be encoded in strings that are both grammatical and contextually appropriate. Users should be able to derive the system's communicative intent and update their own knowledge store accordingly (Stone et al., 2001).

As discussed above, even when considering a single main clause, there are usually many ways to encode some given propositional content. In addition, as noted elsewhere (Bangalore et al., 2000), often it seems that many of these ways may be equally good. Humans choose contextually-appropriate strings from these many ways with little conscious effort and with rather effective communicative results. Unfortunately, so far there is no clear consensus on how this selection happens and how to replicate it an NLG system.

Like much work in the field of natural language processing, previous approaches to clausal word order selection (almost all on English) can be characterized as belonging to one of two approaches, rule-based or statistical. The former approach can be thought of as defining a function F mapping from a set of conditions C to a form f.

In general, the rule-based approaches have attempted to integrate contextual information into the set of conditions that determine the use of a particular form (Stone et al., 2001); (Kruijff-Korbayová et al., 2002); (Geldof, 2000); (Klabunde and Jansche, 1998); (Humphreys, 1995). Unfortunately, for the most part this work has not been grounded in corpus-based research on the discourse function of these forms. In addition, even work based on corpus pragmatics research (Stone et al., 2001) cannot account for the pattern of usage we have seen in Section 1.3 because the functions used are too simple. The set of conditions are only necessary conditions. As such, *whenever* the necessary conditions hold, a special form is always generated.

Such a model will vastly overgenerate given the ubiquity of the necessary conditions and the relative infrequency of the forms in naturally-occurring discourse. As shown in Table 1.1 a search of the trees in the Switchboard and Wall Street Journal corpora in the Penn Treebank shows that these four forms appear with a frequency of about 200 and 850 tokens per million words, respectively.[14] In the corpus used for this project, 58 transcribed oral histories from the on-line Social Security Administration Oral History Archives (SSA), these forms occurred with a frequency of about 850 per 750,000 words.

	WSJ	Switchboard	SSA
IT-CLEFT	66	64	150
WH-CLEFT	124	289	280
LEFT-DISLOCATION	4	406	258
TOPICALIZATION	20	102	155
TOTAL	214	861	850
WORDS	1,000,000	~1,000,000	752,000

Table 1.1: Frequency of non-canonical forms in three corpora

This relative infrequency also poses a problem for purely statistical approaches to NLG. These methods are based on the idea that the most frequently found word order in a corpus is the most likely to be a grammatical string. Statistical NLG algorithms may use counts of n-grams (Langkilde and Knight, 1998a,b) or trees (Bangalore et al., 2000) in a corpus on which to base their selection of a form. The most frequently found form is the one selected. This presents a fundamental problem for incorporation of such a technique into a model for generating the non-canonical word orders examined here. A purely statistical approach would presumably never choose a non-canonical word order instead of a canonical order because the former is so rare. As we saw in Section 1.3.3, this would result in an inability to express the types of meanings that only the non-canonical equivalent can express in some contexts.

---

[14]The category TOPICALIZATION includes focus preposings and topicalizations.

Alternatively, a statistical approach might also function such that all forms would be generated at the rate that they appear in the corpus but without regard for the semantics of the form of the conditioning context. The resulting output would be grammatical but it would in a sense be quite meaningless because these forms would not be tied in any way to the communicative intentions underlying them.

Neither the rule-based nor any statistical approaches as they stand are a good computational model of how human speakers generate different syntactic encodings of propositions. The rule-based models do not take into account optionality or probability in the application of their rules, and their use is based on the use of necessary rather than sufficient conditions for application. The statistical models do not take into account the importance of discourse context, not merely frequency, in the distribution of syntactic forms in natural language data.

The approach taken in this project will incorporate some of the advantages of both in hopes of escaping some of the downfalls each present.

1.5   Structure and summary of dissertation

The purpose of this dissertation is to present a more complete model of when human speakers generate different syntactic encodings of propositions in order to further our understanding of syntactic form selection and to better characterize these forms' conditions of use for utilization in an NLG system.

In this dissertation, first, a more nuanced, but still essentially "rule-based" model of generation will be presented, one that explicitly ties the goals of the communicative agent to the linguistic forms it selects to achieve those goals. In particular, the three types of communicative goals that we claim play a role in motivating the use of these four non-canonical sentence types are (1) attention marking, (2) discourse relation, and (3) information structure focus disambiguation. The evidence supporting this model of how speakers achieve these types of communicative goals using non-canonical syntactic forms will be based on the examination of a corpus of naturally-occurring examples. This same corpus, annotated with low-level information about the discourse context surrounding utterances with non-canonical word order, will then be utilized as the basis for training a statistical model that can approximate some aspects of the rule-based model. The correlations measured by the statistical model are evidence to support the theoretical model of how communicative goals motivate the use of particular syntactic forms. The statistical model is also used as a probabilistic classifier, which is tested on unseen data to give a measure of whether the classifier could be used as a probabilistic way of selecting word order as part of a natural language generation algorithm.

The remainder of the dissertation is laid out as follows. Chapter 2 presents both brief reviews of previous closely-related work and summaries of all the necessary theoretical constructs that are to be used in later chapters. The latter are drawn upon extensively in Chapters 3 and 4. Chapter 3 presents the theoretical model of what type of communicative goals speakers achieve through the use of the non-canonical forms examined here. Then in Chapter 4, we attempt to find empirical support for this theoretical model by creating a statistical model of the discourse contexts where non-canonical forms are found, which could also be used as a probabilistic classifier to select forms based on discourse context. Finally, in Chapter 5, we conclude and discuss avenues for future work.

CHAPTER 2

Background: previous work and relevant theory

An investigation of the discourse function of non-canonical syntactic forms and their role in natural language generation necessarily overlaps and draws from a large amount of previous research. Of particular relevance here is corpus-based research on the discourse function of syntactic forms. This is the topic of Section 2.1, which provides a detailed picture of the necessary conditions for the use of non-canonical syntax posited in the literature. Section 2.2 summarizes and attempts to synthesize several theories of discourse structure in order to provide a framework for the claims made in Chapter 3 about the use of non-canonical syntax to communicate information about discourse structure relations. Section 2.3 is included to clearly delimit the scope of the research undertaken here given its overlap with issues of prosodic encoding of information structure ground and focus. In addition, it provides a framework for understanding the claims made in Chapter 3 about the role of focus disambiguation in the use of non-canonical syntax. The body of work in natural language generation devoted to selecting word order of major constituents in the clause in English, is summarized and critiqued in the final Section 2.4 in this chapter. Altogether, these four sections should provide the reader with the necessary background to understand the motivation for the problem set out in the previous chapter and the solutions to this problem that are presented in the following ones.

2.1   Previously posited discourse functions of syntactic forms

Many syntactic forms allow speakers to indicate their assumptions about the status of the entities, properties, and events with respect to their own and their hearer's mental models of the discourse and real-world knowledge. Previous literature in linguistic pragmatics has provided an account of the discourse conditions relevant for a variety of forms in English and other languages (Prince, 1978, 1986, 1996, 1998, 1999; Gundel, 1974; Green, 1980; Levin and Prince, 1986; Ward, 1988; Birner, 1996; Hedberg, 1990; Delin, 1992); *inter alia*. The current study will focus on topicalizations, left-dislocations, wh-clefts, and it-clefts. Although a large literature has accumulated on each of these constructions in its own right, corpus-based research positing specific functions for these constructions will be of the most use in attempting to formalize a model of syntactic choice. Hence, studies providing this type of characterization for these forms are the focus of the review here.

2.1.1   Constructions involving leftward movement

The research on constructions involving an NP displaced to clause-initial position of most relevance here includes Ward (1985), Birner and Ward (1998), Ward and Prince (1991) and Prince (1986, 1998, 1999). Naturally-occurring examples of both forms, topicalization and left-dislocation, are shown in (21a-21b), respectively.

(21)   a.   She had an idea for a project. She's going to use three groups of mice. One, she'll feed them mouse chow, just the regular stuff they make for mice. Another, she'll feed them veggies. **And the third she'll feed junk food.** (Prince 1999: 17a)

      b.   Contrary to popular wisdom that says most white wines (except sweet dessert wines) and Champagnes do not age well, white Burgundies and premium California chardonnays gain intensity and richness after a few years of bottle age. **And Champagnes, well, they acquire a rich, toasty aroma and nutty flavor that I and the English prefer to the crisp, acidic fruit of a young sparkler.** (Prince, 1998: 10b)

Syntactically, topicalization (shown in (21a)) can be defined as a non-vocative NP in initial, pre-clausal position and coreferential with a gap/trace somewhere in the clause. Prosodically, the tonic stress falls within the clause. A pitch accent may occur on the preposed constituent also, but this is not obligatory. Left-dislocation (shown in (21b)) is similar to topicalization, but the clause-initial NP is coreferential with a resumptive pronoun.

It should be noted that although these constructions involve movement to the left-periphery of the clause, their discourse functions do not appear to have anything to do with traditional notions of topichood (Prince, 1999). In light of the predilection to conflate notions of topichood with the functions of the forms in this section, however, I will define what I take *topic* to mean.

Perhaps the most useful formalization of topichood, in the sense of pragmatic aboutness, is to be found in centering theory (Joshi and Weinstein, 1981; Grosz et al., 1995; Walker et al., 1998), which provides an objective way of characterizing coherent discourse in terms of transitions between local centers of attention at each point in a discourse. Prince (1999) uses the concepts of a backward-looking center, C_b, or preferred center, C_p, as a formal correlate of topichood, in the sense of what a given utterance is about (Reinhart, 1981). In English, the usual ranking algorithm for members of an utterance's list of forward-looking centers (C_f list), a determining factor in what is allowed to be the C_b or C_p of an utterance, is based on grammatical relations, with grammatical subject ranked highest on the C_f list (Brennan et al., 1987). Every non-discourse initial utterance has a C_b, the highest ranked element from the previous utterance realized in the current utterance, and every utterance has a C_p, the highest ranked element on the C_f list. According to the Pronoun Rule, if anything in the utterance is pronominalized, the C_b must be. There appears to be no obvious correlation between the C_b of an utterance and the use of topicalization or left-dislocation. If anything, it seems that the subject of a topicalized or left-dislocated sentence is almost always discourse-old, and the left-preposed NP never appears as a pronoun without a pronominal subject (Prince, p.c.), further supporting the claim that the preposed NP is not C_b and hence not a topic.[1] The actual transitions between centers of attention (or topics) found in these forms will play an important role in Chapter 4. The relevant point for the moment is merely that the displaced NP itself is not a backward-looking center, or topic.

The discourse functions of these forms, left-dislocation and topicalization, are not identical. Both topicalizations and at least one function of left-dislocations depend on the existence of a salient partially-ordered set relation (poset) for felicitous usage. Posets have been shown to be relevant to a variety of linguistic constructions, both syntactic and prosodic (Hirschberg, 1985; Ward, 1985). A poset can be defined as a set defined by a PARTIAL ORDER, one that is reflexive, transitive, and antisymmetric or irreflexive, transitive, and asymmetric. Typical examples of poset relations are IS-A-MEMBER-OF, IS-A-SUBTYPE-OF, and the identity relation.[2] In both topicalization and left-dislocation, the clause-initial

---

[1] The data used in this project further support this claim. Out of 111 topicalizations, 7 had subjects which were not personal pronouns. Left-dislocations are a less uniform class; see discussion below.

[2] In fact, because IS-A-MEMBER-OF and the identity relation are poset relations, essentially any set can potentially serve as a poset relation, and any entity already evoked will be

NP must stand in a salient poset relation with some previously evoked entity or entities in the discourse model.

In topicalization, however, an additional discourse condition must hold. Here, the proposition expressed by the main clause should be structured into an open proposition where the constituent appearing with tonic stress is replaced with a variable. The open proposition should be salient to the hearer at that point in the discourse. For the examples above, then, the discourse conditions that must be fulfilled are as follows:

(22)   a. And the third she'll feed junk food.

       b. POSET P = {SET OF GROUPS OF MICE}; OPEN PROPOSITION = SHE'LL FEED X TO AN ELEMENT Y, SUCH THAT Y $\in$ P; X = JUNK FOOD

(23)   a. And Champagnes, well, they acquire a rich, toasty aroma and nutty flavor...

       b. POSET P = {SET OF WHITE WINES}; CHAMPAGNES $\in$ P

Left-dislocations appear to have several other functions also. Prince (1998) presents a second function for which left-dislocation can also be used in English, the simplifying function, illustrated in (24):

(24)   I was thinking about what we had to work for. I used to work for $1.50 a week. This is five days a week, sometimes six. If you live in the servant

---

in a poset with itself. This apparently vacuous condition makes the restriction of the use of these non-canonical forms even weaker. However, there is some kernel of meaningfulness in these analyses' claims that a salient poset is what makes the use of topicalizations and left-dislocations, among other forms, felicitous.

In my view, the intention behind saying that the set relation should be a poset is that whatever the notion used it must be able to encompass ordering relationships like *none of the Xs* vs. *one X* vs. *all of the Xs*, which should all be members of the powerset of the set defined by the predicate X. In addition, it must not include arbitrary groupings of entities and entities grouped together by functional dependency (*bottle* and *its cork*, *house* and *its roof*, as possible licensers of the use of topicalizations or left-dislocations. (However, see Whitton (2004) for counterexamples to the latter claim.)

Perhaps the only real way to restrict what types of sets allow for felicitous use of these constructions would be through the use of a theory like Sperber and Wilson (1986)'s Relevance theory or Nunberg (1978)'s theory of normal beliefs. Under one of these theories, the acceptability of a set (or powerset) which licenses the use of these constructions will depend on the hearer being able to understand the speaker's intention. For the purposes of the project here, we will simply assume that the existence of some salient set or poset relation is indeed a necessary discourse condition. The exact restrictions on what kinds of sets are acceptable and how hearers recover them are left for future investigation. We will continue to refer to the necessary set relation as a *poset*.

quarter, your time is never off, because if they decide to have a party at night, you gotta come out. **My grandmother, I remember when she used to work, we'd get milk and a pound of butter.** I mean this was pay. (Prince 1998; 6c).

According to Prince (1998) simplifying left-dislocations have a discourse processing effect. They serve to remove discourse new-entities from certain syntactic positions disfavored for NPs with this information status, namely subject and possessive positions. Instead, the discourse-new entity appears in clause-initial position, essentially as part of a separate processing unit. This allows a second reference to it with a pronoun in the subject or possessive position with which it is coreferential.

In a small corpus study, Manetta (2001) found several left-dislocations that did not appear to be either poset or simplifying left-dislocations. Manetta suggests that these particular left-dislocations may be functioning in contexts where the preferred center, C_p, of the previous utterance does not become the backward-looking center, C_b, of the following utterance. Instead, a noun phrase referring to a different entity (either lower-ranked than C_p on the C_f list of the preceding utterance or not on the list at all) appears in subject position.[3] Manetta calls this an UNEXPECTED SUBJECT, and suggests that left-dislocations with unexpected subjects should be collapsed functionally with simplifying left-dislocations.

The final function that Prince (1998) presents for left-dislocations is island-violation-amnestying left-dislocations. These forms appear in cases where the discourse conditions of topicalization hold, but the site where an NP would be extracted would result in an island-violation. Instead of a gap or trace, a resumptive pronoun appears, one which is coreferential with the leftward-displaced NP; thus, the form resembles a left-dislocation. The left-dislocation in (25a) clearly has no topicalization equivalent, as shown by the unacceptable (25b). In addition, the topicalization discourse conditions do apply here.

(25)   a. The book I had I had got from a guy who got it from a very good call girl. We kept a copy of that book in a safe deposit box. The standard procedure was that somebody new gave half of what they got the first time for each number. You'd tell them: "Call so-and-so, that's a fifty-dollar trick." They would give you twenty-five dollars. Then the number was theirs. **My first book, I paid half of each trick to the person who gave it to me.** After that it was my book. (*Working*, Studs Terkel; (Prince, 1998): ex 23)

       b. * My first book, I paid half of each trick to the person who gave ∅ to me.

---

[3]See Gregory and Michaelis (2001) for additional evidence bearing on a need to revise the discourse functions of left-dislocation posited in Prince (1998).

    c. POSET P = { SET OF BOOKS I HAD}; OPEN PROPOSITION = I PAID
        X TO THE INDIVIDUAL WHO GAVE ME Y, SUCH THAT Y ∈ P, X =
        HALF

For the purposes of this project, island-violation-amnestying left-dislocations will be categorized with left-dislocations because in many cases they will be ambiguous in function between poset left-dislocations and island-violation ones. This ambiguity is due to the fact that nearly all left-dislocations will still have a pitch accent somewhere in the core clause. This pitch accent may be marking a salient presupposed open proposition. The open proposition marked with prosody in a left-dislocation may differ from that in a topicalization in saliency; the latter may need to be more salient. Making this distinction, however, is beyond the limits of this project and will be left for future work.[4]

Another form with a close syntactic relation to left-dislocations and topicalizations is focus preposing. Focus preposing has the syntactic structure of topicalization, but the tonic stress falls on the leftmost constituent, as shown in (26):

(26)   She was here two years. [checking transcript] **FIVE semesters she was here.** (Prince, 1999: ex 18)

Like topicalization, a salient open proposition is also relevant for focus preposing. In focus preposing, however, the constituent that should be replaced with a variable is the tonically-stressed clause-initial constituent. The open proposition must express the proposition that a certain attribute holds of a certain entity. The tonically-stressed constituent represents the value that instantiates this attribute (Prince, 1986). Under a file card-type analysis of the discourse model (Heim, 1983), this value will be entered under that attribute, which is already listed on a pre-existing file card for the entity in question. The discourse conditions for (26) are shown in (27).

(27)   OPEN PROPOSITION = SHE WAS HERE A SET OF SEMESTERS WITH
       THE CARDINALITY X; X = FIVE

The potential complexity in the ontology of all these leftward-displacing forms and their functions is simplified to some degree in the present project. As discussed above, island-violation-amnestying left-dislocations will be grouped with left-dislocations due to their potential functional ambiguity. All other left-dislocations will also be treated (for most purposes) as a uniform class. As will be discussed in Chapter 4, in practice it is frequently difficult to distinguish which left-dislocated NP referents are brand-new (Prince, 1981), neither previously evoked nor in an salient inferable relationship with previously mentioned

---

[4]This is due in part to the fact that only the written transcriptions of the oral corpus were available in a form practical for inclusion in this study.

entities, and which are in fact inferably related to other entities in the discourse context. This is particularly the case when a third-party is interpreting a discourse in which they did not participate; differentiating exactly what (the speaker thinks) is known, what is to be accommodated, and what is new is not always straightforward.

This is further complicated by the issue of what *inferably related* means. Prince (1998) claims that for the purposes of poset left-dislocations and topicalizations, only strictly poset relations support the use of these forms. Birner and Ward (1998) list five poset relations found in preposings: SET/SUBSET, GREATER-THAN, PART/WHOLE, TYPE/SUBTYPE, and IDENTITY. Functional dependency relations, another type of inferable relations, do not support the use of a preposing construction. Examples of functional dependency relations are the *a house* and *its door*, *a car* and *its steering wheel*, *a restaurant meal* and *the bill*, *a book* and *its cover*.[5] Birner and Ward describe the salient poset relation in the following way:

> "The preposed constituent must represent a link standing in an inferable linking relation to the 'anchoring poset', a contextually licensed, partially ordered set of items ordered by one of a small number of linking relations." (Birner and Ward, 1998, p.218)

One can see from this definition, and numerous examples in this paper as well, that the speaker can leave a considerable amount of inference to the hearer. First, the relationship between the preposed constituent's referent and its anchoring poset need only be inferable. In addition, the anchoring poset itself need only be contextually licensed, i.e. inferable from the context or extralinguistic knowledge about the context. Birner and Ward claim further that the referent of the preposed constituent must be discourse old, but this category includes elements that have not been previously evoked but instead are only inferentially-related to information evoked previously. In their corpus, which includes both topicalizations and several other types of English preposings, about half of the tokens have preposed constituents which have not been previously evoked (971/2153, or 45%).

Beyond the difficulties that the categorization of inferable entities present for an effort to separate poset from simplifying left-dislocations in practice, the

---

[5]Note that for Prince (1998) and Birner and Ward (1998) these functional dependency relations do not count as instances of the part/whole poset relation. Examples of part/whole that do given by Birner and Ward include {PARTS OF REALITY} and {PARTS OF AN EXAM}. For the former example, the NP referring to the entity in a poset relation was *those parts having the capacity for perception and action*; it stood in a poset relation to the explicitly evoked set *parts of this reality*. The latter example had two related tokens, whose topicalized NPs were *the hard part* and *the historical question*.

existence of left-dislocations which are neither poset nor simplifying, the so-called unexpected-subject left-dislocations, further complicates the separation of the syntactic class into multiple functions. Whether inferable entities should be grouped with respect to their with discourse-old entities or discourse-new entities, is relevant to drawing distinctions between these functional categories. The classification of inferables is much discussed in the literature, in particular with respect to centering theory (Birner, 1994; Prince, 1992; Hahn et al., 1996; Kibble and Power, 1999). This debate is of relevance here because we will investigate the role of these non-canonical syntactic constructions, including left-dislocations, in marking or coinciding with discourse segment boundaries. At the beginning of a new segment, whether an entity is brand-new or not may be of less importance than how salient it is. With respect to the role that left-dislocations play in indicating discourse segment boundaries, inferable entities may be as unsalient as unexpected subjects and brand-new subjects or possessives. This issue will be of particular interest in Chapter 4 when the theory presented in Chapter 3 is tested empirically.

Fortunately, alternative answers to this question of whether to treat left-dislocations as two separate classes for the purposes of natural language generation need not be decided *a priori* but can be put to the test empirically. In general, the intention behind this project is not to resolve the question of the discourse status of inferable entities, but rather to make explicit what choices are made with regard to inferables (both in left-dislocations and otherwise) in order to contribute in small part toward a clearer idea of how such an issue can be dealt with in investigations using naturally-occurring data.

2.1.2 Cleft constructions

Cleft constructions in English, both wh-clefts and it-clefts, have functions related to given open propositions (Prince, 1978). Both types of clefts can be characterized as having a focus-presupposition structure, one where the FOCUS— the post-copular constituent in the wh-cleft and the post-copular, pre-*that* clause[6] constituent in the it-cleft—serves as a variable instantiating the open proposition of the complement clause, or PRESUPPOSITION. According to Prince (1978), the informational status of the open proposition differs crucially in wh- and it-clefts. The majority of the discussion here will follow the line of argumentation she presents for this claim.

In the wh-cleft, the information conveyed in the open-proposition must represent material which the speaker can assume to be in the hearer's consciousness at the time of hearing the utterance. This material may have been explicitly presented in the discourse, as in (28) or it may require some inference on the part of

---

[6]What I refer to as a *that*-clause here may also begin with either a null-complementizer or a wh-word.

the hearer, as in (29–30):

(28) In Haviland and Clark they say that...Certainly **what they are talking about** is...(Prince 1978; 22a)

(29) At first contact he developed a furious hatred for the party of the Social Democrats. "**What most repelled me**," he says, "was its hostile attitude toward the struggle for..."(Prince 1978; 23a)

(30) The fact that pre-eminence of some groups and regions over others shifted frequently is well known...**What is less known or rather not admitted by some who prefer not to look at the staring presence of reality**, is the other fact that...(Prince 1978; 24b)

In (29) the hearer can reasonably be expected to infer from the fact that if the speaker hates something, there are particular causes for that hatred. In (30) the open proposition has a "given" status with respect to the previous linguistic context, where a proposition that expresses the opposite of the material present in the wh-cleft (e.g. X IS WELL KNOWN vs. Y IS LESS KNOWN OR NOT ACKNOWLEDGED) appears.

Often the material found in the pre-copular wh-constituent is assumed familiar and salient to the hearer simply on the basis of the speech situation. Depending on the genre, the speaker can reasonably assume that the hearer is attending to the fact that the speaker has opinions about the topics of the discourse (*what I think is*, *what bothers me about it is*) or to the fact that the discourse is describing a sequence of events (*what happened is*, *what we did was*). This flexibility on the part of the speaker to assume that all of these open propositions are salient is yet more evidence that it is not the salience of the open proposition alone that is the true conditioning factor of when *in particular* the speaker decides to use these forms.[7]

One additional factor in the use of wh-clauses is the relative information status of the pre- and post-copular material. The wh-clause must be (assumed by the speaker to be) more prominent in the hearer's consciousness than the material following the copula, as the following contrast in acceptability illustrates (Prince 1978; 28a):

(31) a. A: Wasn't that incredible when Mary called the boss a pig?
      B: Yeah, it really shocked me that she called him that.

      b. B: ?? Yeah, What really shocked me was that she called him that.

Like wh-clefts, it-clefts also encode a type of 'givenness' in their open proposition. However, like left-dislocations, it-clefts may have multiple functions in

---

[7]Otherwise, we would expect that speakers could felicitously begin every statement of fact with *what I think is* and every sentence describing an event as *what happened was*.

English. Prince (1978) refers to these two types of it-clefts as informative-presupposition it-clefts and stressed-focus it-clefts. The latter have a focus constituent which bears the tonic stress of the sentence. Prince (1978) claims that in contrast with wh-clefts, in an stressed-focus it-cleft, the complement clause need not be something that the speaker may appropriately assume the hearer is attending to at that point in the discourse. Instead, it seems that the clause need only be something that the speaker could assume is inferable by the hearer, as in the following naturally-occurring dialog (Prince 1978; 33c).

(32)   A: Mmm...[eating pieces of fudge]
        B: Aren't those good? It was only sheer will power that kept me from
        eating twelve every night.

Here B can reasonably assume that A could infer that something stopped B from eating the fudge since it was still there, but not that A was actually thinking about what stopped B from eating the fudge.

Contra Prince (1978), Ball (1994) claims that the complement clause in a stressed-focus it-cleft should in fact be salient shared knowledge, i.e. information that the speaker assumes the hearer could appropriately assumed to have in her consciousness at the time of hearing the utterance. In other words, the content of the complement clause is assumed to be under discussion. This clearly contrasts with Prince (1978)'s characterization of the difference between the two types of clefts because for Prince the wh-clause serves as a theme[8] of the current discourse, and the it-cleft complement clause is marked as *not* being the theme. Further corpus-based study of both forms may clarify the difference between these two forms.

The informative-presupposition it-cleft differs from the stressed-focus it-cleft both prosodically and informationally.[9] In these it-clefts, the *that*-clause has normal stress, rather than being deaccented. The constituent that appears in the focus position is usually a subject NP or a scene-setting adverbial (e.g. time, place, or reason). The *that*-clause, rather than expressing a given proposition, expresses a discourse-new proposition, and serves to mark this proposition as a known fact, albeit one that is unknown to the hearer (Prince, 1978). Informative-presupposition it-clefts are illustrated in (33):

(33)   a. It was just about 50 years ago that Henry Ford gave us the weekend.
            (Prince 1978; 41a)

        b. The leaders of the militant homophile movement in America gener-
            ally have been young people. It was they who fought back during

---

[8]By *theme* possibly a backward-looking center-type concept is meant. It is not entirely clear what role propositions (as opposed to entities) play in a centering theory.

[9]See Hedberg (1990) for a very similar distinction between two types of it-clefts, TOPIC-CLAUSE and COMMENT-CLAUSE.

> a violent police raid on a Greenwich Village bar in 1969, an inci-
> dent from which many gays date the birth of the modern crusade for
> homosexual rights. (Prince 1978; 42a)

Prince suggests that this discourse function of marking a known fact makes informative-presupposition it-clefts especially common in written genres like historical narratives.

In their work, Delin and Oberlander attempt to unify the different functional types of it-clefts (Delin, 1995; Delin and Oberlander, 1995). Delin and Oberlander (1995) present a detailed analysis of the functions of it-clefts, one that they attempt to tie quite closely to the syntax and semantics of the form, in particular the presence of the copula as indicating a semantics of stativeness.[10] They make several claims about how it-clefts, both stressed-focus and informative-presupposition, are related to discourse structure. These claims are based in a theory of discourse structure as a hierarchical structure where each new segment is attached via either coordination or subordination to the previous segment. First, they claim that an it-cleft is attached as a sibling with a common parent node to the previous discourse segment (assuming that the previous segment expresses the given open proposition that licenses the use of the it-cleft.) Secondly, they claim that the use of an stressed focus it-cleft closes off the discourse segment to which it attaches as a child; that is, after causing a discourse pop up to the level of the common parent node of itself and its antecedent segment, that segment is complete. In contrast, an informative-presupposition it-cleft leaves the segment to which it attaches open for further elaboration. One additional aspect of this 'discourse pop' effect,[11] according to Delin and Oberlander, is that neither type of it-cleft supports a relation of NARRATIVE PROGRESSION.

This lack of support for a relation of NARRATIVE PROGRESSION is closely tied to the second claim of Delin and Oberlander's of relevance here—that the use of a stressed-focus or informative presupposition it-cleft limits the possible coherence relations that can be inferred between it and the previous discourse. Delin and Oberlander remain agnostic about the particular framework of coherence relations to use, citing (Grosz and Sidner, 1986; Hobbs, 1990; Mann and Thompson, 1987; Moore and Pollack, 1992) among others. For stressed-focus it-clefts they suggest two possible relations that may be relevant, QUESTION-

---

[10]I remain agnostic here on whether the latter effort is desirable and/or necessary. For the purposes of this project, I will refrain from addressing the question of how the truth-conditional semantics are related to the basic discourse conditions and the additional communicative goals outlined in the following chapter. With respect to Delin and Oberlander's claim that it is a range of factors that determine speakers' choice of the best form to fit their communicative goal, however, this analysis is in complete agreement.

[11]Delin and Oberlander claim that a discourse-pop effect is more prevalent with stressed-focus than informative-presupposition it-clefts.

ANSWER and CONTRAST and claim that stressed-focus it-clefts can *only* be attached to the discourse using these two relations. These relations are the intuitive ones that characterize the functions of stressed-focus it-clefts, i.e. the instantiation of a variable in an open proposition, and the instantiation of a previously filled proposition with a different instantiation of the variable, respectively. For informative-presupposition it-clefts, Delin and Oberlander claim, drawing on the claims of Prince (1978), that one of the relevant coherence relations is CAUSE-EFFECT, where the it-cleft is used to present a backgrounded causal event. Additionally, they say that informative-presupposition it-clefts can also be used to report events where a relation of TEMPORAL or NARRATIVE PROGRESSION is not desired, and instead the event denoted by the it-cleft should be understood to have preceded the event denoted by the immediately preceding utterance. Evidence bearing on Delin and Oberlander's claims about it-clefts will be presented in Chapter 3 because, as will be discussed in both the following section and in the following chapter, it appears that non-canonical syntactic forms can be used to communicate information about discourse structure.

This concludes the section providing the necessary background on the discourse functions and conditions of the syntactic forms examined in this project.

2.2   Discourse structure and syntactic form

The term *discourse structure* can be used to mean a variety of different things. It will be used here to express the relation, either syntactic or semantic, between two (or more) discourse segments. In any text made up of more than a single utterance, the semantic relations that hold between utterances are an additional part of the meaning of the text supplementing the meaning that a single utterance contributes. These relations, referred to as *coherence, subject matter, rhetoric* or *semantic relations* hold between two utterances and include, for example, the temporal relation holding between events or a contrast relation holding between propositions (Kehler, 2002; Hobbs, 1990; Halliday, 1985; Mann and Thompson, 1988). Because the linguistic material comprising a text, its clauses and phrases, can be combined into larger discourse segments, these relations may hold between sets of utterances. These groupings of utterances (or the intentions underlying them) can be modeled as a hierarchical tree structure (Grosz and Sidner, 1986; Webber, 1991; Webber and Joshi, 1998).

As mentioned in the previous section, the connection between discourse structure and syntactic form plays a significant role in the model laid out in Chapters 3 and 4, in particular how speakers use the non-canonical forms of interest here to signal particular aspects of discourse structure. This section presents several theories of both semantic and syntactic discourse relations mentioned above. Select aspects of all of them will be utilized in the following chapters to explicate a theory of how intrasentential syntactic choices affect and are affected by intersentential relationships.

2.2.1 Semantic relations between clauses

Rhetorical Structure Theory

Mann and Thompson's Rhetorical Structure Theory is a descriptive framework for characterizing the relations between clauses in a text (Mann and Thompson, 1987, 1988).[12] Two text spans, composed of a single or multiple clauses, can be related in one of many possible rhetorical relations. In most relations, one span is designated as a nucleus and the other as a satellite. The nucleus is somehow more integral to the meaning and function of a text. If it were removed, the text would be altered significantly. In addition, the meaning of the nucleus is crucial to the meaning of the satellite because without the nucleus, the satellite would be a non sequitur. The quintessential nucleus-satellite pair is a main clause and its attached subordinate. A complete RST analysis of a text forms a hierarchical tree structure. Every unit in a text belongs to a text span which is related to some other text span in a rhetorical relation. In addition, only adjacent text spans can be related by a rhetorical relation.

In general, the relations in RST are semantic ones, that is they make explicit how the meaning of the two text spans is related. Mann and Thompson present a large list including the following: CONTRAST, QUESTION-ANSWER, BACK-GROUND, ELABORATION, PURPOSE, VOLITIONAL CAUSE, CONCESSION, and EVIDENCE.

Although the role of rhetorical relations in interpretation is not entirely clear, they can be useful as a meta-level characterization of a discourse segment's purpose. As such, much use has been made of them in text planning in natural language generation systems (Marcu, 1997; Hovy, 1990, 1988; McKeown, 1985).[13] In such cases, the text plan is essentially a rhetorical tree-structure which is filled out with information relevant to the communicative goals that the plan is intended to achieve.

Coherence relations (Kehler, 2002)

Mann and Thompson explicitly state that the set of relations in RST are not a closed list, but instead are "an open set" which is potentially extendible. In contrast, building on Hobbs (1990), Kehler (2002) presents a theory of a small set of discourse coherence relations. He then demonstrates the role of these relations in

---

[12]Mann and Thompson (1988) specify that their own analyses consider the basic units of text to be the clause, excluding restrictive relative clauses and complement clauses.

[13]See Hovy (1993) for a thorough summary of the role of rhetorical relations in text planning.

a variety of linguistic phenomena. Kehler claims that the process of coherence establishment is a general cognitive function which plays a role in the process of determining the coherence of any situation comprised of varied objects and events, including a discourse. In order to establish the coherence of a discourse, the interpreter must "recover the implicit 'coherence structure' of a sequence of utterances communicated to them."

Kehler attempts to provide a theory of basic types of coherence relations that can comprise a coherence structure and the inference processes that are the basis for establishing these relations. For example, of the following two passages, (35) is less coherent than (34) because in the latter the inference can be made rather easily that the institution of a Medicare drug benefit would require the revelation of the true costs. Thus, the second sentence is an EXPLANATION of the first. Example (35) is a less coherent passage because it is more difficult to establish an intended relationship between the meaning of the two sentences.

(34)   The domestic pharmaceutical industry fears the institution of a Medicare drug benefit. They do not want to reveal the true costs of their proprietary medicines.

(35)   The domestic pharmaceutical industry fears the institution of a Medicare drug benefit. Newt Gingrich has been campaigning for George W. Bush.

Once a coherence relation between two text segments has been established, the relation imposes constraints that then play a role in language interpretation. Some of the many phenomena that are affected by coherence relation establishment are VP ellipsis, gapping, and pronoun resolution.

Kehler presents three classes of coherence relations, RESEMBLANCE, CAUSE-EFFECT, and CONTIGUITY. These relations differ both in what types of arguments they apply to and what type of inference process underlies this application.

The class of RESEMBLANCE relations includes PARALLEL, CONTRAST, EX-EMPLIFICATION, GENERALIZATION, EXCEPTION, and ELABORATION relations. The key factors in resemblance relations are similarities and differences among sets of entities and events. A resemblance relation P is a common (or contrasting) relation that subsumes two relations p_1 and p_2; each pair of corresponding arguments (elements) of p_1 and p_2 share a common property. For example in (36), the common relation is CONSUME, which takes a consumer (*Cookie Monster, Big Bird*) and a thing consumed (*cookies, bird seed*).

(36)   a.   Cookie Monster eats cookies.

       b.   Big Bird snacks on bird seed.

(37) P: CONSUME; p_1: EAT; p_2: SNACK ON

(38)   MUPPET: *Cookie Monster, Big Bird*; FOOD: *cookies, bird seed*

In order to establish a resemblance relation, the hearer must identify the common relation P, the number and identity of its arguments, and which arguments of p_1 and p_2 correspond to each other. Often syntactic parallelism between the two sentences involved in the relation facilitates this identification.

The CAUSE-EFFECT relation class includes RESULT, EXPLANATION, VIOLATED EXPECTATION, and DENIAL OF PREVENTER. For these relations, two propositions P and Q should be inferred from the two sentences whose meanings are related, S_1 and S_2, respectively. In order to establish a cause-effect relation, the hearer must infer that $P \rightarrow Q$. There is no need to establish subclausal syntactic parallelism.

For the final class of relations, CONTIGUITY, Kehler includes only OCCASION. An OCCASION relation is relevant in descriptions of a sequence of eventualities centered around a system of entities, in other words a narrative.[14] In order to establish such a relation, the hearer must infer from the two sentences (or segments) S_1 and S_2, that these two sentences describe a change of state of the system of entities where S_1 describes the initial state, and S_2 the final. Establishing contiguity usually requires much extra-linguistic knowledge about the world, such as how events are related to each other and which events count as separate events. Temporal progression alone is inadequate to establish this relationship.

Kehler claims his principles are rooted in small set of basic cognitive methods for establishing relationships between ideas. Ideally, coherence establishment could be done automatically with an algorithm using logical abduction, as discussed in (Hobbs et al., 1990). However, an unlimited number of facts about the world (axioms) might be relevant in establishing relations, and so implementing such an algorithm in an unlimited domain could be nearly impossible.

Partial evidence for Kehler's claims about the relationship between coherence relations and linguistic interpretation comes from the meanings of connectives because one can use connectives as diagnostic tests to identify the existence of particular coherence relations. However, Kehler warns that there is a many-to-many mapping between connectives and coherence relations.[15] Some connectives can be thought of as underspecified with respect to the connective with which they can be associated. For instance, *but* may mark a CONTRAST or a VIOLATED EXPECTATION. Kehler notes that coherence relations are independent of the connectives used (or not used) to signal them because their establishment depends on semantic relationships between the arguments, not just the use of a connective.[16] As such, in order to identify coherence relations, we are left only

---

[14]I will use NARRATIVE, CONTIGUITY, and OCCASION interchangeably to describe this coherence relation.

[15]In addition, a discourse segment may simultaneously satisfy more than one coherence relation.

[16]Mann and Thompson (1988) make a similar claim that the definitions of relations 'do not rely on morphological or syntactic signals,' like the presence of a particular connective.

with our intuitions to apply constraints dictated by relation definitions. This process can be helped along by using conjunctions as paraphrases.

Narrative structure (Labov, 1997)

In the theory of coherence relations outlined in (Kehler, 2002), the relation with the least detailed description of its meaning and establishment is the CONTIGUITY relation, essentially the relation that holds between utterances in a narrative. In order to get a clearer idea of what this relation is like, we will examine some work on narrative structure, in particular that of presented in Labov (1997) and Labov and Waletzky (1967).

Labov (1997) defines a formal framework to describe and analyze the quintessential narrative genre, narratives of personal experience. He defines NARRATIVE OF PERSONAL EXPERIENCE as a report of a sequence of events in the biography of a speaker presented as a sequence of clauses in the order in which the original events occurred. The "point" of a narrative of personal experience can be regarded as the most highly evaluated action or the most reportable event in the narrative. The latter is a relative concept depending on the context and audience of the speaker's presentation of the narrative. The most reportable event should be the least common event in the narrative and have the greatest effect upon the participants in the narrative (the latter explaining why it receives the highest degree of evaluation.) Labov argues that on the basis of the claim that a narrative is centered on the most reportable event, a narrative can be viewed as a presentation of a causal chain of events leading up to this most reportable event. The beginning point of the narrative, or ORIENTATION is the situation that does not require an explicit cause.[17]

A TEMPORAL SEQUENCE is defined in Labov and Waletzky (1967) as a sequence of clauses whose order cannot be changed without changing the inferred sequence of events in the original interpretation. Crucially, to be a narrative, the units of the narrative must be ordered in the same way as the original events. So, the verbal sequence of clauses must match the sequence of events that actually occurred. Only independent (main) clauses are relevant in establishing the temporal sequence. Subordinate clauses do not effect the temporal order of the chain of events; in other words, if the subordinate clause were detached from the clause where it originally appears in the narrative and placed elsewhere, it would not change the stream of events.

Because the correspondence between events and clauses is not clear cut, Labov and Waletzky (1967) define how to establish a temporal sequence. Clauses must be assigned to one of several classes based on how and where they can be displaced with respect to the other narrative units without altering the meaning of

---

[17]The relation between causal chains of events and narratives suggests that perhaps Kehler's two categories CAUSE-EFFECT and OCCASION may often overlap.

the narrative.

- FREE CLAUSES: can be displaced anywhere within a narrative

- NARRATIVE OR BOUND CLAUSES: cannot be moved without changing the temporal sequence that makes up the narrative.

- COORDINATE CLAUSES: a set of clauses with identical displacement sets, i.e. they can be freely interchanged with each other within a specified range in the text.

- RESTRICTED CLAUSES: have a wider range than narrative clauses but can only be displaced in one direction (either before or after their current position, but not both.)

Two clauses will be TEMPORALLY ORDERED with respect to each other if their displacement sets do not include each other (although the sets themselves may overlap). A TEMPORAL JUNCTURE is then defined as the point that separates two clauses that are temporally ordered with respect to each other. The definition of narrative clause can then be specified formally as a clause that cannot be displaced across a temporal juncture. Narrative clauses cannot have as part of their displacement set two clauses that are ordered with respect to each other. A narrative then is *any* sequence of clauses that contain at least one temporal juncture. However, a narrative without an evaluation section will be difficult to understand because it "lacks significance: it has no point." Evaluative material can be spread throughout a narrative but is often concentrated just before the most reportable event which has the effect of suspending the forward movement of the action.

Both Labov (1997) and Labov and Waletzky (1967) discuss types of linguistic structures that are related not to the reporting of a particular causal event in the chain of events but instead to the evaluation of the most reportable event. These devices are used in restricted or free clauses. They include emphasis, perfect tenses,[18] parallel structures, comparatives, modals, negatives, and futures. The last three are particularly relevant as ways to talk about what did not but might have occurred, and as such play an important role in evaluating the narrative. The combination of Labov's formalization of a NARRATIVE with Kehler (2002) ontology of coherence relations provides us with a small set of relatively clearly defined semantic relations between discourse segments in which to frame our own discussion in Chapter 3 of the relationship between non-canonical syntactic forms and coherence relations. This small taxonomy of coherence relations

---

[18]The use of past perfect tense in a 'flashback' function has not been found to occur in narratives of personal experience, according to (Labov, 1997). When the past perfect is used, it is only to report events that the narrator knew at the time in the temporal sequence in which they are reported.

should not be taken as an independent theory of coherence or coherence establishment, it is merely a reasonable way to divide up the domain of semantic relations between discourse segments. The relations which we will make most use of—NARRATION/OCCASION/CONTIGUITY, RESEMBLANCE and its subtypes, including ELABORATION—will presumably be distinguished in nearly any theory of the semantic relations between discourse segments, and so using them even in lieu of a larger theory of how discourse participants establish coherence is not unjustified.

We now turn to a discussion of several different theories of syntactic discourse relations because the relationship between non-canonical syntactic forms and syntactic discourse relations will also be an important part of the discussion of the communicative goals motivating the use of non-canonical syntax in the next chapter.

2.2.2 Syntactic relations between clauses

Rather than concentrating on the semantic relations between segments of a discourse, some theories of discourse structure focus on the syntactic relations between segments. This section outlines three theories of the syntax of discourse structure.

Grosz and Sidner (1986)

Grosz and Sidner (1986) argue for a model for coherent discourses which has three substructures: a LINGUISTIC STRUCTURE, an INTENTIONAL STRUCTURE, and an ATTENTIONAL STRUCTURE. The linguistic structure is the actual linguistic material comprising a text, a sequence of phrases and clauses. The linguistic structure can be subdivided into discourse segments. Segments may or may not contain adjacent parts of the text, i.e. two non-adjacent utterances may belong to a single segment.

The intentional structure is a hierarchical structure composed of discourse purposes. Each individual DISCOURSE SEGMENT PURPOSE (DSP) specifies how the segment contributes to the purpose of the discourse as a whole. Two relations determine how the structure is organized. A DSP may be related to another DSP by SATISFACTION-PRECEDENCE or by DOMINANCE. A purpose satisfaction-precedes another when it must be satisfied before the other can be satisfied. A purpose dominates another purpose when it is in part satisfied by satisfying the other. The dominance relation forms a hierarchical structure over the discourse segment purposes of a text.

The third component of discourse structure is the attentional state. It can be modeled as a stack of focus spaces. Each discourse segment has a corresponding focus space containing the currently salient discourse entities (objects, properties, and relations) and that particular segment's DSP. When a segment begins, its focus space is pushed onto the stack on top of any other incomplete segments. When the segment ends, the focus space is popped off the stack.

In Grosz and Sidner's model, the hierarchical structure of the text is identical to its intentional structure. A speaker's goal in uttering a segment and how that segment fits into the larger discourse are inseparable. Hearers make use of this isomorphism when they make hypotheses about the speaker's intention underlying a segment. Although there is an unlimited number of possible DSPs, or intentions, there are only a small number (i.e. the two above, satisfaction-precedence and dominance) of relations between segments. Recognizing the relevant structural relationship among segments, and thus their DSPs, can help in identifying the DSP itself.

Grosz and Sidner's framework then differs from a model of discourse structure like Mann and Thompson (1988) where the relations between segments come from a theoretically unlimited set of possible relations. Grosz and Sidner suggest that although rhetorical relations can provide a meta-level description of a discourse, their role in interpretation of a discourse is not clear and in fact could possibly be derived from a combination of domain-specific information and their own more general framework. This is contra a position like Kehler (2002)'s, for whom understanding the meaning of a discourse depends on establishing its coherence, which in turn depends on identifying the specific coherence relations which hold between its parts.

From a generation perspective, where we are interested in the factors that motivate a speaker's selection of a form, it seems that it is neither necessary nor desirable to neglect semantic relations between discourse segments in favor of syntactic relations. Certainly, for natural language generation purposes, concepts like rhetorical relations can play a useful role in planning a discourse. In most applications, the system will not have an infinite set of possible intentions for contributing an utterance. A limited number of discourse segment purposes or rhetorical relations may in fact be all that is needed in a limited domain. Ideally, we will be able to investigate the potential role of both syntactic and semantic relations in selection of non-canonical syntactic forms. In addition, as will be discussed below in the section on DLTAG, retaining the simplicity of Grosz and Sidner's syntactic model of discourse structure does not necessarily preclude the addition of a layer of semantic representation where relations beyond just dominance and satisfaction-precedence may play a role.

Webber (1991)

Webber (1991) outlines a theory of how demonstrative pronouns can refer to segments of the discourse. As part of this, a formal analogue of text processing is presented, in particular an algorithm for creating a tree structure corresponding to how the discourse model grows as a text progresses.

Webber says there are three structures relevant to her model:

1. the text structure made up of discourse segments

2. the discourse model made up of various regions (i.e. file cards)

3. the tree structure which records how (1) and (2) progress

The tree structure records two relations between segment nodes. The first is the PARENT-OF relation where the claim made by child provides evidence for parent. Second, the RIGHT-SIBLING-OF relation where the two linearly ordered claims provide evidence for the same conclusion. These two relations closely correspond to Grosz and Sidner (1986)'s dominance and satisfaction-precedence relations.

Trees can be grown with two operations, ATTACH and ADJOIN. Attaching (as a rightmost daughter) adds a single node to the tree's right frontier. The region of the discourse model "comprising the entities, properties, and relations conveyed by the new clause" is included in the same region of the model as those associated with the rest of the segment. Attaching corresponds to pushing a new element onto the focus stack.

In contrast, adjoining adds two nodes to tree. The newly adjoined node and the node adjoined to both become children of single new parent node. Here the newly adjoined node is taken to be contributing jointly with the adjoined-to node to some single common purpose or meaning represented by the parent node. Adjoining corresponds to popping all the stack elements corresponding to the segment adjoined to and pushing the elements of the adjoined-in node onto the stack. The choice of operation depends on which relationships between the new node and the previously attached nodes, RIGHT-SIBLING-OF or PARENT-OF, are desired, i.e. the new node should be attached such that it will be a sibling with other nodes that provide evidence for the same conclusion and it will be a child of the node for which it provides evidence.

The elements in focus are always those in the regions taken to be in focus, i.e. those regions in the discourse model on the right frontier of the tree structure. This procedural model of building up a discourse structure as the discourse progresses is extended in the framework of tree-adjoining grammar to be discussed in the next section.

Discourse Lexicalized Tree-Adjoining Grammar

In recent work, Webber and her colleagues present a lexicalized tree-adjoining grammar for discourse, DLTAG (Webber and Joshi, 1998; Webber et al., 1999; Creswell et al., 2002; Webber et al., 2003). In DLTAG, the tree structure for the discourse is created by performing the operations of TAG on smaller structures (i.e. discourse segments) anchored by discourse connectives. DLTAG is a grammar to build (or specify well-formedness of) discourse structures rather than sentences. The trees in DLTAG are lexically anchored with discourse connectives, subordinating or coordinating conjunctions, or so-called empty connectives. The semantics of the anchors and the arguments substituted into them is that of a predicate-argument relation. The discourse connective (or conjunction) is the predicate which takes the interpretation of discourse segments as its arguments. A flat semantic representation corresponding to the DLTAG can be defined such that the hierarchical discourse tree structure for a text can then be mapped to its semantics (Stone et al., 2001; Kallmeyer and Joshi, 1999; Kallmeyer et al., 2003).

In the case of the lexical connectives and conjunctions, the semantics of the relation is at least partially specified. For example, in its use as a sentential coordinate conjunction *and* may encode a narrative relation or a parallel relation. In the case of empty connectives, i.e. when a sentence contains no explicit discourse connective, there is no lexical realization of the predicate. The predicate relation that they "encode" must be derived inferentially. The default relation assumed is simply that the new segment is related to the previous discourse structure as a continuation of the description of the same entity as that to which it is adjoined.

The elements substituted and adjoined into the DLTAG trees are clauses (or larger trees). As in other TAGs, there are two types of elementary trees, initial and auxiliary. Elementary trees encode basic predicate-argument relations, where the lexical anchor is the predicate (functor) and the substitution nodes (in the initial trees) or the foot nodes (in the auxiliary trees) correspond to the arguments. Recursion is possible due to the two combining operations of substitution and adjoining. The anchors for initial trees are subordinating conjunctions. Auxiliary trees can be anchored by coordinating conjunctions, discourse connectives, or empty connectives. The semantics of auxiliary trees varies. In some cases, the left argument of the connective is found structurally, that is it must be the leftmost daughter in the tree, i.e. the node to which the auxiliary tree is adjoined. This is true for coordinating conjunctions. In other words, a coordinating conjunction can only relate two adjacent discourse segments. In the case of most adverbial discourse connectives, however, the left-hand argument can be inferentially derived from antecedent material in the preceding discourse, material which is not necessarily adjacent to the adverbial connective. This is illustrated in the discourse in (39) where the coordinating conjunction *so* relates the propositional content of S_2 and S_3, and the adverbial *nevertheless* relates S_1 and S_3.[19]

(39) S_1: Max is a committed user of public transportation and couldn't possibly justify owning a car himself.
S_2: Last month his friend Jack bought a car.
S_3: So, nevertheless, Max has thought about giving up his bus pass for a new set of flashy wheels.

The DLTAG theory differs from Mann and Thompson's RST because two segments which have a semantic relation need not be adjacent in the discourse

---

[19]For a similar example utilizing a subordinate conjunction see Creswell et al. (2002).

structure. Their semantic relation may be resolved anaphorically. In general, DLTAG is a combination of some of the more purely syntactic or semantic approaches discussed above. The syntactic representation is closely tied to the syntactic formalism used for intrasentential syntactic phenomena and is quite specific. Conceptually, however, it is clearly the descendant of approaches like Grosz and Sidner (1986) and Webber (1991). The innovation of the DLTAG approach, lies in the fact that it also has a semantic representation which is transparently derivable from the syntactic representation, and as such the semantics of a discourse are also tied to its linguistic realization. In this, DLTAG also differs from RST because the linguistic forms themselves determine a highly specific and strictly limited amount of information about intersentential discourse relations. All additional meaning must be derived inferentially.

The DLTAG theory of discourse structure is relevant to this project for two reasons. First, although DLTAG has thus far not been utilized in any natural language generation systems, the potential usefulness of TAG for NLG has been recognized since Joshi (1987) (See Bangalore et al. (2000) for discussion.). An NLG system that already uses LTAG formalism like SPUD (Stone et al., 2001), to be discussed below, could be extended relatively straightforwardly to incorporate the discourse version of the grammar. In such an extension, a text plan consisting of multiple related communicative goals could then be encoded not merely as a sequence of individual trees but instead as a hierarchical discourse tree structure, whose arguments would themselves be trees encoding subgoals. Because DLTAG bridges the gap between syntax at the sentence level and at the discourse level, it can serve a useful purpose in an NLG framework.

The second reason for DLTAG's relevance here is that throughout the rest of the project we will assume a DLTAG-type analysis of discourse structure, one where the syntax is simple and well-understood and the semantics is relatively underspecified. Most information on the semantic relations between two segments must be derived inferentially in lieu of a specific lexical connective signifying the semantics. The addition of a new utterance to a discourse will be regarded in the following way. A new utterance (a main clause and its subordinates which will be joined into a single elementary tree) must be adjoined to the right frontier of the previously built discourse structure. The particular node to which the speaker intends it to be adjoined must be inferred by the hearer. In addition, the particular semantic relation holding between the utterance must also be determined inferentially by the hearer. As we will see in the following chapter, it is precisely these two inferential processes in which the use of non-canonical utterances can assist the hearer and which motivate the use of these forms by the speaker.

2.3 Focus and information structure

2.3.1 A brief overview

All of the forms under consideration here appear to have some relationship with the variety of topics grouped under the concept of *focus* in the linguistic literature. Focus is a notoriously vast and messy topic. Gundel (1999) and Hockey (1998, chap. 2) present far more thorough introductions to the topic than that presented here. Nonetheless, the forms presented above have an intuitive relationship to the many (interrelated) aspects of focus:[20]

- information-structure concepts of focus (rheme) and ground (topic/theme) (Vallduví, 1990a; Sgall et al., 1986; Lambrecht, 1996; Steedman, 1991);

- phonological or syntactic theories of focus placement relating to the distribution and meaning of pitch accents in English (Selkirk, 1995; Scharzschild, 1998; Rooth, 1985, 1992; Pierrehumbert and Hirschberg, 1990);

- focus-presupposition structure of propositions (Chomsky, 1972; Jackend-off, 1972)

- alternative sets of related entities (Prevost, 1995; Theune, 2000)

Given this relationship, some commentary attempting to clarify it with respect to the focus literature is necessary. The discourse functions discussed in Section 2.1 appear to relate to two aspects of focus—given open propositions (all forms but left-dislocations) and sets of related entities (topicalizations, left-dislocations). We will attempt to elucidate both of these aspects here. They are related to each other, of course, because the open proposition may often be instantiated with a member of some salient set of related entities.

Given open propositions

Hockey (1998)'s discussion of prosodic focus distinguishes three subconcepts: the marking of discourse-new (vs. discourse-old entities); the information structure of an utterance, where the informative focus is marked prosodically as a nuclear accent; and the concept of relevant non-uniqueness, i.e. discourse entities which share common properties and are in some sense interchangeable with one another. Hockey finds that only the information structure subconcept correlates significantly with any prosodic features in English, in particular, with an increased duration and amplitude that is realized over an entire focused constituent

---

[20]The lists of references naturally do not begin to do justice to the literature here and are meant only as a rough guide to each subcategory of the focus literature.

(and not just its syntactic head.) By information-structural focus, Hockey means the part of an utterance that corresponds to the instantiation of the missing constituent in a wh-question with that utterance as the answer, as exemplified by the all-capitalized constituents in the following paradigm (Gussenhoven, 1984):

(40) *What's happened?* PAPA HAS GIVEN TOMMY A GUN.

(41) *What's Papa done?* Papa HAS GIVEN TOMMY A GUN.

(42) *What happened to Tommy?* PAPA HAS GIVEN Tommy A GUN.

(43) *What's Papa done to Tommy?* Papa HAS GIVEN Tommy A GUN.

(44) *What's Papa given Tommy?* Papa has given Tommy A GUN

The non-capitalized constituents are the ground. In discourses where there is no explicit wh-question, the structuring of an utterance into focus and ground can be regarded as being relative to an implicit question (van Kuppevelt, 1995; Roberts, 1998; McNally, 1998).

Another formalization of this focus-ground concept utilizes a file card metaphor (Heim, 1983; Vallduví, 1990a,b). In this model, information structure is regarded as a set of instructions to the hearer about how to update his knowledge store, a set of file cards labeled with discourse entities and containing propositions. The focus is the information to be added, usually the instantiation of an unbound variable; the ground tells the hearer where and how to enter the focus, in other words on which file card the hearer should enter the information presented as focus.

Because wh-questions can be analyzed as denoting a set of propositions related but for a different instantiation of the answer "slot" (à la Kartunnen (1977)), the information-structural ground of an utterance has a close relationship with the salient open proposition relevant to the discourse conditions of the non-canonical forms above. Nonetheless, it seems that speakers must prosodically mark this focus-ground structure on *every* utterance. But the syntactic forms considered here are clearly optional. Why would language users need to use the special syntactic forms at all? We will return to this question in Section 2.3.2.

Sets of alternatives

In addition to possibly marking an open proposition as given (Pierrehumbert and Hirschberg, 1990), the placement of a prosodic focus can indicate that the focused constituent is one member of a set of related potential instantiations of the predicate (Rooth, 1992; Prevost, 1995; Vallduví and Vilkuna, 1998; McNally, 1998). Whether the instantiation of the variable *must* have some set of related alternatives or whether this is some sort of secondary effect arising only under the condition that an appropriate set of alternatives is present in the context remains unresolved. Vallduví and Vilkuna (1998) claim that the notions of informational RHEMATICITY (= Hockey's information-structural focus) and quantificational KONTRAST should not be unified under a single concept; the tendency to do so, they suggest, is merely the result of the fact that in English, these concepts often coincide structurally. Using evidence from Hungarian, Finnish, and Catalan, they argue for a separation.

Another variation on the focus vs. contrast issue can be found in Prince (1998). She argues that contrast is not a primitive notion, but one that arises when alternate members of some salient set are evoked in a discourse and there is a *salient opposition* in what is predicated of them. With respect to the forms examined here, the notion of contrast, as defined by Prince, does not play a crucial role. The sets of entities needed to felicitously use a topicalization or left-dislocation must stand in a poset to one another. What is predicated of an entity from one of these sets does not necessarily need to stand in a salient opposition to what is predicated of any others.

Perhaps the most relevant aspect of the alternative set conception of focus is that the type of information one needs to keep track of to generate pitch accent placement could be useful when generating the special syntactic forms investigated here. For example, Prevost (1995) uses what he terms an ASET, or set of alternative entities in a discourse model that belong to the same class, to generate pitch accent placement for both rhematic (i.e. information structure focus) and contrastive use of intonation. This type of information could be used for keeping track of salient posets.

2.3.2 Focus marking: prosody vs. non-canonical syntax

We now return to the question of why similar information structure constraints can be indicated in both prosody and syntax, and how this redundancy affects the intended course of study here. The explanation for redundant focus-marking may be multidimensional. First, language is a system that utilizes redundancy extensively. A simple example is the morphological marking of agreement in some languages, including English, on both nouns and verbs. So there is no *a priori* reason that two formal correlates of a single function cannot exist. The null hypothesis then may simply be that prosody and syntax have identical functions.

In addition, prosody is necessarily a verbal form; writers can typically utilize prosodic-like highlighting in only a very limited way through the use of special orthographic devices to mark emphasis (e.g. all capitals, italics, underlining). Possibly, these special syntactic choices could be compensatory strategies used primarily in written vs. spoken genres.[21] The frequency counts of non-canonical

---

[21] Unfortunately, despite numerous studies of the differences between spoken and written language (see Biber et al. (1999); Biber (1986a) for references), the question of how users of English indicate prosodic distinctions in writing has, surprisingly, not been investigated in any depth. Of the forms of interest here, Biber's own work examined only

forms found in two spoken corpora vs. a written corpus, as presented in Table 1.1 above, do not lend strong support for this conclusion, however.

Besides coinciding in some cases with the information structure of an utterance indicated by the syntax, in some contexts the functions of prosody appear to be orthogonal to information structure altogether. Delin (1995, 1992) discusses this discrepancy in her analysis of the interaction between prosody and syntax with respect to it-clefts. She cites Rochemont (1986)'s presentational sentences as paradigmatic instances of a case where the tonic stress placement does not trigger an inference that an open proposition is given in the discourse, as in (45), where there need not be a presupposition that X ARRIVED FOR YOU.:

(45)   A LETTER arrived for you.

(46)   It was a LETTER that arrived for you.

In contrast, Delin claims that (46) *does* presuppose such a proposition, demonstrating this by embedding each under *Why do you think that...?* The entire content of example (45) falls under the scope of question; in (46), however,

---

wh-clefts and it-clefts (Biber, 1986a,b, 1989). He examined the incidence of 41 linguistic features across 15 text types; on the basis of a multi-variable analysis he grouped the features into 4 dimensions on which texts could vary. Some features did not appear to group closely enough with other features to be included in any dimension; some features appear in multiple dimensions. The text types fell in various places along each dimension; only one dimension seemed to categorize the various types along the lines of written vs. spoken. It-clefts were found more in written texts which grouped at an endpoint for this dimension (termed by Biber situational vs. abstract content type; written being more abstract). They were also more frequent on the opinionated end of the opinionated vs. objective style dimension. Academic prose was a text type characteristic of this pole. Wh-clefts were not considered an important linguistic feature for characterizing any of Biber's dimensions. However, they seemed to pattern with it-clefts on the dimensions of situational vs. abstract content type, interactional vs. informational focus of text (both were more interactional, with wh-clefts more so than it-clefts), and reference to a distant vs. immediate context (both more immediate). In contrast, wh-clefts were slightly more related to the objective style factors than the opinionated style.

The differences Biber found with respect to these two forms, though interesting and perhaps relevant for a characterization of the goals speakers have in using the forms, do not appear to shed much light on whether these forms can be used to indicate prosodic information in a written domain. Even the seeming greater frequency of it-clefts in the written and academic prose domain is not particularly helpful for what we are attempting to investigate here. Biber did not distinguish between different types of it-clefts, i.e. stressed focus and informative-presupposition. Given that the latter are reported by Prince (1978) to be more frequent in written discourse and are used to present known facts, the patterning found in Biber's texts could be explained as telling us only about this type of it-cleft.

only *what* arrived is in question.[22] Delin explains this by distinguishing the types of information contributed by pitch accent placement and by syntax. She claims that pitch accent placement indicates "a speaker's assumptions about the state of a hearer's knowledge and model of the discourse"; while the syntactic form[23] "indicates a speaker's requirements as to what information should be present in the hearer's knowledge."

Birner and Ward (1998) make a separate but related comment about the difference between the information status requirements on being referred to by a preposed constituent and being deaccented (lacking a pitch accent). According to them, the requirements on being deaccented are stricter than those on being preposed. Deaccenting can only occur when it is applied to linguistic content which has been *explicitly* evoked in discourse. In contrast, for preposing, the discourse-familiarity requirement need only be met *implicitly*. In other words, prosodic deaccenting depends on the degree of salience of the information's connection to the previous discourse, not just on whether the connection can be established.

Delin's analysis of it-clefts leads her to an additional important point about the relationship of prosodic focus to syntactic forms with focus-related functions. Prosody does not necessarily trigger the same sorts of inferences as the use of syntactic forms, and this is possibly the result of the fact that prosody is obligatorily marked on constructions while these non-canonical syntactic forms are optional. As Delin says, it-clefts "operate in relation to the goals of the speaker to achieve certain effects, rather than being produced out of constraints imposed by the current state of some model of the discourse." These goals and effects are exactly what are of interest in this study and explaining them will be the topic of Chapter 3.

2.3.3 Structuring information structure

The previous discussion has taken into account only a very simple model of the interaction between prosodic prominence and focus-ground marking. Prominence, that is the presence of a pitch accent,[24] marks information structural focus; lack of prominence, ground. Such a model is of course a gross simplification of the interaction between accent placement and information structure. In order to investigate where prosody and non-canonical syntax diverge functionally, we need a richer analysis of the correspondence between prosodic marking and its semantic function. An approach which can provide such an analysis is that of

---

[22]Delin supports her argument through additional evidence from informative-presupposition it-clefts.

[23]To be precise, Delin in fact attributes the function of the syntactic form to PRESUPPO-SITION. By this she means the syntactically-indicated, logically-presupposed (not pragmatically presupposed) material in a construction.

[24]Or, in many theories the presence of capitalization in constructed example sentences.

Ladd (1996). His theory provides the necessary framework to examine the limits of prosody in order to see where speakers may be utilizing non-canonical syntax to compensate for these limits.

Ladd claims that more basic than the assignment of sentence accent positions is the division of the utterance into prosodic phrases. He phrases this difference as the difference between two questions: *Why is the main prominence in this sentence on word X rather than on word Y?* vs. *Why is this sentence divided up into phrases the way it is?* Evidence he uses to support his claim comes from comparing focus/accent languages like English with languages like Japanese and Korean. In the latter, the use of DEPHRASING patterns like the use of deaccenting in English.

According to Ladd, the final accent in a phrase has a special status in signaling focus. Although there is no evidence to show that it is phonetically more prominent (and it does not have to be especially prominent), it nonetheless is the crucial factor in whether a broad focus interpretation (vs. a narrow focus) is possible. If the final accent in the phrase is not in a position that allows broad focus interpretation, broad focus is not possible. The converse, however, is not true. If there are accents present other than the final accent, broad focus interpretation is still possible. Ladd says that the number of these non-final accents may depend on deliberateness of speech or other factors.

The reason for the special status of the final accent is that it indicates the location of phrasing. Ladd presents a theory of sentence stress based on overall prominence rather than the placement of individual pitch accents. In Ladd's theory, abstract tune patterns are imposed on the metrical structure of a sentence, the phrasing of which is determined by context. Then, the placement of non-final accents can be derived from the metrical structure. In Ladd's words, "Ultimately [...] accents do not respond directly to focus, but arrange themselves according to the demands of the metrical structure."

In a sentence (phrase) with broad focus, the final accent is associated with a designated terminal element (DTE), which is the peak of prominence in a metrical structure (Liberman and Prince, 1977). The DTE is determined by the overall metrical structure, the relative strength and weakness between the nodes in a binary-branching tree. Because the strength-weakness relation is defined at every level in a metrical tree, and because broad focus corresponds to a weak-strong (rather than a strong-weak) pattern, the rightmost accent of the largest phrase ends up being the DTE for the structure as a whole.

Ladd shows that accent patterns depend on the length of sentences. Intermediate phrases are limited in length. In a short sentence, the subject and predicate may form a single intermediate phrase. In longer sentences, the two may form separate intermediate phrases, and the relative strength of predicate and subject may be different than in a shorter version, as in (47) and (48), where *died* is the DTE for the sentence as a whole in the latter, even when the context is held constant:

(47) [JOHNSON$_s$ died$_w$]

(48) [[[Former$_w$ President$_s$]$_w$ JOHNSON$_s$]$_w$ [[unexpectedly$_w$
DIED$_s$]$_s$ today$_w$]$_s$] (Ladd's 6.37)

In some cases, deciding whether to separate a sentence into more than one
intermediate phrase depends on more than just phonological heaviness. Some
sentences appear to have more than one "default" accent pattern, as in the classic
underground sign, (49):

(49) a. DOGS must be carried.

     b. Dogs must be CARRIED.

Rather than analyzing this as two different accent placement patterns, Ladd
analyzes it as a choice between a single intermediate phrase or two intermediate
phrases. In the case of a single intermediate phrase, because of the rules for
accenting predicates and arguments in English, the subject is the DTE. In the case
of two intermediate phrases, both subject and predicate have their own DTE, and
so each may have a pitch accent, but the full sentence has broad focus, and so the
predicate receives the main accent. The decision to separate a sentence into two
intermediate phrases in this case rests on whether it forms a single unit of new
information, (49a), or whether the subject should be a separate information unit,
(49b).

Ladd says an additional factor in forming an intermediate phrase is contrastive focus, but does not expand on this.

2.3.4 Summary

To summarize the discussion in this section, it is clear that the choice of a prosodic
form will depend on some of the same conditions as the choice of a syntactic
form. In light of Hockey (1998)'s findings, it seems that prosodic focus (i.e.
increased duration and amplitude) most likely is an indication of information
structure, that is the division of the utterance into a given component and an
instantiation of that given part.[25] However, the relationship between prosodic
focus and information structure focus is not a simple one, as made clear in Ladd
(1996). In any case, explaining the distribution and meaning of the prosodic
patterns does not entail an explanation of the syntactic forms because the two
phenomena are distinct. The use of prosody in English can be either redundant

---

[25]One aspect not touched upon here is the fact that the type of pitch accents that ap-
pear on focal material can vary and the meaning associated with them will vary as well
(Hirschberg, 1985; Ward and Hirschberg, 1985; Pierrehumbert and Hirschberg, 1990;
Hirschberg and Ward, 1995).

or orthogonal to the factors involved in the selection of syntactic form which justifies the examination of syntactic choice by itself undertaken here.

2.4   Syntactic choice in NLG

This section will review previous work on generating non-canonical syntactic forms in English. Although the approaches differ in many respects, all of them attempt to integrate contextual information into the process of choosing a particular form. Three approaches I will discuss briefly are Geldof (2000), Klabunde and Jansche (1998), and Humphreys (1995). I will then examine in more depth the approach taken by Stone et al. (2001) in the SPUD system because the theoretical basis for this system is the most compatible with the theory to be presented in Chapter 3.

2.4.1   Geldof (2000)

The goal of Geldof (2000) is to generate sentences that are linked to the attention space of the hearer. Her generation system is to be used in a device that provides the user with helpful information situated with respect to the user's spatio-temporal context. Almost all sentences this device generates will be uttered "out of the blue" as if to answer the hearer's question *What is appropriate for me (=the hearer) to do now?* For example, if the hearer was wearing the device at a conference, the device would have knowledge of the conference schedule, the wearer's schedule, and the identity of people and events in the wearer's immediate vicinity. As such, the type of information the machine will present the hearer with is statements like *Professor X, who works on topic Y, is nearby* or *A talk on topic X given by Y begins in five minutes.*

Geldof's goal is to situate this information with respect to the hearer's knowledge base by using particular syntactic forms and by including deictic references to the current time and place. She uses a simplified version of Lambrecht (1996)'s theory of information structure as her model of the relationship between discourse and syntactic form. Sentences will have an optional topic and an obligatory focus on either the predicate, the subject, or the entire sentence. This focus corresponds to a particular pattern of pitch accent; informationally, it appears to correspond to either discourse-new information status or rhematicity, i.e. "the unpredictable part of an utterance." She uses *topic* to refer both to something roughly equivalent to backward-looking center of an utterance, i.e. an unaccented pronoun in subject position, but also to any part of an utterance that "links the message to the context in a broad sense." In this way, even a reference to the hearer's current time and location can count as topical.

Geldof presents the following algorithm. It takes an input structure with information presented in propositional form and produces an output after comparing the contents of the input structure with the previous linguistic context (i.e. what it uttered in previous messages) and with what the machine knows about the hearer's physical context and interests. For each step in the algorithm, I have provided an adaptation of Geldof's example sentence that illustrates the output of that step.

- **Step 1:** If the input structure has a time or location that is close to the user's time or location, make this the first NP[26] and give it a prosodic accent. Then put a focus on the predicate also.

  (50) Please note that within FIVE MINUTES, you have to give a presentation on NATURAL LANGUAGE GENERATION.

- **Step 2:** Else if the input structure has an entity that is in the user's attention space (physically or virtually) make it the topic. If it is something that has been referred to in the immediately preceding discourse context, use an unaccented pronoun. If it is only present in the physical context, use a left-dislocated constituent.

  (51) MARY SMITH, she will give a presentation on KNOWLEDGE SYSTEMS.

  (52) She will give a presentation on KNOWLEDGE SYSTEMS.

- **Step 3:** Else if one of the entities in the input structure is something that the user is interested in and the "physical context also allows for a topic shift" (i.e. the user is not engaged in some other activity at the time of utterance) then introduce this new topic and then use an "argument focus structure."

  (53) Someone interested in AGENTS is in your neighborhood. It's JOSEP ARCOS.

- **Step 4:** Else, use a sentence focus structure, i.e. place pitch accents on both the subject NP and within the VP.

  (54) MARY SMITH proposes to MEET you to talk about NLG AND CONTEXT.

---

[26]Geldof's own phrasing here is "let the time expression be the topic, opening the sentence and carrying a prosodic accent." This seems to contradict her formal criteria for topichood, that topics should not carry a prosodic accent, as well as part of her informational criteria for topichood as "what an utterance is about."

The purpose of Geldof's generation system is a highly specific. Even though her goal is to link her utterances contextually, it seems that most of the system's utterances will be discourse-initial. She attempts to overcome this factor by referring to hearer-old entities and concepts. However, no solution will alter the fact that nearly everything her device wishes to talk about will be discourse-new. Although the use of left-dislocation to introduce a discourse-new entity appears correct, in general her use of prosodic form to encode what the machine knows about the hearer's discourse model results in odd-sounding constructions, in particular in the results of Step 4. This is probably due in part to the fact that she is implementing the placements of pitch accent placement without having grounded it in a larger theory of prosodic phrasing.

An empirical study of the prosodic form of discourse-initial utterances would quite possibly disconfirm many of her strategies. In addition, the source of the syntactic structure generated in Step 3 using an indefinite pronoun and what appears to be an abbreviated it-cleft, is unclear. Overall, because her approach focuses primarily on pitch accent placement rather than syntactic form, Geldof's work offers few useful precedents to the present project.

2.4.2   Klabunde and Jansche (1998)

Klabunde and Jansche (1998) use abductive reasoning, reasoning from conclusions to premises, to select a syntactic form based on contextual knowledge. One goal of their work is to generate three different syntactic forms that have the same information structural partitioning but are appropriate in different contexts. The three forms they are concerned with are canonical SVO order, as in (55); left-dislocation, as in (56); and what they refer to as a *hanging topic*, as in (57).

(55)   Die Vitrine   steht   rechts von der Lampe.
      the showcase stands right of   the lamp
      'The showcase is standing to the right of the lamp'

(56)   Die Vitrine,   die steht   rechts von der Lampe
      the showcase it   stands right of   the lamp
      'The showcase, it is standing to the right of the lamp.'

(57)   Was die Vitrine   betrifft, die steht   rechts von der Lampe
      what the showcase concerns it   stands right of   the lamp
      'As for the showcase, it's standing to the right of the lamp.'

They assume that the functions of these three syntactic forms are "more or less identical for German and English," and describe the forms' discourse functions as follows:

- Canonical order: The subject is the unmarked topic.

- Left-dislocation: This form indicates a topic shift, i.e. signaling that the dislocated NP's referent is changing its discourse status from inactive to active à la Lambrecht (1996). In addition, the form gives rise to the pre-supposition that another individual exists which does not have the property expressed by the matrix clause. The referent of the dislocated NP must also be "in some way related to a previously established set which it is a member of."

- Hanging topic: This form indicates a topic shift where the new topic is a one of a set of previously established set of referents in the discourse.

The discourse conditions given here for left-dislocation, in fact, appear to be a conflation of those of topicalization and left-dislocation in English described in Prince (1998) and Ward (1985), except that in the latter frameworks, the variable in the presupposed proposition is not instantiated by the left-displaced NP, but rather by whatever bears the tonic stress in the main clause. The hanging topic conditions appear to be similar to those claimed to hold of poset left-dislocations in English (Prince, 1998). Without some corpus study of these constructions in German, it is unclear whether the discourse functions are the correct ones. They nonetheless do not appear to correspond exactly with the conditions based on corpus-based studies of English.[27] Without providing explicit prior contexts, it is also difficult to discern what Klabunde and Jansche mean by a shift in topic.

In addition to these three forms, Klabunde and Jansche's system also generates locative inversions. According to them, the discourse condition on this form is that the NP appearing in the clause initial PP must be "accessible," which appears to mean discourse-old but not necessarily salient.[28] They do not discuss a case where two entities are both accessible, and so it is not clear how their conditions here would compare to those of English locative inversion (Birner, 1994).

Their generation algorithm uses rules based on the above definitions to determine the surface realization of the input. The input includes various propositions

---

[27]In addition to their claims about the discourse conditions, Klabunde and Jansche also claim that all these forms have *die Vitrine* as their topic. In light of Prince (1999)'s examination of clause-initial dislocated NPs and the support for her claim that given a clear definition of topichood, (one where topic is defined as a backward-looking center according to centering theory), these NPs are unlikely C_b's in either English or Yiddish, it is highly unlikely that these NPs are topics in German either. Quite probably the discourse functions of these forms do differ from their functions in English. The conditions for preposing to clause-initial position in German may be less constrained than preposing constructions in English.

[28]This may be the equivalent to Gundel et al. (1993)'s *familiar* (the addressee has a representation of the referent in memory) category of cognitive status. Klabunde and Jansche also utilize a category of information status "active"; this appears to correspond to Gundel et al. (1993)'s *in focus*.

about the discourse status and location of discourse entities; these are their *assumptions*. Because Klabunde and Jansche's system only generates statements about location, the possible main verbs can be chosen on the basis of the assumptions alone. In addition, the algorithm can use propositions either present or derivable from the knowledge base. From these propositions, a sentence is generated as the result of an abductive proof. If more than a single sentence is provable, the proof that uses more "proved literals," i.e. propositions derivable given the starting conditions, is best. This would seem to give the result that the form with the most specific conditions satisfied is the preferred form (cf. Stone and Doran (1997)).

The problems with Klabunde and Jansche's system are twofold. One, the conditions on the usage of the forms they generate are unsubstantiated, and given research on related languages (e.g. English and Yiddish), are likely to be at least partially incorrect. Two, even if their rules were replaced with more accurate conditions of usage, their model treats necessary discourse conditions as sufficient conditions for the purposes of generation. Hence, the problem of overgeneration would very likely occur in Klabunde and Jansche's system also.

2.4.3 Humphreys (1995)

Humphreys (1995) attempts to model the choice of syntactic form through the characterization of speaker intentions at a level detailed enough to map directly from intentions to syntactic form. In addition, he has a larger purpose of generating forms that can communicate some of the same meaning distinctions through written language that are communicated through intonation in spoken language. His model of syntactic choice includes the generation of several different forms in English, canonical sentences, it-clefts, wh-clefts, reverse wh-clefts, and topicalizations. In his model, *speaker intention* means a speaker chooses a form based on what he assumes about the status of a particular proposition in a hearer's discourse model. If the hearer's discourse model is empty, then the illocutionary act performed by uttering any proposition is an ADDITION to the model. The appropriate form to use is a canonical sentence. If the speaker assumes that the hearer has some form of the proposition, e.g. an open proposition with an uninstantiated variable, then the speaker uses a wh-cleft. Here the act is also an ADDITION but the addition of a single entity into a pre-existing open proposition.

On the other hand, if the hearer's model is assumed to include a full proposition that is identical to one in the speaker's model but for the instantiation of a single variable, an it-cleft should be generated as a CORRECTION the hearer's model. An it-cleft would be appropriate as the answer to a yes-no question where the answer is no (e.g. *Did Sandy kiss Jamie at the party? No, It was Fred who Sandy kissed.*) Humphreys claims that reverse wh-clefts can be generated under the same conditions as it-clefts, but suggests that some additional "syntactic factors play a role in choosing between the two." Topicalizations are also appropriate

in this situation, according to Humphreys, but only when they are in RETRAC-
TION of a particular entity referred to explicitly in the discourse.[29] To choose
between it-clefts and reverse wh-clefts, Humphreys' model simply selects the
least recently used form in the discourse. In addition, whenever a non-canonical
form can be used, it is.

Whether or not Humphreys' characterizations of the discourse conditions of
these forms is entirely accurate, his model suffers from the same shortcoming as
Klabunde and Jansche's above in that it cannot account for the behavior of actual
speakers who sometimes choose not to use a non-canonical form even when they
may reasonably assume the conditions for its use hold.

2.4.4 The SPUD system (Stone, et al, 2001)

The Sentence Planning Using Description (SPUD) system (Stone and Doran,
1997; Stone et al., 2001) is similar to the other systems described above because
its basis for selection of syntactic choice cannot explain the set of facts laid out at
the beginning of the proposal. It deserves a more detailed look, however, because
it is based on a theory of language generation grounded in a speaker's intention
to achieve explicit communicative goals. This idea will underlie the theory of
why speaker's choose particular forms to be presented in Chapter 3. In addition,
in its current state, SPUD bases its syntactic choice on the pragmatic conditions
described in section 2.1.1. Also, unlike Geldof (2000) and Klabunde and Jansche (1998), it does not simply conflate topichood and the discourse functions of
syntactic forms.

Natural language generation has traditionally been split into two primary
components *what to say* and *how to say it*. The continuum between these two
ends stretches from content determination to more detailed sentence planning
and then to deciding the surface syntax of the sentence input. From there, issues of morphology and then text-to-speech implementation are dealt with. The
sentence planning stage is where "high-level abstract semantic representations
are mapped onto representations that more fully constrain the possible sentential realizations."(Prevost, 1995) The inclusion of such a stage is computationally
useful because it reduces the need for feedback between higher and lower level
stages. Many NLG systems have separate sentence planning and surface realization stages; after content generation and sentence planning are complete, a surface generation phase translates the semantic representation into a surface string.
In contrast, SPUD combines both sentence planning and surface realization—
choosing words, semantic representation and syntactic structure simultaneously.

---

[29] In other words, although he cites no work on topicalization and does not explicitly
say that the topicalized entity must belong to a salient poset in the discourse, Humphreys
does seem to have an intuitively correct characterization of the discourse conditions of
some possible contexts of its use.

Utilizing the concept of ontological promiscuity, SPUD treats sentences like referring expressions. Rather than just referring to what we might normally think of as an entity, these expressions can be used to describe states and events also. Given a set of entities to describe and a set of intentions to achieve in describing them, operators are applied to a description until the content is enriched enough to satisfy the given intentions. These operators are the elementary trees of a lexicalized tree adjoining grammar (Joshi et al., 1975; Schabes, 1990). They have syntactic, semantic, and pragmatic properties and are lexicalized, in other words anchored with a particular lexical item. As such, they are tied to the lexicon in a way that a strict semantics-only representation is not.

The meaning of a tree is the conjunction of the elementary trees that are used to derive it. Each syntactic node in the tree supplies information about an entity or collection of entities; substitution and adjunction are only possible when the nodes have the same label (e.g. in a node labeled [NP↓: book19] only an elementary tree whose top node is about book19 can be inserted.) For any given "meaning" that needs to be incorporated into the description, there will be a family of operators that are possible expressions of this meaning. To choose between these operators, SPUD uses pragmatic and semantic knowledge.

SPUD chooses the "most marked licensed form," i.e. the form, or operator, with the most specific pragmatic and semantic conditions that are fulfilled. With respect to choosing between different syntactic forms for the main clause, SPUD can select from a form with canonical word order, topicalization, left-dislocation, and locative inversion. It utilizes the discourse conditions for the use of these forms posited in Ward (1985), Prince (1997), and Birner (1992). In order to generate these forms in the appropriate contexts, the knowledge base keeps a record of both what is referred to as *common knowledge*, i.e. the system's assumed beliefs about the hearer's beliefs, and the *speaker's knowledge*, i.e. the system's private set of beliefs. In addition, the information status (discourse- and hearer-oldness) and salience of particular entities, poset relations, and open propositions are kept track of within a model of the discourse. The discourse model can then be searched in order to decide which conditions are fulfilled when a form must be selected.

SPUD's overall approach is one where communicative goals and the discourse context are connected through patterns of linguistic form. The choice of syntactic form based on pragmatic conditions implemented in SPUD, however, is only as complex as the theories on which it is based. Because the pragmatic theories provide only necessary but not sufficient conditions for the use of a particular form, SPUD's model of syntactic choice of main clause word order suffers from the same problems as those theories.

2.4.5 Statistical approaches

In the last several years, a new approach to natural language generation has emerged, one that hopes to build on the success of the use of probabilistic models in natural language understanding (Langkilde and Knight, 1998a,b; Bangalore and Rambow, 2000; Bangalore et al., 2000; Ratnaparkhi, 2000). Building an NLG system is a highly labor-intensive project. For the system to be robust, large amounts of world and linguistic knowledge must be hand-coded. The goal of statistical approaches is to minimize the amount of hand-coded knowledge and rules and instead rely upon information which can be automatically extracted from linguistic corpora when selecting a linguistic realization of some conceptual representation.

One of the first of these statistical NLG systems is the NITROGEN system (Langkilde and Knight, 1998b,a). The input to the NITROGEN system is a semantic or conceptual representation which can be highly underspecified. NITROGEN has a lexicon, with mappings from words to conceptual meanings with sense frequency information, a morphological knowledge base, and a grammar, with mappings from word lattices to conceptual roles and relations (e.g. agent, patient). These are used in mapping the conceptual representation to a word lattice of possible renderings. The more specific the conceptual representation is, the smaller this lattice will be; the more general, the larger the number of possible renderings. For example, the input may not have information about number or specificity on a concept like DOG, and so this concept has the possible realizations of *a dog*, *the dog*, *dogs*, or *the dogs*. Then, based on unigrams and bigrams extracted from a corpus, all paths through the lattice are ranked. The highest ranked path is chosen as the sentence(s) which best expresses the meaning. So, for any single word and any particular pair of adjacent words, the most frequently seen token in the corpus (out of the set of tokens which are possible renderings of some part of the underlying meaning to be expressed) is selected. Because the system relies only on unigrams and bigrams, longer distance dependencies like subject-verb agreement are not captured in cases where the head noun of the subject and the inflected verb are not immediately adjacent.

Bangalore et al. (2000) present a conceptually-similar NLG system, FERGUS, which overcomes some of the disadvantages of Langkilde and Knight (1998b)'s system. The primary advantage of the FERGUS system is that it incorporates knowledge of hierarchical syntactic relations by utilizing tree-based representations. The input to FERGUS is a dependency tree with each node labeled by a word (lexeme).[30] The sister nodes at each level are unordered.

---

[30]Although the particular dependency trees FERGUS utilizes unrealistically include all function words and have fully-inflected words as their node labels, this is simply an artifact of the way the system is set up. Dependency trees can be used simply to encode a simple flat-semantic conceptual representation. In such a case separate modules to insert function

The first step in converting the dependency structure into a surface realization is to choose a syntactic structure for each node. The structure chosen for each node is a tree anchored by the node label, an elementary tree in a tree adjoining grammar (Joshi et al., 1975). The choice of a tree for a node is made to depend only on itself and its daughter nodes, that is a tree must incorporate its own node label and that of its daughters. It must be compatible with its mother node (i.e. it must be able to be adjoined or substituted into the tree chosen for its mother node.) The choice of a tree is stochastic and based on a tree model derived from 1,000,000 words of the Wall Street Journal. For example, the tree chosen for a noun N will be the most frequently found tree in the corpus headed by N. After trees are chosen for each of the nodes, the structure is "unraveled" to produce a word lattice similar to that in Langkilde and Knight (1998a)'s system, one which encodes all possible strings permitted by the partial derivation structure created by choosing trees. Multiple strings are possible because things like order of adjuncts are not determined when trees for node labels are chosen. The best path is then determined by using a trigram language model also based on 1,000,000 words of the Wall Street Journal corpus.

The primary difference then between the FERGUS model and the NITROGEN model is the use of tree representations and a stochastic tree model in FERGUS. These allow FERGUS to capture long-distance dependencies and also to utilize grammatical information that is not stochastic, such as head-argument ordering.

Problems with statistical approaches

Both FERGUS and NITROGEN operate under the same assumption, as expressed in Bangalore and Rambow (2000):

> "[T]he whole point of the stochastic approach is precisely to express the input in a manner that resembles as much as possible the realizations found in the corpus (given its genre, register, idiosyncratic choices, and so on)."

In other words, in generating a form, a string of words, to express an input, one wants to maximize the probability of the string (or in the case of Bangalore and Rambow (2000) the trees and the string). In examining the training corpus (either strings of words or a treebank), this is precisely the probability that is being calculated, $P(form)$. However, with respect to a natural language generation task, in fact, the probability we really need to be calculating and then maximizing is $P(form|meaning, context)$, i.e. the probability that a particular form is used given a meaning that is to be expressed and the context in which it will be used.[31]

---

words and morphology would be used, as Bangalore et al. (2000) discuss.

[31]This probability, $P(form|meaning, context)$, is, of course, the mirror image of the probability to be maximized in probabilistic natural language understanding; that is

Because of the lucky coincidence that statistical NLG has been primarily used on English, a language where possible surface realizations are relatively limited, the problems with selecting word order based only on a calculation of $P(form)$ are not immediately obvious. As discussed in Section 1.4, this approach will certainly fail to ever select very infrequent forms like the non-canonical sentences of interest here. But in general, it seems that the most frequent tree might indeed express a given truth-conditional meaning adequately. But even with a slightly closer look at English word order, we can see that a model based on $P(form)$ quickly becomes problematic. For example, in English, the double object and dative alternations, illustrated in (58), occur with about equal frequency (Snyder, 2003).

(58)   a. I gave the book to the boy.

        b. I gave the boy the book.

As such, statistics alone are not useful in selecting which form, the double object or the dative should be generated. In fact the use of the form is almost entirely predictable from the relative size of the object NPs and their relative information status (Snyder, 2003). An NLG system which chooses the order based purely on frequency counts in a corpus cannot encode this difference.

In comparison with English, this problem is magnified many times for languages with relatively freer word order. In such languages, the relative frequencies of possible trees for a single head verb might not be one-to-one, as with the double-object/dative alternation in English, but they will be greater than the 1 to 200 ratio of non-canonicals to canonicals that we find for the forms of interest to this study. In addition, in cases where word order alone, and not morphological marking, encodes information status of NP referents, native speakers will judge the use of the wrong form infelicitous and odd, and a text incorporating several wrong forms in succession will become incoherent (Kruijff-Korbayová et al., 2002). The most frequent form may end up being infelicitous in the majority of contexts.

The point here, however, is not that statistical NLG is fundamentally flawed. Attempting to generate natural language so that it mimics as closely as possible a corpus of naturally-occurring human-generated language may be the most feasible strategy with the most natural output for solving the engineering problem of designing robust, scalable systems. However, human language is not just a system for stringing together lexical items (or assembling trees) to create grammatical outputs. In other words, human speakers do not put constituents in a certain order simply because the words they are using to express the constituents have been frequently put in that order in the past. They put constituents (and thereby

---

$P(meaning|utterance, context)$ (Manning, 2003).

words) in particular orders because those orders can reliably indicate aspects of meaning and context they wish to communicate.[32]

Therefore, statistical generation systems must take into account, not just grammaticality but felicity. And to do this, one must take into account the fact that two identical strings do not necessarily mean the same thing in two different contexts. A single string of words can be fine in one context and nonsensical in another. Ultimately then, we need to provide a statistical generation system with an augmented representation from which to learn. Not just strings, or even trees, but pairings of linguistic forms, contexts, and meanings. This project is a very preliminary attempt in the direction of utilizing statistical models of language which incorporate meaning and context. In particular, Chapter 4 will explore the possibility of building an probabilistic model of discourse context which can then be used to play a role in selecting the order of major constituents at the clausal level.

---

[32]This selection may very well depend on the frequency of such successful association of form and meaning in the past of course, just not on the frequency of the forms alone.

CHAPTER 3

A goal-based model of syntactic choice

3.1 Introduction

Chapter 1 demonstrated that the distribution of non-canonical forms does not correlate one-to-one with the presence of the necessary conditions posited in the literature, and in some cases these optional forms play a crucial role in the meaning contributed by an utterance.

In this chapter we will describe a model for characterizing the conditions motivating the use of a non-canonical form. Like the SPUD system described in Chapter 2, this model will explicitly connect the communicative goal and discourse context of an utterance with the linguistic form realizing the goal.

By using non-canonical forms, speakers make explicit their assumptions about the discourse model, including which entities are in poset relations and which open propositions are currently salient or presupposed. Making these assumptions explicit can trigger further inferences (as shown in Section 1.3.3). Therefore, an algorithm for syntactic choice must incorporate goals characterized by a speaker's desire to trigger these inferences.

This chapter describes what these goals are like and illustrates them using naturally-occurring examples from a corpus study of non-canonical syntactic forms. The pairing of naturally-occurring data with constructed data allows us to gauge the communicative goals of particular forms in particular contexts based on native speaker intuitions.[1]

---

[1]Unless otherwise noted, all corpus examples used in this chapter are from the SSA

3.1.1   Contributing more than truth-conditional meaning

As discussed in Section 2.4.4, an utterance generated by the SPUD system can be characterized in part by the update to the conversational record that the utterance is intended to achieve. These are the ASSERTIONS of the utterance. In Stone et al. (2001), only the assertions of an utterance affect the conversational record. The choice of main clause syntactic form is related only to the PRAGMATICS. For example, a transitive verb will be associated with multiple trees, a canonically-ordered tree, a topicalization tree, a wh-cleft tree, etc. The tree with canonical order can be chosen in any context. The tree with, for instance, a topicalized order will be associated with some additional special pragmatic requirements and will be selected when these requirements are fulfilled. Any tree, canonical or non-canonical, associated with the verb will achieve the same update to the conversational record.

Based on the current corpus study, I claim that the update of the conversational record that an utterance with non-canonical syntax can achieve is in fact different than that of canonical syntax. In terms of a SPUD-like model, trees with non-canonical syntax should be associated with not just the assertions of their canonical counterpart and some necessary pragmatic conditions but must also be associated with a richer set of potential assertions that they achieve by virtue of the fact that they can be used to fulfill some additional communicative goals.[2]

In this chapter I present three additional types of goals: ATTENTION MARK-ING, goals of manipulating the saliency of discourse entities referred to in the clause; DISCOURSE RELATION, goals of indicating the syntactic and semantic relations between the clause and the previous discourse structure; and FOCUS

---

oral history corpus. Particular examples are marked with the name of the interview file from which they come.

  [2]By *assertions* here, I do not mean that the additional meaning should be regarded as part of the truth-conditional semantics or entailments of the non-canonical form. I am using the term as it is used in Stone et al. (2001) to mean the update that the use of such a form is intended to effect upon the conversational record. As will be discussed below, such effects might best be considered to have the same status as pragmatic presuppositions in that they can be thought of as conditions that should be fulfilled, and if not, may be added to the conversational record through accommodation (Lewis, 1979). I will leave the precise status of the additional goals posited here as entailments/assertions, semantic presuppositions, or pragmatic presuppositions undetermined here. There is a good deal of debate on defining these categories in the literature (Grice, 1975; Sadock, 1978; Morgan, 1978). My claim is merely that the additional meaning associated with these forms is conventionalized, (to some degree) arbitrary, possible to accommodate, and holds constant when embedded under negation or propositional attitudes. The label that should be assigned to such a phenomenon is left for the reader to determine.

DISAMBIGUATION, goals of limiting the way the discourse model can be updated with the propositional content of the clause. The latter two types of goals, discourse relation and focus disambiguation, will in fact be derived from the most basic additional goal that using these non-canonical forms can achieve, the attention marking goals. [3]

In this model, the choice of a syntactic root clause word order will not be a simple function mapping static discourse conditions to form, where the form is determined by the context. Instead, the choice of word order will be a complex piece of overall text planning and sentence planning, dependent upon how the speaker wants to affect the discourse context.

3.2 Marking attentional structure

The attentional structure of a discourse can be modeled as a stack of focus spaces or a finite cache that contains the individuals—entities, properties, and relations—salient at each point in a discourse (Grosz and Sidner, 1986; Walker, 1996). Although the pragmatic constraints on the use of non-canonical forms in SPUD require certain entities (posets and open propositions) to be salient, in fact the use of the form is often better characterized as licensing an inference that this entity is salient at a particular point in the discourse. Speakers can use a non-canonical form to efficiently indicate which discourse entities are currently salient in order to have the hearers' model of the discourse match their own more closely.

In essence then, static rules like (11), repeated here, must be greatly revised to play a role in a generation model.

(11)   If condition C does not hold, then the use of form f is infelicitous.

Rather than having pragmatic conditions that require that certain individuals (i.e. entities, sets, and propositions) are present in attentional structure in order for the use of a particular form to be felicitous, each form will be associated with a dynamic meaning, such that it will be an instruction to the hearer about how to update her current information state.

The choice of a particular non-canonical form will then correspond to a particular communicative goal fulfilled through the use of the form. This goal will

---

[3] As such, the discourse relation and focus disambiguation goals might be best considered as resulting from conventions of usage (Morgan, 1978), i.e. conventions governing the use of meaning-bearing expressions on certain occasions, for certain purposes. Therefore, although these additional goals can be calculated from the more basic contribution of the form, the attention marking goals, their association with a particular non-canonical form results from the fact that the use of the form has been conventionalized as a strategy to convey this additional meaning. The lack of a need to be consciously calculated is what Morgan refers to as a *short-circuited implicature*.

be to manipulate the attentional structure[4] such that after the use of the form, the hearer will recognize that the speaker believes the relevant individual is salient and has updated his own version of the attentional structure of the discourse accordingly.

The discourse conditions discussed in Chapter 1 still play a role in the choice of form. If they are neither already fulfilled or accommodatable, then the hearer will be unable to successfully update her own version of the conversational record without entering conflicting beliefs.

Based on the conditions in the previous literature, then the use of the forms will have the following corresponding goals, where P is the denotation of the utterance Q used to communicate the goal:

(59) **Canonical order:** COMMUNICATE(P)

(60) **Topicalization:** COMMUNICATE($P \land$ IN-POSET(a,S) $\land$ SALIENT(X)), where a is the referent of the dislocated NP in Q, X is the open proposition created from the tonic stress placement in Q, and S is some contextually-recoverable poset

(61) **Left-dislocation:** COMMUNICATE($P \land$ IN-POSET(a,S)), where a is the referent of the dislocated NP in Q and S is some contextually-recoverable poset

(62) **Wh-Cleft:** COMMUNICATE($P \land$ SALIENT(X)), where X corresponds to the denotation of the presupposition constituent of Q

(63) **It-Cleft:** COMMUNICATE($P \land$ SPEAKER-BELIEVES($\exists x.X(x)$)), where X corresponds to the presupposition constituent of Q

A sample prose translation then of (61) is: uttering a left-dislocation Q will fulfill both the goal COMMUNICATE(P), where P is the truth-conditional semantics of Q, and the additional goal, COMMUNICATE(IN-POSET(a,S)), where a, the referent of the dislocated NP, is a member of the salient (po)set S. The speaker intends for the hearer to update the conversational record with both P and IN-POSET(a, S).

As such, at the point where Q is uttered, IN-POSET(a,S) need not be explicitly part of the current attentional state of the conversational record. It may in fact only be inferable from the conversational record up to the point of Q's utterance. In such a case, the utterance of Q can be interpreted as an instruction to the hearer to take the extra step of making that inference.

In other cases, the additional propositions may be part of the current attentional state; in which case the hearer will probably infer that the speaker must

[4]Utilizing a model like that of Webber (1991) or Grosz and Sidner (1986), I presume that both the current and former states of the attentional structure are recorded as part of the conversational record, such that by affecting the attentional structure, one then affects the conversational record and the discourse model.

have uttered Q with some other communicative goal in mind. Such an inference follows from the hearer's assumption that the speaker will not intend to make uninformative contributions in a cooperative exchange (Grice, 1975).

The speaker's attention-marking goals in both of these situations are closely related to the goals achieved through the use of other informationally-redundant utterances (IRUs) (Walker, 1993; Jordan, 2000). In particular, Walker's Attention IRUs are used with purposes similar to those outlined here. Attention IRUs are used to manipulate the locus of attention of discourse participants by making particular propositions salient.[5] In order to coordinate in creating a discourse model, speakers and hearers must make sure they are attending to the same concepts. Because of the limits on attentional capacity, they cannot attend to everything simultaneously. Therefore, the ability to direct the hearer's attention to particular discourse entities is crucial to successful communication. The use of non-canonical forms to achieve attention-marking goals is one aspect of this ability.

The additional attention-marking communicative goal must not be in conflict with the contents of the conversational record at the point, and in most cases will probably easily follow from information already in the conversational record.[6]

In a system with these complex communicative goals, the choice of form is now based on whether that form would contribute to achieving a communicative goal of the speaker. There is no automatic selection of a form based on the fact that the discourse conditions that license its felicitous use hold. The conditions need to be known to hold or be easily inferred to hold, but this alone does not motivate the choice of the form.

To illustrate this selection process with a very simple constructed example, we will look at how the left-dislocation in (64b) may be generated.

(64)   a.   COMMUNICATE(GRILL($m1,s2$) $\wedge$ IN-POSET($s2$,TYPE-OF-MEAT))

---

[5]Walker's category of CONSEQUENCE IRUs are those IRUs used to "augment the evidence supporting beliefs that certain inferences are licensed." This is similar to the case discussed above where the additional communicative goal's content is not already part of the discourse model and must be accommodated. However, in the latter, the non-canonical form is used to instruct the hearer to draw an inference which corresponds to that additional content. In the case of a Consequence IRU, the purpose of the IRU is to draw some inference which the IRU is evidence for.

[6]If this were not the case, then there would be no reason to match these discourse conditions that hold for all felicitous uses of the non-canonical forms with the use of the form. Nonetheless, the fact that the speaker can manipulate the use of the forms with respect to different levels of saliency of the discourse conditions makes the fact that language learners at some point learn an association between these forms and the conditions (i.e. extra information they communicate) a more difficult problem to explain. See Whitton (2004) for a discussion of examples of topicalizations where the basic discourse conditions do not appear to hold in the context of a diachronic study of topicalization in English.

b. Steak, Myra grills it.

Given the goal in (64a), the speaker will make numerous decisions in realizing the goal as a linguistic form. When selecting a root-clause form, the agent will choose the root clause that will communicate the maximal information present in the goal to be achieved. In this case, choosing a topicalization would express more information but the additional information is not part of the goal to be achieved, and so the left-dislocation form is the best candidate because it will achieve all of the updates in the relevant goal, but no more.[7]

We will now look at some examples where the non-canonical form is used to license the additional inference that the form contributes. For example, in (65), the topicalization licenses the inference that the poset {ASPECT OF PRESS BEING DISCUSSED} is relevant here; i.e. the speaker is only making a statement about a single member of the poset (i.e. *press* means 'news stories') not any others. In (66), the speaker at the point of the first topicalization is indicating the salience of the poset {BLACKS}, i.e. black steelworkers, black intellectuals. The use of the second topicalization introduces an entirely new poset, that of {INTELLECTUALS}, i.e. black intellectuals, white intellectuals, etc. Until the use of the topicalization, the poset {INTELLECTUALS} is not salient.[8]

(65)   Q: Would you discuss your relations with the press and its attitude toward Social Security over the years?
Altmeyer: I don't know what you mean by the press. **The press, insofar as news stories are concerned, I don't think had much influence one way or another.**(SSA, ajaoral2)

(66)   "This is why even on, yeah I guess, sure, on the black thing...I can't really hate the colored fella that's working with me all day. **The black intellectual I got no respect for. The white intellectual I got no use for.** I got no use for the black militant who's gonna scream three hundred years of slavery to me while I'm busting my ass."(Studs Terkel, *Working*)

In addition, we can now explain cases seen in Chapter 1 where the discourse conditions posited in the literature hold, but the use of the form is odd. These will be cases where the most plausible additional communicative goals to be achieved

---

[7]Clearly, the difficulty in this problem then reduces to answering the question, *what goals should an agent want to achieve?* As a linguist, I will perhaps too conveniently leave this question unanswered.

[8]The concept INTELLECTUAL is presumably salient here, but the concept of INTELLECTUAL as a set made up of different subsets of intellectuals presumably is not. This statement applies to the example (65) also. Although the concepts of THE PRESS, and MEANING OF *the press* are salient, the concept that MEANING OF *the press* is a set of possible meanings that the interviewer might intend is only salient upon the use of the topicalization.

from the use of the non-canonical form licensed by those conditions are too difficult to discern. In other words, cases where the hearer cannot easily infer why the
speaker would possibly intend for them to update their version of the conversational record with anything more than the proposition that the utterance denotes.
The following two examples are repeated from Chapter 1.

(15) *(Subject: Re: Need Help Selecting a Laptop)*
      I would recommend a Toshiba. I just bought the 5105-S607 model and
      am quite pleased with it. (comp.sys.laptops, May 2, 2002)

    (15a)   ?? A Toshiba I would recommend.

    (15b)   ?? A Toshiba I would recommend it.

(16) And when I landed, they assigned me to a very, very bad transit camp on
      the other side of the river. And I couldn't stand it. It was muddy, difficult.
      I said, "I'm not going to stay here." I walked out. I was lucky, because
      I was wearing bars on my shoulders, so I could get away with it. And
      I asked around and found out that there were a number of officers and
      other people sleeping at the Grand Hotel, right opposite the race course,
      right in the center of Calcutta. So I went over there. **And I found a bed.**
      And that's where I stayed in Calcutta as long as I was there.
      (http://fas-history.rutgers.edu/oralhistory/addison.htm)

    (16a)   ?? And what I did was find a bed.

The oddness of (15a–15b) can now be explained as uses of non-canonical
forms when achieving their additional communicative goals are unnecessary.
Given the context of the utterance, the membership of *a Toshiba* in the set LAP-
TOPS is salient and assumed. Also assumed is the fact that someone responding
to a message entitled *Need Help Selecting a Laptop*, is likely to be explaining
what they would recommend doing. In such a context a cooperative speaker
will not normally have a goal of communicating either of these propositions, A
TOSHIBA ∈ LAPTOPS or SALIENT(SPEAKER WOULD DO X).[9] In the absence
of normal beliefs (Nunberg, 1978), the hearer will probably attempt to attribute
some additional reasons in order to interpret the speaker's contribution, but this

---

[9]Possibly it would also be rude to expect the hearer in this context to update their
discourse model with either the fact that it is salient that the speaker would do X or the
fact that there is something that the speaker would recommend. This explains why both
the wh-cleft and it-cleft versions of (15) seem presumptuous if not outright infelicitous:

(1)   What I would recommend is a Toshiba.

(2)   It's a Toshiba that I would recommend.

The point here being that there are limits on what one can demand of one's hearer for both
social and cognitive reasons.

additional inferential burden certainly impinges on the quality of such utterances in this context.

The wh-cleft in (16a) is also unnecessary in its redundancy. In the context of an oral history narrative, the implicit question at every point is *What did the speaker do next?* To point out this implicit question must result in the hearer doing some additional work to infer *why* the speaker is pointing this out at this point. There is no particular reason to point it out here and thus the wh-cleft is infelicitous.[10]

3.3   Indicating discourse relations

As discussed in Section 2.2.1, in any text made up of more than a single utterance, the semantic relations that hold between utterances are an additional part of the meaning of the text, which supplement the meaning that each single utterance contributes. These relations, referred to as *coherence, subject matter, rhetorical* or *semantic relations* (Kehler, 2002; Hobbs, 1990; Halliday, 1985; Mann and Thompson, 1988), hold between the denotations of two utterances and include, for example, a temporal relation holding between two events or a contrast relation holding between two propositions. Because the linguistic material comprising a text, its clauses and phrases, can be combined into larger discourse segments, these relations may hold between sets of utterances. These groupings of utterances (or the intentions underlying them) are often modeled as a hierarchical tree structure (Grosz and Sidner, 1986) as discussed in Section 2.2.2.

Speakers can use non-canonical forms to communicate information about both coherence relations and discourse segmentation, as illustrated in Chapter 1 in example (18) and here in (67). In (18), the use of a left-dislocation changes the time interpretation of the event in the second sentence. This can be expressed in terms of the semantic relation between the meaning of the two clauses. The left-dislocation instructs the hearer that the relation between the left-dislocated clause and the previous is not NARRATIVE, but PARALLEL. The second clause is not a subpart of the event described by the first, but an additional separate event. The augmented goals fulfilled by the left-dislocation in this case would be COMMUNICATE($P \land$ PARALLEL(P,Q)), where Q is a previous proposition in the discourse context.[11]

---

[10]In fact, it seems that points in the discourse where it is felicitous to have used a wh-cleft have been to some degree conventionalized. We will examine these types of uses in the next section where the relationship between these non-canonical forms and discourse relations is discussed.

[11]Possibly, any such Q appearing in a communicative goal of this type should be restricted to being on the right-frontier of the discourse; this remains an unresolved empirical issue.

(18) "The first time was 1968, just to get out of my dad's house," she says. **"Second guy, I just met him and didn't have anything else to do.** Didn't work out...Third and fourth times were business partners. We got married for business reasons." (*Philadelphia Inquirer, p. 4-J, 7/3/88*)

In (67), the use of the it-cleft occurs after some intervening discussion of a separate topic marked by the hearer as an aside; it allows the speaker to mark his question as related to the previous discussion because it marks the existential closure of the open proposition, YOU GOT TO MICHIGAN STATE AT TIME T, as his belief. In a tree structure of this discourse, the cleft will correspond to an instruction to "pop" the intervening material between the point p_i at which YOU GOT TO MICHIGAN STATE (AT TIME T) was added to the discourse (in italics in (67)) and the point p_j at which the speaker asks the question. In terms of the segmental structure of the discourse, this can be interpreted as attaching the subsegment corresponding to the utterance of the it-cleft to the discourse tree at a higher node on the right frontier, at p_i instead of the node created at point p_{j-1}, i.e. the utterance of the sentence immediately before the it-clefted question.

(67) G: So for two years, I served as a project officer for grants and contracts in health economics that that agency was funding. I decided to go to academia after that and taught at Michigan State in economics and community medicine. *One thing I should mention is that for my last three months in government, I had been detailed to work on the Price Commission which was a component of the Economic Stabilization program. [Multi-sentence description of work on Price Commission intervenes]* B: **In what year was it that you got to Michigan State?** (SSA, ginsberg)

The augmented goals fulfilled by the it-cleft in (67) are shown in (68), where N is the non-terminal node on the right frontier of the discourse tree sharing the same attentional focus space as P.

(68) COMMUNICATE($P \wedge$ ATTACH(N,P))

These additional goals of communicating information about discourse segmentation and about coherence relations are closely related to the attention-marking goals discussed in the previous section. For both, it is the marking of part of the information communicated in the non-canonical utterance as having a salience that is given (or should be treated as such through accommodation) that allows them to serve these additional goals. We will examine this relationship in more detail in the following two sections.

3.3.1 Discourse segmentation

Because of the necessary discourse conditions that license the use of a non-canonical form, in many cases the open proposition or poset are already part of a focus space that was at the top of the attentional-structure stack previously. In such a case the non-canonical form evokes the old proposition or poset and thus reactivates the salience of that focus space. Because each focus space is associated with a discourse segment in a Grosz and Sidner-type discourse model (Grosz and Sidner, 1986), reactivating the salience of the focus space reactivates the salience of the discourse segment also. The discourse segment associated with the non-canonical utterance can then be taken as a segment that should be attached at the same level as this reactivated discourse segment. The intervening segments should be closed off; in terms of the focus space stack, this means these segments' focus spaces should be popped off the stack.

Example (67) above illustrates this segment-closure/pop use with an it-cleft. Examples (69), (71), (73), and (75) illustrate similar discourse structure effects with the other three forms, topicalization, wh-cleft, and left-dislocation. In these examples, the embedded segment which is "closed off" through the use of the non-canonical form is shown in italics. In each example, the canonical counterpart used in the same context results in a more difficult to understand, less coherent discourse; this shows that the canonical counterpart does not as easily serve the same segment-closure signaling function.

In addition, in both (69) and (71), the topicalization is also an Informationally Redundant Utterance, (IRU); the IRU antecedents are indicated in small caps. As shown in Walker (1993), IRUs can be used to indicate the location of discourse segment boundaries.[12] The status of the non-canonical utterances as IRUs here supports the claim that they are used to close off an embedded segment and pop back to a higher level in the discourse structure by directing the hearer's attention to that higher level. This function is additionally indicated through the use of the cue words *but anyway* in (69) and *so* in (71).

(69)   Do you have anything else on your list that we haven't covered? [...]
        Clark: No, I think we've done it all. There was one–oh, Edward R. Murrow. This was fascinating because I LISTENED EVERY NIGHT TO EDWARD R. MURROW. *Gerrick Utley-the one that's on TV–his father used to be professor at the University of Chicago, and he was on every Sunday night, and I used to listen to him. During World War II, they took five English children to live with them, all during the war.* **But anyway, Edward R. Murrow, I never missed.** So I read that he had come back. (SSA, fbane)

(70)   But anyway, I never missed Edward R. Murrow.

(71)   I didn't go around trying to push my own ideas, but the Republican members frequently would ask me what I thought and I would say what I

---

[12]In fact, several of the examples of attention IRUs discussed in Walker (1993) are topicalizations.

thought. When minor things came up I WOULD SOMETIMES TRY TO PUSH THEM. For example, like Social Security coverage of employee contributions to 401K plans, *which is a minor matter from a policy standpoint. But this was something that was just opening up at that time and it was a big loop hole. So the Commission did recommend that we require these contributions to count for Social Security even though they didn't for income tax purposes.* **So maybe technical things like that I might push,** but I didn't try to push my own views. (SSA, meyersorl)

(72) So maybe I might push technical things like that.

In (73), the segment closed off by the use of the wh-cleft is background material which will make the speaker Failla's explanation of what happened in the 1970s easier to understand. At the end of the parenthetical background segment, in italics here, he returns to the main thread of the present discourse of what changes occurred in the 1970s.

(73) Q: In terms of the role of ORS, I have the impression that in the early years the research that you folks were doing to a considerable degree was driving policy in the Agency. Then somewhere down the road that became less the case, and the research became somehow more abstract and less connected to policy drivers. Is that correct?
Failla: That is correct.
Q: Is it part of the same change that you were just talking about? Or did it happen later?
Failla: I think THAT ALSO STARTED TO HAPPEN IN THE 1970S and the telling blow was in the 1980s. Let me see how I can put this delicately. *Part of the reason for the research was that there's more than one bill being considered in the Congress at any given time. We had a very close relationship with the Hill. A lot of the research was done to show where we should be going—studies about people who were above and below the poverty line, for example. I can't forget Molly Orshansky. Ida, in her wisdom, early on had a woman who was working for her named Molly Orshansky. Oh, what a character–brilliant, and I loved her office. She had steel racks with computer printouts all over the place. Molly developed the poverty index. [discussion of poverty index and its use...] It [=poverty index] was used on the Hill every time we had new pieces of legislation. How many people lived at the poverty level, etc., all came from this kind of an organization. Sometimes findings were not popular.* **I think what happened in the 1970s is somebody felt that people were doing their own thing.** The original founding fathers of the program really had a design of where this program should be when it reached maturity. Obviously the political process doesn't work that way. (SSA, failla)

(74)   I think in the 1970s somebody felt that people were doing their own thing.

In (75), the speaker asks a question using a left-dislocation and, as a result, returns the interviewee to primary topic of that portion of the interview, an outline of his career. The use of the left-dislocation serves the speaker's purposes in multiple ways. It marks the NP *your first job as a field assistant* as not salient enough to serve directly as an NP subject (having not been on the C_f list of the previous utterance at all), as well as marking it as part of a salient set JOBS OF INTERVIEWEE. The fact that the dislocated NP is an unexpected subject and marked as such alerts the hearer that this utterance is part of a different segment than the previous sentence.

(75)   Question: If possible, just your career first.
Mr. Kopelman: Career first, okay. Well I was a field assistant from September '39 to May of '41. *A year before that field assistants had been reclassified to a grade 4. I played a role in bringing this about. I was selected by the union in New York along with a representative of the union in Philadelphia to present the case for reclassification of this position. Bernie Dubin, the Philadelphia representative, and I represented the field organization in negotiations with Mike Shortley who then headed the whole field organization. We had to meet him in Baltimore and I became the leading spokesman and negotiator and was hailed by the field assistants and the union for my success in persuading Mike Shortley that our jobs deserved upward reclassification. But, in May of '41 I was jumped two grades over the heads of men with a lot more seniority than I by Hugh McKenna, who was the man who originally hired me and was then the regional representative of what was then called the Bureau of Old-Age and Survivors Insurance.*
Question: That was in New York, wasn't it?
Mr. Kopelman: That's the SSA in New York, right. He picked me over men with a great deal more seniority than I, and I was made administrative assistant ("third man" was the unofficial title) of the Borough Hall Field office, which was then called Brooklyn I. It was one of the three largest offices in the New York area, the other two were the Midtown and Downtown Field Offices.
Question: **When you began in '39, your first job then as a field assistant, was it in New York?**
Mr. Kopelman: Yes, it was as a field assistant in New York. (SSA, dkoral)

(76)   When you began in '39, was your first job as a field assistant in New York?

Actually, however, it is not entirely clear in this example, where in terms of a discourse structure, the interviewer's question should be attached. Possibly, it could be treated as a follow-up to Mr. Kopelman's statement *I was a field assistant from September '39 to May of '41.* In addition, it might be better thought of as a way to close off the smaller segment beginning with *But, in May of '41 I was jumped two grades over the heads of men with a lot more seniority than I by Hugh McKenna* and adjoining as this statement's sibling.

The ambiguity here illustrates the inherent complexity of the task of shared management of the construction of a discourse structure between multiple discourse participants. Attachment ambiguity is a pervasive problem for the concept of parsing a set of discourse segments into a hierarchical structure. The non-canonical syntactic forms here can to some degree assist in resolving this ambiguity. Although we have shown evidence for their role in this process here, we will not propose a specific mechanism for how this takes place.

One possibility is that the mechanism used is an instance of a more general psychological process of manipulation of the locus of attention. This approach is used in Walker (1993) to explain the role of IRUs in discourse. Walker finds evidence for both cognitive and conventional functions of Attention IRUs in indicating discourse segment boundaries and making particular propositions salient. Speakers may rely on particular conventions to convey instructions on how to augment the discourse structure, or hearers might automatically retrieve previously salient material (i.e. the content of the IRU), and the salience of entities and propositions related to this material will also have elevated degrees of salience.

From a computational point of view where one actually wants to formalize the role of these forms for use in a natural language understanding and generation system, associating each of these forms with an entirely conventionalized meaning might be the most practical approach. Here, each form would have, as a basic part of the meaning that it could communicate, an instruction, like (68), for attaching it to the discourse at a particular node, as suggested above for the example in (67), both repeated here.

(67)   G: So for two years, I served as a project officer for grants and contracts in health economics that that agency was funding. I decided to go to academia after that and taught at Michigan State in economics and community medicine. *One thing I should mention is that for my last three months in government, I had been detailed to work on the Price Commission which was a component of the Economic Stabilization program. [Multi-sentence description of work on Price Commission intervenes]*
B: **In what year was it that you got to Michigan State?** (SSA, ginsberg)

(68)   COMMUNICATE($P \wedge$ ATTACH-AT(P, N)), where N is a non-terminal node on the right frontier of the discourse tree

Then, because we would not want N to remain a free variable, its value would somehow be bound to the location in the discourse structure of the focus space containing the 'old' material in the utterance. For example, in (67), the location in the discourse structure of the content of *(I) taught at Michigan State in economics and community medicine* will be the point N where *In what year was it that you got to Michigan State* should be attached. At that point, N, the it-cleft's presupposed complement clause G GOT TO MICHIGAN STATE AT TIME T was at the top of the focus stack and salient.

At first glance, it might appear that this problem would be quite trivial from a generation point of view because one could simply specify the identity of the non-terminal node N. For understanding, however, we would need to figure out a way to resolve this variable.[13] But in fact, even from a generation perspective, if we do not know how the attachment resolution proceeds at the understanding end, then we cannot be sure that any goal will be fulfilled in using it. In other words, there is no problem that is interesting purely from either a generation or an understanding perspective, because there is little point in generating linguistic material whose meaning and effect on the hearer is not understood. This is essentially the same claim that was argued for in Section 2.4.5 that generation systems should be arranging constituents (and thereby words) in particular orders because it is known that there is a reliable association between those orders and the aspects of meaning and context to be communicated.

To sum up this section then, the claim here is that non-canonical syntactic forms can serve an additional communicative goals related to discourse structure. Specifically, this is a goal of instructing the hearer to attach the utterance's semantic content to a node on the right frontier of the discourse structure higher than the leaf node, in order to close off embedded segments and continue a previously unfinished segment. Presumably, there must be an association between this non-leaf node and the segment in which the "old" content of the non-canonical utterance was salient. The details of how hearers infer this additional goal from a basic communicative goal, like those presented in Section 3.2, remain, however, for future work.

3.3.2 Coherence relations

The second important communicative goal related to discourse-level relations is that of communicating information about the coherence relation between the content of the non-canonical utterance and some other proposition (or propositions) in the conversational record.

The coherence relation-type goals are related to the attention-marking goals in two ways. First, the use of a non-canonical form communicates that some aspect of the information communicated in the proposition is already salient.[14] In

---

[13]For example there might be multiple parts of P that are old, i.e a salient poset and an open proposition, which were salient at conflicting times, or a single part may have been salient at multiple times.

[14]That is, it is either actually salient or its status as salient should be accommodated by

the case of left-dislocations and topicalizations, it is the existence of a poset that is salient; in the case of topicalizations and wh-clefts, it is the status of an open proposition; for it-clefts, the information communicated is that some aspect of the information communicated is a known fact, in particular the existential closure of the open proposition. This use of "old" material helps overrule the default coherence relation of CONTIGUITY because it makes a contiguity relation less likely. Secondly, the use of old material and a structured proposition enhances the hearer's interpretation of a relation of RESEMBLANCE.

As discussed in Section 2.2.1, a CONTIGUITY relation is essentially the basic relation that makes up a narrative. The utterances in the most prototypical narrative will describe a sequence of events that happen in the same sequence as that of the utterances used to describe them. Labov (1997) claims that the events should be causally related and lead up to a MOST REPORTABLE EVENT. Kehler (2002), following Hobbs (1990), claims that the eventualities should be centered around a system of entities, and that each event described should correspond to a change of state for that system.

In the simplest case then, we can think of a narrative as a sequence of clauses that describe the events that happen to some main character. Each clause adds some additional new point of information about what happens (or happened) to that character. In such a case, the grammatical subject refers to that main character, and the predicate adds the new information, an event in which the main character is an argument.[15] By identifying an entity a referred to in utterance U_j as the same entity referred to in U_i and by identifying the time of the event referred to by U_j, as following the time of the event in U_i (among other things) a hearer will most likely infer that U_i and U_j are contiguous. And, of course, the hearer may use extralinguistic knowledge about how types of events are related to each other to infer that U_i and U_j are contiguous and therefore identify the anaphoric relationships between the entities and times in the two utterances.

In contrast, inferring a RESEMBLANCE relation between two utterances depends on very different type of information, in particular on the identification of "old" information. As laid out in Section 2.2.1, in order to establish a resemblance relation, the hearer has to identify the common relation R that will relate two propositions and also the number and identity of their arguments, and which arguments correspond to each other (Kehler, 2002). Resemblance relations include PARALLEL, CONTRAST, EXEMPLIFICATION, GENERALIZATION, EXCEPTION, and ELABORATION.

---

the hearer.

[15]This pattern of reference and predication is supported by evidence from pronoun resolution preferences. The preference for resolving pronouns to the previous sentence's subject is correlated with there being a CONTIGUITY relation between the two sentences. When a PARALLEL relation holds, this preference does not hold, as discussed in Kehler (2002, 1997); Kameyama (1996).

In all of the non-canonical forms considered here, the more basic attention-marking communicative goals are ones that will enhance the inference of a resemblance relation and detract from inferring a relation of narration. This is for two reasons. First, given the use of the non-canonical form N, the speaker is communicating that something about the propositional content is already salient; that is, the entire proposition is not going to add a fully new piece of information to the discourse.[16] In establishing a narrative relation, the hearer tries to interpret the meaning of the utterance as a description of some new event in which the current topic/center-of-attention plays a main role which can be added to the discourse model. A non-canonical form, however, is not going to be expressing a new event; some of the material it contains is old. In particular, at least one of the relations in its denotation is not going to be a new addition to the discourse model. This relation may either be the one expressed by the main predication in the sentence, or it may be the relevant poset relation, or both. In such a case, the utterance expressing this old information is not suitable for a coherence relation of contiguity.[17]

The second reason that the use of a non-canonical form enhances the inference of a resemblance relation is that because the information in the utterance is partly old, the process of identifying what that common relation R is is made easier.[18] In wh-clefts, it-clefts, and topicalizations, the form itself structures the information in such a way that it marks part of the proposition as the given (or believed closure of) open proposition and part as the instantiation/identity of a particular variable. In the case of topicalizations and left-dislocations, the form identifies which entity is in a poset relation to another set of entities.

Both of these types of structuring, which I will refer to as predication structure and poset structure, respectively, help the hearer in the task that is necessary to identify a resemblance relation. The resemblance relation must hold between two propositions, P_1 and P_2, whose main predicates are either identical ($R_1 = R_2$) or negated ($R_1 = \bar{R}_2$) versions of each other and thus have the same number of arguments as each other.[19] Predication structuring helps the hearer

---

[16]By which I mean a new piece of information about possibly discourse- or hearer-old entities.

[17]In the simplest case, this is true. Of course, as Kehler and others point out, there are cases where a hearer may plausibly infer more than a single coherence relation between two utterances; hence, there are certainly context and utterance pairings where either or both a contiguity and a resemblance relation could be intended to be inferred. For the purposes of the present exposition such complex cases will be ignored.

[18]This use of a non-canonical form to structure the presentation of a proposition such that the recovery of a common relation underlying the denotation of the proposition described here is identical to the process as originally described for gapping in Levin and Prince (1986).

[19]The equalities presented here are also a great simplification. As Kehler (2002) ex-

identify that the relation itself is old. In addition, it marks which argument should be compared with the argument in the other proposition; an argument in a focus position can only be the paired element for another argument in a focus position. The poset structuring also assists in argument identification; two arguments are in parallel positions only if they are both members of the same poset.

In constructed examples like (77a) of the type usually used to illustrate coherence relations, it is easily discernible which arguments and predications are related (*me* and *me*, *hot dogs* and *not-dogs*, *bring to party* and *leave home*) and that the coherence relation between the two sentences is one of contrast with no help from syntax or prosody.

(77) a. I brought hot dogs to the party.
         I left the not-dogs at home.

      b. CONTRAST ((BRING(ME, HOT DOGS, PARTY)),(LEAVE(ME, NOT-DOGS, HOME)))

In naturally-occurring discourse, things are often more complex. Identifying that the proposition the speaker is adding to the discourse stands in a resemblance relation with another proposition may be difficult. The use of a non-canonical form can facilitate the hearer's identification. This is illustrated in (78) where the use of the topicalization makes it clear that the speaker's statement is PARALLEL to his commentary about Jessie Lynn.

(78) a. But his ARRs [Assistant Regional Representatives] were something else again. I don't think some of them are alive today. But, Jessie Lynn was from Beltbuckle, Tennessee. He used to put on a accent about being a country boy. **Irv Allen, I remember particularly.** He was a nice guy. (SSA, simermeyer)

      b. ?? I remember Irv Allen particularly.

In the canonical equivalent, even with the tonic stress on *Allen*, the sentence is an incoherent continuation to the discourse. The hearer will be lead to ask

---

plains, the actual relations (predications) in the propositions P_1 and P_2 may only be similar to each other, that is they are both variants of the single common relation R. For example, in identifying the PARALLEL relation between the utterances in (1), the hearer needs to realize that the common relation in question is PREPARE FOR VISITORS.

(1) The visitors were to arrive the next day. Max vacuumed. Mike gave the dog a bath.

As such, it is the number of arguments of PREPARE FOR VISITORS that must be the same, not the number of arguments of the particular instantiation in each propositional argument in the relation. The limits of the generality of the common relation, that is how closely related the parallel predicates must be, are important but cannot be pursued here.

how REMEMBER (SPEAKER, IRV ALLEN) fits with the previous text. Because of the topicalization however, the utterance also contributes the proposition IN-POSET(IRV ALLEN, S) and SALIENT (REMEMBER (SPEAKER, IRV ALLEN, X DEGREE).[20] The most plausible currently salient poset is presumably the set {ARRs}. With a salient open proposition, the hearer can infer then that the issue *to what degree the speaker remembers members of the poset, the ARRs*, is "on the table." This statement then is likely to be in some resemblance relation with propositions added to the discourse earlier. In this case the relation can be either an EXEMPLIFICATION with the utterance *But his ARRs were something else again* or a PARALLEL with the implicit proposition *I remember Jessie Lynn well (enough to make statements about him)*, where *Jessie Lynn* refers to the previously discussed member of the set of ARRs. What might otherwise have been a very difficult to understand utterance about a hearer-new, discourse-new entity can be processed and attached to the discourse with little difficulty.

Identifying which arguments should be paired with which other arguments may also be difficult. The additional communicative goal of the non-canonical form, i.e. the basic discourse conditions, once again can assist with this. This is illustrated in (79). Because of the use of the left-dislocation, the hearer knows that the referent of *a lot of the doctors* is in a salient poset. By identifying the set {PROFESSIONAL PEOPLE} as that poset, the hearer can realize that the information being added about *a lot of the doctors* is going to be in a resemblance relation of EXEMPLIFICATION to the previous statement about professional people in general, that they began to think of themselves as disabled.

(79) a. During the Depression an awful lot of people began to think of them-selves as disabled, especially professional people, who depended on clients whose business was on a cash basis–there was no credit, this was a universe without credit cards. **A lot of the doctors, they were doing an awful lot of charity work.** They couldn't support them-selves. They'd have a little heart attack. They'd have disability in-surance. They went on the insurance company rolls. A lot of doctors had disability insurance and a lot of others too. A lot of the insurance companies stopped underwriting disability insurance. They couldn't afford it.

b. A lot of the doctors were doing an awful lot of charity work.

Without the left-dislocation, being able to identify the pairing relationship between professional people and doctors would be quite difficult here. A pre-ferred interpretation of the canonical sentence would be that the doctors were

---

[20] Alternatively, because of the ambiguity of prosody focus marking on a verb phrase in this case, the salient open proposition may also be X (SPEAKER, IRV ALLEN), where X is some predicate.

doing charity work for professional people who had no credit cards. This would still have a relationship with the previous discourse, but it is likely to have been in a CAUSE-EFFECT relation with only the previous two utterances. The proposition denoted by *this was a universe without credit cards* would be in a cause-effect relationship with the effect denoted by *the doctors were doing an awful lot of charity work*. Because of the left-dislocation, the cause-effect relationship holds, but in addition, a resemblance relationship with the proposition *people began to think of themselves as disabled* holds too.

In the previous section, we discussed how the basic communicative goals of non-canonical syntactic forms allow hearers to infer additional goals about where to attach utterances to the discourse structure but left the detail mechanisms of the inference process for future work. Here too we will not provide an explanation of how and where particular relations can be inferred from the use of a non-canonical syntactic form. Despite much discussion in the literature, the problem of how human language users resolve coherence relations remains unsolved. We have argued here that the use of non-canonical syntax can play a crucial role in this resolution and suggested reasons for why this is so. The problem of coherence relation resolution itself, however, is beyond the scope of the current project.

Types of resemblance relations

The set of resemblance relations given in Kehler (2002) are all possible resemblance relations for the forms of interest here, PARALLEL, CONTRAST, EXEMPLIFICATION, GENERALIZATION, EXCEPTION, and ELABORATION. Using Kehler's notation, for all of these relations, there is a subsuming relation R that holds of the two relations, R_1 and R_2, whose resemblance is to be inferred. Relations R_1 and R_2 each have as arguments a set of entities $a_1, ...a_n$ and $b_1, ...b_n$, respectively. These two sets of corresponding entities are related by what Kehler terms a *property vector*, q, where each q_i is the common property relating a_i and b_i. In the case of the relations PARALLEL and CONTRAST, the corresponding entities will be members of the same poset (e.g. *Fido* and *Rex*); the corresponding relations, R_1 and R_2 will also be in a poset relationship. In the case of EXEMPLIFICATION, GENERALIZATION and EXCEPTION, the corresponding entities will be in a subset-superset relationship; this too means that they will be members of the same poset (e.g. *Fido* and *all dogs*). For these latter relations, the corresponding relations will also be in a poset relationship.[21] Because all of these relations involve poset membership, all of them are possible resemblance relations that are found with left-dislocations and topicalizations.

---

[21]The ELABORATION relation is a special case where the corresponding entities a_i and b_i must in fact be identical. Identity too is a possible poset relation because a partially-ordered set relation is reflexive.

The following examples illustrate each:

(80)   EXEMPLIFICATION: It worried us at the time because everything worried us. We were very insecure. The benefits hadn't started. This was in the late '30s, and as a result we were on trial. **The cost of administration, for example–nobody seemed to get on that,** but they could have really taken us apart on that because the cost of administration of old age benefits before anything except a small lump sum of benefits were paid probably did exceed the benefits. (SSA, ajaoral2)

(81)   EXCEPTION: I think we were fortunate in the kind of leadership we had, generally. **Some of them, as you know, I'm not enthused about,** but generally speaking, the quality of our leadership was quite high. (SSA, davidkoral)

(82)   GENERALIZATION: When I came back from my surgery I found that the job had been filled by Helen from Payroll. I went in to see Mr. Tyssowski, Joseph Tyssowski. He was a tough individual, but I enjoyed working with him. When he said it was black it was black, if he said it was white it was white. I liked Mr. Tyssowski, and I went in to speak with him. "Why was I passed over?" And he said, "Well, Helen had so many years in statistics." I was able to better it. **Everything he said about Helen, I could better,** in fact, to the point where her name was in a statistical book, mine was too, because when I worked at the Army Chemical Corp I helped the G.I.s on a study, and they put my name in as being one of the assistants. (SSA, lsoral)

(83)   PARALLEL: And she [=Ellen Woodward] was like a best friend. **Some of my friends–like Ruth Appleby who I told you about who died in 1996-I considered best friends.** And I would say Ellen Woodward was my best friend. (SSA, fbane)

(84)   CONTRAST: We were not allowed to make allowance decisions, they didn't trust us. They were afraid we'd be too liberal. **And the states, Congress figured they'd be careful.** Little did they know. (SSA, hboral)

The given open proposition of the wh-cleft and the known existential closure of the open proposition of the it-cleft make both of these forms well-suited for expression the resemblance relations of CONTRAST:

(85)   Were you aware beforehand–you and Secretary Perkins–of how antagonistic the AMA leadership would be to Drs. Sydenstricker and Falk. Or did this come as a surprise to you? And am I correct that the opposition to the medical advisory committee seemed to be focused on these two individuals?

Altmeyer: If it hadn't been Sydenstricker and Falk, it might have been somebody else that they would focus on. **What came as a surprise was that the AMA leadership was so strongly antagonistic to the idea of considering a health insurance program.** (SSA, ajaoral3)

(86)   As a matter of fact, you probably recall that it was started in Germany in the late 19th century as an antidote for socialism by Bismarck. Under socialism there would be no need for social insurance. **It's in a system of free enterprise, competitive private enterprise, production for a market that social insurance becomes necessary for the protection of the individual.** (SSA, biggeoral)

Both it-clefts and wh-clefts can also be used to express parallel relations, as in the following examples:

(87)   I think it is inevitable that if it is true that 25 years from now the confidence of this institution continues to be lower and lower and lower and more people become more and more skeptical, then there will be radical change to the system, because a big institution such as this needs to have broad-based legitimacy across generations and income groups over time. So there needs to be broad-based legitimacy at a fundamental level, and that is why it is so important that we're not sitting here 25 years from now, or 35 years from now on the verge of the next 1983 situation which would be a lot tougher than 1983 in terms of shortfalls. **If we're sitting here 35 years from now, it won't just be your kids, it'll be their kids and it could even be their kids that have the same kind of doubts.** (SSA, apfeloral)

(88)   Q: What about the Committee on Economic Security? Do you have any impressions of the Committee's work? It's very difficult for somebody who comes at it from a historian's point of view being able to read through documents that were published after the fact and historical materials now available...
Mulliner: Have you seen Ed Witte's publication...?
Q: Yes, I have. But I'd like to evoke the impressions of somebody who was an outsider...
Mulliner: I wasn't close enough to be able to do that for you. Wilbur Cohen could do it for you. Frank Bane was on one of those committees, he could do it for you.
Q: **But what I'm looking for too is the impressions of somebody who was an interested bystander, who wasn't on the inside.** What were the impressions from the outside of what was going on? (SSA, mulliner2)

The use of these forms in parallel relations seems more common for wh-clefts than for it-clefts. This may be related to the so-called 'uniqueness presupposition' of it-clefts (Delin, 1992), which would presumably make them better suited for a resemblance relation where a contrasting relation *p* holds of the focused entity in the it-cleft, but does not hold of the entity in the related predication.[22]

The final type of resemblance relation that appears frequently with one of these non-canonical forms is ELABORATION. The form used to communicate this relation is the wh-cleft. Kehler describes elaborations as restatements where the particular relation and entities involved are the same, but described from a different perspective or at a different level of detail. The hearer must infer the identity of the event and entities being described in the two segments related by ELABORATION. In the following example (89), the wh-cleft expresses a more detailed version of the proposition presupposed by the previous statement *she knew there was a problem out there*.

(89)   But she knew THERE WAS A PROBLEM OUT THERE. There was a GAO report, from New York I think, that showed that the phones weren't getting answered, that people were getting busy signals. Most of us, in our own personal life who had friends that knew that we worked for Social Security, they would ask us "could you get me a local number. I can't get through to this Teleservice Center. I can't reach them." **What was going on out there was that when people got to know the local DO's phone number they changed the number.** Because they didn't want people to call. (SSA, failla)

The wh-cleft is well suited to this function because it marks an open proposition as salient and something the hearer should be attending to. As discussed above, from this the hearer can infer that the speaker is not making a statement about an entirely new event, but rather re-explaining the same event at a different level of detail. This new level of detail will contribute new information to the conversational record, but with the use of a wh-cleft expressing an elaboration relation, the hearer will have an easier time integrating and organizing that information. Often, re-explaining an event in more detail requires multiple clauses. In this case, the wh-cleft often serves to begin this new embedded segment; as such it can be regarded as a marker of a PUSH discourse move. This move is an instruction to the hearer to add a new focus space to the top of the attentional stack and begin an embedded segment in the discourse structure.

In addition, as discussed above in the attention-marking section, wh-clefts can be used to make it known that a speaker regards a particular open proposition as salient, and that the hearer is licensed in inferring from the previous discourse that a particular open proposition is relevant. This is illustrated in (90). Here, the speaker is discussing an administrative problem. The fact that a solution to

---

[22]In fact, the uniqueness presupposition has been posited for all types of clefts in English, it-clefts, wh-clefts, and reverse wh-clefts, so in fact, the relative lack of it-clefts used for PARALLEL may very well be due to some other cause.

the problem was needed is only implicit. In such a case, the ELABORATION will not hold with the content of any particular prior utterance, but instead it will hold with a proposition that the speaker expects the hearer to have inferred from the prior discourse.

(90)   My participation in those decisions was the greater because the Board in these years never really had confidence in the people who successfully headed that Bureau. And as a consequence they were really relying on the Executive Director's Office, of which I was part, to exercise a close surveillance and give them some assurance that things were going the way they should go. That is an unfortunate administrative situation whenever it exists. **Now, what was needed was someone in the Bureau Director's job who had the confidence of the Board,** and that was lacking for that period of years. (SSA, corsonoral)

In fact, sometimes it is only the wh-cleft alone that can mark this ELABORATION relation. Even though the canonical equivalent is identical in its truth conditions, inferring an elaboration relation only happens when the wh-cleft with its given wh-clause is used. In (91), the use of a wh-cleft yields an interpretation of the clause as stating a conclusion that the speaker has been leading up to; the wh-cleft is an IRU at this point. Without the wh-cleft, the utterance is most naturally interpreted as a new piece of information; given the context, the hearer knows this is not of course the case; hence, the canonical is bizarre here.

(91)   a.   Q: So at this point that you're talking about now, Svahn has not been confirmed as Commissioner, is that correct? This is a transition team.
Failla: It was a transition team. In fact, we didn't know he was going to be Commissioner, the scuttlebutt was that one of them would be Undersecretary, Dave Swope or Jack Svahn, and one of them would be Commissioner; but nobody knew at that point which way it was going to end up . **And eventually what happened was that Swope became the Undersecretary and Svahn became the Commissioner.** (SSA, failla)

   b.   And eventually Swope became the Undersecretary and Svahn became the Commissioner.

Because the wh-cleft is a signal of an elaboration, it will often only be a single detail in the more detailed account. As such it becomes the marker of the beginning of an entire new segment of the discourse. In such a case, the presupposition part of the clause should really be equated with multiple clauses, not just the single clause that follows it, as seen in the following two examples:

(92)   So my first question is was that [=starting the Health Care Financing Administration] your idea?

Califano: Yes. **What happened was after I was appointed, I started.** I did two things from Christmastime until January 20th, which was to focus on people. I was interviewing maybe 10, 15 people a day and looking at the way HEW was organized: where the money was, where the people were, what the functions were. We put together a series of charts that started with the department and then took each piece of the department. (SSA, califano)

(93)   Our job was to do all of the administrative stuff for ORS. **What that meant was you did the budget.** You did all of the personnel work. You wrote new job descriptions, and you set up new organizational structures, and you went to the Civil Service Commission when we identified somebody at the university we wanted to pick up. (SSA, failla)

This use has been conventionalized to the extent that in some cases, the presupposition and the focus components can not actually be combined into a canonical equivalent, as in (94)

(94)   Levine: I came back to BHI. And they gave me a job which involved the teaching physicians. Do you know about teaching physicians?
Q: I know what they are, but I don't know what we had to do.
Levine: They were just taking money and not doing anything. They were really strong. **What they would do was the teaching physician would go into a hospital, like a county with all-charity patients.** The physician would put his name on the form; he is responsible for this patient. Dr. Jones never saw the patient. The resident or an intern saw the patient. And then they would file a claim for every day of service. But Dr. Jones never saw the patient. (SSA, ml)

We can see further evidence of the non-OCCASION nature of many wh-clefts because they do not carry an inference of the passage of time, as illustrated in example (95).[23] Here, the best paraphrase of the wh-cleft is a canonical sentence with past perfect tense. The simple past equivalent makes it seem as if the forgetting is taking place after the calling. The wh-cleft and the perfect tense order the forgetting before the calling.

---

[23]This example might be best classified, along with several other wh-cleft examples as an incidence of CAUSE-EFFECT in particular EXPLANATION. The difference between the explanation and elaboration relations is somewhat fuzzy. One subtle difference is that of temporal progression. In an explanation relation, there should be a temporal juncture, a la Labov (1997), between the the explanation segment and the effect segment. In elaboration, there should be no temporal juncture between the two segments. In some cases, however, it can be difficult to decide whether a temporal juncture holds.

(95) a. There are all sorts of other things concerning the early days of HCFA
that are fascinating, including a telephone call to John Brademus
who was on his honeymoon in Paris. Califano wanted to tell him
about it and so he called him, **but what he forgot was that it was
four o'clock in the morning in Paris.** (SSA, mcfee)

   b. (But) He had forgotten that it was four o'clock in the morning in
Paris.

   c. But he forgot that it was four o'clock in the morning in Paris.

As noted in both Labov (1997) and Kehler (2002), the use of perfect tense is
not compatible with the semantics of narrative (bound) clauses. Its similarity in
meaning here with the wh-cleft supports the claim that this non-canonical form
is used to indicate that a narrative relation should not be inferred.

This canceling of the 'forward' movement of time also seems to be a possibility with the use of topicalizations. Webber (1988) illustrates the fact that a
sequence of simple past tenses can allow the 'backward' movement of time with
a topicalization, as in (96) (Webber's 11a-b):

(96) a. For an encore, John played the "Moonlight Sonata."

   b. The opening movement he took rather tentatively, but then...

Finding a naturally-occurring example of this tense effect however is not possible
because topicalizations are rarely used in contexts where the semantics are such
that the possibility of having a temporal juncture even occurs.

3.4   Disambiguating focus structure

In the previous two sections, we have seen that non-canonical forms can manipulate the attentional structure and the discourse structure through the type of
communicative goals that their use can fulfill. Now we will look at a third and
final type of communicative function that these forms serve, the disambiguation
of information-structural focus.

As discussed in Section 2.3.2, in English, focus-ground structure correlates
significantly with the prosodic effects of duration and amplitude (Hockey, 1998).
The information structure focus marks the part of an utterance which would correspond to the instantiation of the missing constituent in a wh-question with that
utterance as the answer (Gussenhoven, 1984; Vallduví, 1990a). In other words,
focus-ground structure is relative to an implicit question that the utterance is answering (van Kuppevelt, 1995); (Roberts, 1998);(McNally, 1998).

Although speakers must prosodically mark focus-ground structure on *every*
utterance, this prosodic focus marking is often ambiguous because a single sentence final pitch accent may potentially correspond to multiple focus structures
(Ladd, 1996). In addition, depending on its heaviness, even a single constituent

may be realized with multiple pitch accents. How these additional pitch accents effect focus-ground partitioning is still a matter of debate.[24]

Because of the more basic communicative goals they are used with, the non-canonical forms that contribute information about how the proposition is structured—topicalizations, wh-clefts, and it-clefts—are also suited to the additional goal of marking focus-ground partitioning unambiguously and independently of an utterance's prosodic form. This allows them to be used in contexts where they contribute crucially to the information structure of the sentence. Using one of these forms can also allow the speaker to move constituents into and out of the focus and ground parts of an utterance—in some cases to avoid presuppositional effects and in other cases to create them. We will look at examples of all of these functions.

Wh-clefts are useful in disambiguating the focus-ground partitioning of an utterance, particularly when it has large constituents which receive multiple pitch accents. For example, in (97a) the focused object NP can be realized with multiple prosodic phrases each with its own primary accent; its canonical counterpart in (97b) would at the least be ambiguous with respect to whether the object or the entire VP were in focus (Ladd, 1996).

(97)   a.   There are those that would argue that **what we need is a quick and dirty decision at the state level based upon whatever information that was to come in the door**...(SSA, apfeloral)

b.   There are those that would argue that we [$_{VP}$ need [$_{NP}$ a quick and dirty decision at the state level based upon whatever information that was to come in the door.]]

The prosodic structure of this example is further complicated by the fact that the wh-cleft is doubly-embedded inside a complement clause in a relative clause. Broad focus on an utterance like this one could in fact span 39 syllables from the highest VP to the end of the most embedded clause. Although it would be difficult to argue for what the exact focus-ground structure in a complex sentence like this one is, it is clear that whatever it is, prosody will not do much to rule out alternative structures here. The wh-cleft however can clearly mark that the NP *a quick and dirty decision...* is not given, and the subject and verb of that clause are.

Wh-clefts are also useful for placing large constituents which would normally have to be segmented into focus and ground themselves, such as entire propositions, into the focus slot, as in (98).

(98)   Essentially what happened was that they agreed to go ahead and do this sometime in March. (SSA, fullert)

---

[24]See Ladd (1996) and Steedman (2000) for discussion.

The focus of the wh-cleft can also allow the speaker to shift material that should not be interpreted as given or presupposed into a position where it cannot be. In (99), the use of the wh-cleft, with the proposition THAT I WOULDN'T MAKE IT in the non-presupposed focus position, prevents the (bizarre) inference, that the 87-year-old writer did *not* make it. This inference is triggered in the canonical and extraposed versions in (99b)–(99c).

(99)   a. I've courted death ever since I was six. I was an asthmatic child
          [...] That plus a couple of bouts with mastoiditis, head swathed in
          bandages made my awakening the next morning a matter touch and
          go. **What troubled me was not that I wouldn't make it,** but that I
          would no longer enjoy the whimsical care of my father and my two
          brothers." (Studs Terkel, *Will the circle be unbroken?*)

       b. That I wouldn't make it didn't trouble me.

       c. It didn't trouble me that I wouldn't make it.

Using clefted forms can also allow the speaker to communicate the opposite goal, namely that the forms can allow presupposed material to escape a position where the default broad focus intonation would mark them with an inappropriate information status. In (100a), the speaker can make the distinction between just figuring out one of several items important to the beneficiaries, and figuring out *the* important thing. With the wh-cleft, the entire VP can escape focushood. Even a prosodic focus on *the exempt amount* does not yield quite the same interpretation here. Similarly, in (101a), the speaker is only indicating that his lack of awareness is with respect to the instantiation of the variable X as Bryce Stewart in the open proposition X WAS THE FOCAL POINT OF THIS, not a lack of awareness of the entire embedded proposition.

(100) a. I ascertained, and I honest to gosh don't think anybody has moved
          that research much further forward, that **what was really important
          to the beneficiaries was the exempt amount,** that is, how much
          they can earn without losing any benefits. (SSA, ksander)

       b. I ascertained that the exempt amount was really important to the ben-
          eficiaries.

(101) a. Q: **Well, I wasn't aware that it was Bryce Stewart who was the
          focal point of this.** I was under the impression that there were sev-
          eral people who were in opposition to the federal-state cooperative.
          (SSA, ajaoral1)

       b. I wasn't aware that Bryce Stewart was the focal point of this.

This ability to escape the scope of a higher verb is also illustrated, in (17), repeated from above. Without the it-cleft the hearer would conclude the speaker was uncertain about whether the president was at the conference. With the it-cleft, however, the uncertainty can only be about the cause of the president's absence because the remainder of the clause is marked as presupposed.

(17)   The conference was to take place in November. [...] We managed to bring it off in November—just when the President had his gall bladder surgery. **I think it was his gall bladder surgery that kept him from being there,** but the thing came off OK. (SSA, lee)

   (17a) I think his gall bladder surgery kept him from being there.

Topicalizations too allow a speaker to disambiguate what prosodic form alone could not communicate. The default broad focus pattern for English has a weak-strong phrasing on the verb and object, as in (102), with the DTE for the entire intonational phrase on the object. Whenever the object is deaccented, it must be semantically "light," i.e. either given or the type of NP that is deaccented in English (indefinite pronouns, words like *man, thing, stuff*, non-contrastive personal pronouns), as in (103).

(102) $[\text{Roberta}]_w$ $[[\text{bought}]_w$ $[\text{a CAR}]_s]_s$

(103) $[\text{Roberta}]_w$ $[[\text{BOUGHT}]_s$ $[\text{one}]_w]_s$

As such, an object, such as the generic NP *fish*, can only be deaccented when narrow focus is wanted on the verb, as in (104). When there is a pitch accent on the object, the interpretation can only be one with narrow or broad focus on the object. In a short sentence like *They eat fish*, even with a pitch accent on the verb, as shown in (105)—no matter what type or strength of pitch accent it is—if there is a pitch accent on the object, only that final pitch accent can affect the prosodic phrasing, as shown in the metrical structure in (106). With two pitch accents on the VP, the interpretation can only be broad focus; with one, either the verb or the object must be weak.

(104) $[[\text{They}_s]_w$ $[\text{EAT}_s$ $\text{fish}_w]_s]$

(105)   They eat fish
            H* H*-LL%

(106) $[[\text{They}_s]_w$ $[\text{eat}_w$ $\text{FISH}_s]_s]$

In a topicalized sentence, however, the object and the verb can be in separate intermediate phrases; the object can be a DTE at a more embedded level of metrical structure. And so, a "double" focus with both the verb and the object being accented is possible. The verb's accent marks the verb's status as the information structure focus; the object's accent, like that in (107), marks the object's membership in a poset (Pierrehumbert and Hirschberg, 1990).

(107)   Fish,   they eat
            (L+)H*   H*-LL%

(108) [[Fish$_s$]$_w$ [they$_w$ eat$_s$]$_s$]

The position of the subject in (108) is not crucial. It can either be part of the verb's intermediate phrase or the object's; either way it will be interpreted as the relatively weaker element.[25] In addition, the type and prominence of the pitch accent on the topicalized NP is not crucial to its interpretation. If it forms a single intonational phrase with the subject and verb, it need not have a pitch accent at all. If it forms its own intonational phrase, it may have a pitch accent of nearly any type. Accent types that correspond to that used for posets (L+H*) will often be preferred. This optionality corresponds directly to the structural description given in Prince (1998) for topicalizations. Topicalizations may or may not have an accent on the topicalized NP, but crucially there is always a main sentence accent somewhere in the remainder of the sentence.

Topicalizations can then be used when the speaker wants two primary sentence accents and are especially useful in cases where the sentence is not long enough to be broken up into multiple intonational phrases.

We can illustrate this with an naturally-occurring example, (109a):

(109) a. And some he destroys. And some he keeps. (Switchboard corpus)

     b. He KEEPS some.

     c. He keeps SOME.

The default prosody on the canonical sentence is with a pitch accent on *keeps*, as in (109b). The information structure here is relative to the question, *What does he do with them? He KEEPS some.* The canonical order with a pitch accent on *some* is a narrow focus; its scalar implicature is that 'he doesn't keep all.' Only the topicalization (with or without two pitch accents, one on *some* and one on *keeps*) can communicate a more complex information structure—that for an element y (=*some*) in the poset P, he will do X with y; X should be instantiated with *keep*.

This goal of focus disambiguation will be the most difficult to simply append to a goal-based generation system like SPUD. The need to disambiguate the focus structure of an utterance is conditioned not only by a speaker's goal COMMUNICATE($P \land$ FOCUS-PARTITION($P,G(f)$)), where G is the ground and f is the focus, but by the formal options and requirements the speaker has when realizing this goal prosodically. An implementation would require choosing among not only alternate syntactic trees but also prosodic realizations of those trees. Clearly, a system where discourse, syntactic, and prosodic choices are made in tandem is crucial.

---

[25]This prosodic weakness is unsurprising in light of the fact that nearly all subjects in topicalizations are non-contrastive pronominals.

3.5   Summary and remaining issues

A speaker's choice of forms is a complex piece of discourse and sentence planning. Rather than a simple function from a discourse condition to a form, it depends on the speaker's intention to communicate information beyond just the truth-conditional content of a proposition. This chapter has presented a theory of the additional communicative goals that the use of four non-canonical syntactic forms can contribute. The most basic type of these goals is communicating information about the the attentional status of open propositions and posets of entities in the discourse model. This additional information is essentially the equivalent of the discourse conditions posited by previous analyses of the pragmatics of these forms. The other two types of goals—relating the meaning of one utterance to another and disambiguating focus structure—follow from these basic goals. The attentional status goals allow the speaker to communicate additional information about how the utterance relates syntactically and semantically to other discourse segments. The fact that attentional status goals structure the propositions communicated in particular ways also allow speakers to communicate the information structure unambiguously in a way that prosody alone cannot.

The multiple intentions that a single utterance can achieve when realized with non-canonical syntax make syntactic choice a useful communicative tool. However, there remain several problems with making it a practical tool for NLG systems. First, any simplistic implementation of the theory is still likely to overgenerate. This is partly due to a second primary problem. Even given a set of goals that forms can achieve, it is not clear when a system should intend to achieve such goals. Additionally, there exist multiple means of achieving the types of goals included here. For example, discourse connectives can contribute information about discourse relations, and prosody can communicate information about how to structure an utterance's focus-ground partition. We are also faced with the problem that none of the above goals are exclusive; multiple goals can be achieved with a single form. A speaker may in fact intend for multiple communicative goals to be achieved. Given a context and a non-canonical utterance, how do hearers reconstruct which goals to update their discourse model with?

In the following chapter we will make a preliminary attempt to resolve some of these difficulties. With the use of a corpus annotated with low-level linguistic properties that correspond to some of these goals, a statistical model of the local discourse context surrounding these non-canonical forms is developed. This statistical model can then be used as a classifier trained to choose, based on context, which form is a best fit. The classifier could then serve as a simple module to be added to a larger NLG system for selecting a syntactic form for a root clause. This selection will be indirectly based on some of the types of the communicative goals examined here and to some degree will allow us to test the viability of incorporating these goals into the generation process.

CHAPTER 4

An empirical study of discourse structure and non-canonical word order

4.1 Background and motivation

In order to support the theory of the interaction of communicative goals and syntactic form presented in Chapter 3 and to be able to implement it as part of a NLG system, additional support beyond native speaker intuitions on the appropriateness of particular forms in particular contexts is needed. Ideally, one would take a corpus annotated with communicative goals and measure the correlations of each goal with the non-canonical forms of interest here. Then, this statistical model of goal-form pairings could be used in a generation system as a way to select the best form to use given the communicative goal to be achieved.

As will be discussed in the next section, however, this plan relies entirely on the ability to annotate a corpus with communicative goals. The problems with such a task will be discussed in the following section, Section 4.1.1. The approach taken here will be a different one which is intended to circumvent these difficulties. First, in order to get a measure of the correlation between communicative goals related to discourse and attentional structure, I use a set of features to create a very low-level approximation of the discourse context surrounding each form. The features were selected both because they are somewhat more easily and objectively annotated than communicative goals and because they are known to correlate with discourse structure. Then, a logistic regression statistical analysis of the correlations between these contexts and the non-canonical sentence types is performed.

The logistic regression model fulfills two goals. One, it can give a measure of how well these feature-approximations of discourse context correlate with the forms, and so it can provide a (partial) statistical model of the context where these forms appear. Two, the logistic regression model can also be used as a probabilistic classifier which, given a context (i.e. a set of features and their values), can select the form that best fits that context, based on what it has learned from the corpus of training data. Such a classifier could be used in a generation system as one step in the selection of a root clause word order, given a discourse plan where the values for the features conditioning the selection have already been determined.

The goals of this chapter then are also twofold. One is to demonstrate that the features examined here do in fact display interesting patterns of correlation with particular non-canonical forms that support the claims of the theory outlined in the previous chapter. The second is to explicate how these patterns could be utilized in an NLG system to improve the performance of the system with respect to choice of root clause word order.

The chapter is arranged as follows. First, background and motivation for the approach taken here is presented, including the problems with annotating communicative goals directly, previous attempts to model discourse structure statistically, and the use of logistic regression as a model of linguistic variation and a classifier. Then, in Section 4.2, the corpus and annotations used to create the data are described. Section 4.3 presents the framework, predictions, and results of the logistic regression model. Next, Section 4.4 is devoted to the use of this model as a classifier, with measures of its accuracy on the data used for this project and an explanation of how it could be utilized in an NLG system. Section 4.5 presents conclusions and suggests directions for future work.

4.1.1   Annotating communicative goals

Given a discourse, identifying the communicative goals that the participants intend to achieve and the linguistic forms associated with those intentions is a highly subjective task. In addition, conversational agents may attempt to achieve multiple goals on multiple levels at a single time. For example, in uttering (110), the speaker may simultaneously have the goal that the hearer identifies the referent of *the 7-11*, the hearer believes (that the speaker believes) of the 7-11 that it is closed, and then depending on the greater context, any number of other goals: that the hearer provide the speaker with the name of an alternative store she can go to, that the hearer believe that the speaker was unable to procure him a drink, that the hearer believe that the speaker was unable to hold up the 7-11, etc.

(110)   The 7-11 was closed.

In annotating a corpus for communicative goals, determining the relevant level at which to annotate goals is crucial, but quite difficult. For the purposes of this project, testing the correlation between non-canonical syntactic forms and the communicative goals presented in the last chapter, it seems only lower-level goals are relevant: to identify discourse entities including individuals, relations, and propositions; to indicate properties of the discourse context, including the relationship between discourse entities and the discourse context, i.e. the information status of entities and information structure of propositions.

Unfortunately, there are few corpora annotated with even these types of lower-level goals, which are essentially the semantic and pragmatic meaning of the discourse or properties of the discourse context. Semantic annotation of corpora is far rarer than syntactic annotation. In addition, semantic annotation is usually only a translation from a syntactic tree structure into a flatter logical form equivalent or annotation of lexical semantic properties and predicate-argument structure (Kingsbury and Palmer, 2002). Annotation of pragmatic knowledge has concentrated either on coreference between entities or speech acts (Jurafsky et al., 1997). Annotation of discourse structure, either intentional or attentional, is notoriously difficult and unreliable to annotate, particularly in the vicinity of segment boundaries although recently some efforts have been put forth (Creswell et al., 2002; Marcu et al., 1999). Information structure is also difficult to annotate although attempts have been made, in particular for corpora in languages which seem to more directly encode information structure in their syntax (Hajičová and Sgall, 2001).

Task-oriented corpora would appear to be ideal for use in annotating speaker goals. However, the frequency of special syntactic forms in the most well-known task-oriented corpora (e.g. TRAINS (Allen et al., 1995), Map Task (Anderson et al., 1991), and Coconut (di Eugenio et al., 1998)) is too low to allow investigation of the discourse contextual properties of the use of these forms. This may be the result of several factors unique to the task-oriented conditions under which these dialogs were collected. First, when the domain of the discourse participants is highly structured and generally unambiguous, the participants may have little reason to use more complex forms. Prince (1981) describes a text (or discourse) as "a set of instructions from a speaker to a hearer on how to construct a particular discourse model." The discourse model includes discourse entities, attributes and links between entities. When it is clear what entities exist, which attributes they have, how the entities are related to one another, and what the participants' goals in creating this discourse model are, speakers will not need to re-emphasize these facts. Highly-task-oriented dialogs with very limited domains will put relatively less strain on the participants ability to coordinate their discourse models.[1] Other factors, like time constraints on syntactic planning, may also affect the use of more complex structures (Kroch and Hindle, 1982). So, although task-oriented

---

[1] Although it will likely require a greater degree of coordination between their models.

dialogs with a limited set of goals will make annotation of speaker intentions easier and more reliable, these same parameters are likely to interfere with the frequent use of more complex syntactic structures and, therefore, are not suitable for the present study.

Rather than a highly task-oriented corpus, I use the same corpus used in the previous chapter, the online Oral History Archives of the Social Security Administration. The relative frequency of the non-canonical forms in this corpus, its goal-directed content, and its only semi-dialog exchanges where the turns of the interviewee are each relatively lengthy and uninterrupted makes it more well-suited to the type of factors I am most interested in investigating.

So, to summarize, annotating communicative goals directly in order to find their correlation with syntactic form is far too difficult, and in most cases too subjective to be reliable. In addition, in corpora where communicative goals may be more transparent, the syntactic forms of interest are too rare. Unfortunately, even annotating the low-level type of communicative goals of interest here, that is the attentional structure, discourse relations and structure, and information structure of a text, is difficult and bound to be fraught with unreliability. As such, rather than attempting explicit annotation of these structures for my corpus, in this project I circumvent these difficulties by only indirectly deriving a picture of the structures of interest in the corpus by annotating their known correlates.

The types of communicative goals I concentrate on here are those relating to attentional structure and discourse structure, and discourse relations. This is not to downgrade the importance of information structure in a speaker's selection of non-canonical syntactic forms. Considerations of information structure clearly play a significant role in some instances of the use of non-canonicals as discussed in Section 3.4. However, because the corpus I use is a transcription by non-linguists, it has no systematic indication of prosodic features.[2] As such, it is difficult to investigate the interaction of prosody and syntax with the current body of data. At best, one can conclude that for many of the tokens in the corpus here, the need to indicate particular prosodic phrasings and hence prosodic structures through manipulation of the syntactic form did affect the speaker's choice of a non-canonical form. The exact degree of that effect would best be measured in a study of the focus-ground structure comparing canonical and non-canonical utterances in a systematic way. The statistical model used to analyze the data here has as one its underlying assumptions that the contribution of any factor to the overall model is independent from all others. Although this assumption would need to be tested empirically, it is not an unjustified one with respect to

---

[2]The recordings that the transcriptions are based on are available for researchers at the Social Security Administration's archives in Baltimore; however they are not digitized or aligned with the transcription in any way, and so are not in fact in a format which allows reasonably efficient searching for particular strings of text in order to compare the prosodic structure with the syntactic structure.

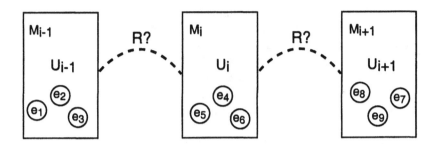

Figure 4.1: Approximating discourse relations (R) between utterances (U) by examining lexical discourse markers (M) and referential connections between entities (e).

the independence of information structure factors, such as size of constituents and ability to bear a prosodic focus which unambiguously marks the information structure of the utterance, and the discourse structure and attentional state factors which are investigated here. Therefore, given the assumption that these aspects of prosodic form are independent of the factors I am examining here, then separate studies of each are justified. Nonetheless, ultimately, if one's goal is to get the best possible model of choice of syntactic form, such a model would need to incorporate both of these sets of factors. As the focus of my project is not prosody, however, a detailed study of how these prosodic factors should be incorporated into a model of syntactic choice remains for future research.

Instead, this project concentrates on the syntactic and semantic relations between utterances that comprise the structure of a discourse. Because these discourse relations are difficult to annotate directly, low-level and relatively objective linguistic correlates will be used to approximate them. These correlates are intended to give an indirect picture of the discourse relations which hold between each token utterance (U_i) and the immediately adjacent utterances which precede and follow it, as shown schematically in Figure 4.1. The particular correlates utilized here are 1) coreferential and inferential links between entities referred to in the text, including centering transitions across utterance boundaries and 2) the presence and type of lexical discourse connectives.

These correlates clearly do not form an exhaustive set of the properties that can serve as indicators of the type of communicative goals of interest here, i.e. goals of communicating information about discourse-level semantic and structural relations. However, these features do share one crucial property that makes them of such utility here: they are relatively easy and straight-forward to annotate. In Section 4.3 we will present in detail what we can infer from these low-level correlates about discourse structure and, most importantly, about the relationship between discourse structure and non-canonical syntactic forms.

An additional benefit of investigating the relationship between these properties and the choice of syntactic form is that the choice of syntactic form will then be closely tied to other aspects of discourse which have already been used for NLG, including rhetorical relations (McKeown, 1985; Hovy, 1993; Marcu, 1997) and centering theory (Kibble and Power, 1999; Rich and Sidner, 1997; Passonneau, 1996). In an NLG system where information about rhetorical relations and centering transitions is incorporated into the procedure of generating the linguistic content of a text, choices of which entities to refer to in which utterance and how or whether to lexically encode rhetorical relations must already be being made. Once we have a model of how those choices relate to the choice of syntactic form, we can utilize that model when selecting syntactic form.[3]

4.1.2   Statistical models of discourse

Previous attempts to model discourse structure–and thus attentional state and discourse relations–statistically can be grouped into two major types of approaches, lexical and multi-source. I present examples of each approach in this section.

The two approaches are relevant here for different reasons. Although the lexical approach presented in Kozima (1993) will not be used here, it does provide an idea of some other factors which could be utilized in future studies. More importantly, it illustrates the concept that the discourse structure of a text might be extrapolated from data about points of greater and lesser cohesion; the points of least cohesion being the most likely points for segment boundaries to be located. The multi-source approach of Passonneau and Litman (1997) is heavily drawn upon as an example of how a set of simple (mostly) binary features can be utilized as a way to model a linear segmentation of discourse. A subset of the features examined by Passonneau and Litman (1997) will be used in the experiments presented in Sections 4.3 and 4.4.

---

[3]It is clear, for the most part, that the identity of entities to be discussed in an utterance must be part of the representation of the content of that utterance to be encoded linguistically, and as such, this information can be drawn upon in a procedure for selecting the word order for that utterance. It is less obvious how information about the presence and type of lexical connectives in an utterance could be utilized in a procedure for selecting the syntactic form used in the utterance. The discourse connectives used with an utterance do presumably encode aspects of the content of that utterance which have to do with the discourse relations that utterance enters into. So, an algorithm for syntactic choice could be implemented such that it takes place after selection of discourse connectives. Alternatively, the underlying content of the lexical connectives could be reconstructed, and from this knowledge of the relation between the lexical connectives and the syntactic forms, one could ultimately derive the relationship between the underlying content of the connectives and the syntactic forms. Then, this information could be used in the syntactic form selection process instead.

Kozima (1993)

Kozima (1993)'s approach is based on the assumption that words in a text are linked together in a lexical cohesion relation. Within a segment, two words are more likely to be more strongly cohesive than if they were in separate segments. To be lexically cohesive, words may either be identical or related in a semantic network; this cohesiveness can be a given a numeric value. Kozima's approach uses a numeric value derived from spreading activation on a semantic network constructed from an English dictionary. After computing a text's lexical cohesion profile (LCP), that is the degree of lexical cohesion for each possible segmentation of the text of a particular window length, one can examine a plot of the LCP (by window) for peaks and valleys, i.e. points of greater and lesser cohesion. The windows with the least degree of cohesion are the mostly likely to be containing segment boundaries.

To evaluate his approach, Kozima compares an LCP plot of a short story with a histogram of boundaries indicated by 16 human subjects for the same story. The story was presented without paragraph boundaries. Based on visual inspection of the overlay of the two plots, Kozima claims that the valleys of the LCP "correspond mostly to the dominant segment boundaries," that is segment boundaries indicated by more than 2 (or more) subjects. Kozima attributes the existence of valleys that do not exactly correspond to segment boundaries to the fact that lexical cohesion is not solely responsible for the coherence of a segment; potentially a lexically cohesive text could be incoherent. He claims that LCP valley computation could be used to segment text for use in anaphora and ellipsis resolution and for analysis of hierarchical text structure.[4]

The ability to entirely automate Kozima's approach makes it intuitively appealing. However, without stronger support for how it corresponds to human annotators of discourse segmentation, it is difficult to say how useful the boundaries it finds would be in tasks that depend on an analysis of discourse structure. In particular, the lack of detail about the instructions given to the human annotators is a handicap here. Ideally, one would like to see an application of Kozima's approach to the dataset described in Passonneau and Litman (1997) in the next section to truly evaluate how it compares to human subjects' ideas about discourse segments. Rather than apply Kozima's approach, we will take from it only the idea that by looking for local maxima and minima in coherence one can approximate the location of discourse segment boundaries. Rather than using lexical coherence as the measure of the degree of coherence, however, we will build on the results of Passonneau and Litman (1997) presented below and use referential coherence.

---

[4]Apparently, Kozima does not wish to collapse these two activities as part of a single natural language understanding task.

Passonneau and Litman(1997)

In contrast with Kozima (1993), Passonneau and Litman (1997)'s approach to discourse segmentation is explicitly intended to facilitate comparison with human annotation, and in fact the resulting segmentation algorithms are designed to mimic the performance and preferences of human subjects.

Passonneau and Litman (1997) create a data set using human annotation of discourse segment boundaries in a corpus of 20 transcribed oral narratives (in total the narratives have about approximately 2,000 prosodic phrases and 13,500 words). Naive (non-linguist) annotators were told to segment linearly rather than hierarchically. Each was given a discourse transcribed with a single prosodic phrase per line. The beginning of each line was a potential discourse segment boundary. Agreement across the segmentations by seven naive annotators was found to be reliable and significant. In particular, agreement that a particular point should be designated as a boundary by three or more of the seven annotators was significantly different than a pattern of agreement by chance only.

Passonneau and Litman (1997) then try to determine if boundaries designated as such by three or more annotators correlate well with particular linguistic features. Each inter-prosodic phrase point, p, was coded for several linguistic features. First, the phrase final prosody preceding the point p was coded for whether it had a SENTENCE FINAL CONTOUR.[5] In addition, the point was coded for the presence of a pause, and if +PAUSE, the length of the pause was recorded.

Besides prosodic features, the first two lexical indicators of boundaries were also annotated as $+/-$CUE$_1$ and $+/-$CUE$_2$, and if $+$, the value for WORD$_1$ and WORD$_2$ were also recorded.[6] A combined cue-prosody, $+/-$ COMPLEX, feature was also recorded; it was assigned $+$ if both SENTENCE FINAL CONTOUR and PAUSE were $+$ and as long as both WORD$_1$ and WORD$_2$ were not *and*.

When the prosodic phrase following p began a new functionally independent clausal unit, C_j, three binary features related to coreference relations between NPs were annotated. The feature COREF was assigned $+$ if C_j contained an NP that coreferred with an NP in C_{j-1}. The feature INFER was assigned $+$ when C_j contained an NP whose reference could be inferred from an NP in C_{j-1} on the basis of a pre-defined set of inference relations. Finally, a feature dependent upon the assignment of boundaries by an algorithm was defined, GLOBAL.PRO. The positive value of GLOBAL.PRO indicates that C_j contains a definite pronoun

---

[5]This feature is based on the original transcription of (Passonneau and Litman, 1997)'s corpus by Chafe; rising and falling sentence final intonations were distinguished from phrase final intonation.

[6]The possible values for WORD$_1$ were *also, and, anyway, basically, because, but, finally, first, like, meanwhile, no, now, oh, okay, only, or, see, so, then, well,* and *where;* for WORD$_2$, *and, anyway, because, boy, but, now, okay, or, right, so, still, then.* These lists were based on the results from Hirschberg and Litman (1994).

whose referent is mentioned in any previous clause intervening between C_j and the last boundary assigned by the algorithm.

Passonneau and Litman used these features in simple algorithms using only a single feature (+CUE$_1$, +PAUSE), or the combination of all the NP features, (−COREF, −INFER, and −GLOBAL.PRO), to determine whether to assign a boundary and compared the results of each with human performance. Then, they separated 15 of the narratives into ten training (which had previously been used as the test set for the simple algorithms) and five test narratives. First, they developed a hand-tuned algorithm through error analysis of the simple algorithms. This Error Analysis algorithm used two criteria to hypothesize a boundary point, either the absence of any referential connections or a positive value of the feature COMPLEX described above. They then incorporated what was learned from the Error Analysis algorithm and used these modified features as inputs to a machine learning algorithm (C4.5 decision tree). The Error Analysis and decision tree algorithms both improved over the best simple algorithms and their additive combinations.[7] The human performance reported by Passonneau and Litman is an average of each measurement taken over all the subjects. In the table below, all results shown are given with respect to a "gold standard" of the set of boundaries marked by at least four human annotators.[8] *Recall* and *precision* are used with their standard meanings here. *Summed deviation* is a sum of the deviation from their ideal values of the four measurements Passonneau and Litman use, recall, precision, fallout, and error. The best possible value for this metric is 0.

	recall (%)	precision (%)	summed deviation
Averaged Human	74	55	.91
CUE	72	15	2.16
PAUSE	92	18	1.93
NP features	50	31	1.53
Pause + NP	47	42	1.42
Error Analysis (train)	70	47	1.05
Error Analysis (test)	60	37	1.30
C4.5 (train)	53	77	.77
C4.5 (test)	39	52	.79

Table 4.1: Passonneau and Litman (1997)'s results

---

[7] An additive algorithm is one that assigns a boundary only if all features it is considering would assign a boundary separately. The best additive algorithm combined information from PAUSE and the NP features. It appears in the fifth row of Table 4.1.

[8] Because there is variation in which and how many points subjects mark as boundaries, one can compare each human to this gold standard, then average over their errors.

The C4.5 algorithm[9] actually surpasses both the hand-tuned Error Analysis algorithm and average human performance on the summed deviation measure. However, the standard deviation across different narratives was consistently higher for the C4.5 algorithm, both in comparison to the Error Analysis algorithm and human performance.

Among Passonneau and Litman (1997)'s conclusions are that the incorporation of more information is better when making hypotheses about potential boundaries. The NP algorithm which utilizes three features was an improvement over both PAUSE and CUE features alone. The Error Analysis and C4.5 algorithms which incorporated a great deal of information improved over the best additive algorithm. Guessing boundary sites is a process fraught with variance. Human performance differs across subjects. Boundaries themselves seem to be somewhat fuzzy, that is they may in fact be larger than the point between two utterances. Particular narratives in the corpus used for the study seemed more difficult for all algorithms, suggesting that how particular speaker's indicate boundaries may vary. Finally, one important difference between the C4.5 algorithm and the others is that the former appears to underclassify boundaries, the precision (actual boundaries out of everything hypothesized to be boundaries) outweighs recall (boundaries labeled correctly out of all actual boundaries). That is the machine learning algorithm is a more conservative boundary guesser. It does not posit boundaries correctly as often, but in general when it posits a boundary there is one there.

From Passonneau and Litman (1997)'s results we can conclude that algorithms can be developed to detect boundaries between discourse segments automatically, but not necessarily that well. This is due in part to the fact that even human annotators show much variance in performance on this task. Nonetheless, even simple linguistic features can be used to give a very rough picture of where discourse segments begin and end. Several of these features will be incorporated in a somewhat adapted form into this study, including the presence and type of discourse connectives and the inferential and coreferential connections between entities in different utterances.

4.1.3   Machine learning and classification tasks

Statistical techniques and machine learning algorithms have been applied to a large variety of tasks in natural language processing, including part-of-speech tagging, parsing, word-sense disambiguation, coreference resolution, and, as seen above, discourse segmentation (Manning and Schütze, 1999). Often these tasks are approached as a type of classification task. An instance of the problem needs a label, and the algorithm must provide the correct label. For example, in a coref-

---

[9]Passonneau and Litman actually report the results of two different C4.5 learned algorithms. The one discussed here is the one with the best performance.

erence task, the algorithm's input is a pair of noun phrases, NP_1 and NP_2. As an output, the algorithm should be able to answer YES or NO, where YES means NP_1 and NP_2 corefer to the same entity, and NO means there is no coreference. In a part-of-speech tagging task, the classification algorithm is given a word as its input and should output a label, NOUN, VERB, ADJECTIVE, etc. as its output. For each of these tasks, the algorithm is provided with a set of features which characterize an instance and which the algorithm can then take into account when making its decision. In the case of the coreference task, these features may include the lexical head of each NP, the syntactic role within the sentence, whether the two NPs appear in the same sentence, or how many words separate them. For a part-of-speech task, in contrast, the set of features may include such things as the lexeme in question, the previous and following words, the most common part-of-speech the word is found with, and so forth.

The task that will be relevant to this project can be characterized as an algorithmic procedure which will take as its input a discourse context, represented by a list of attribute-value pairs, and will output a label which is one of several possible syntactic forms (topicalization, left-dislocation, wh-cleft, it-cleft, or canonical).

The development of a classification algorithm for syntactic form selection need not of course involve machine learning or probabilities. However, given the stochastic nature of human language use,[10] a system which incorporates these two aspects will likely be more robust, more accurate, and more easily adaptable to different domains of language use. Machine learning algorithms are particularly useful in poorly understood domains "where humans might not have the knowledge needed to develop effective algorithms."(Mitchell, 1997) The task at hand is particularly suited to this type of analysis because the choice of syntactic form is not a categorical one; it depends on many factors, and the weighting of those factors cannot be transparently observed simply by examining the corpus. Even given a theory of the relationship between the types of communicative goals that motivate a speaker's choice of a non-canonical form in place of a canonical one, like the one presented in Chapter 3, developing an algorithm that can map from a goal and a context to a particular form is a very difficult and poorly understood task.[11]

In the next section we will present the particular statistical approach to be used here, logistic regression analysis of variable rules. This approach is well known in the sociolinguistics community as a highly successful technique for analyzing language variation. Variable rule analysis has much in common with other statistical machine learning approaches to classification tasks and is well-

---

[10]See Abney (1996) or Manning (2003) for discussion.

[11]This is not to say that the theory in the previous chapter is not worth anything, only that is based on an analysis of choices which have already been made by speakers and does not extend transparently to a algorithm that can make that choice itself.

suited to the project at hand, as will be discussed in the following section. Unfortunately, however, it is not well-known outside the community of sociolinguistics and has for the most part developed quite separately from the development of statistical techniques for use in computational linguistics.[12] A brief discussion of machine-learned classifiers is provided here in order to facilitate an understanding of variable rule analysis as a type of machine learning classification algorithm. This discussion is based primarily on Mitchell (1997), but by necessity it is only a very abbreviated, simplified version of this large topic, and the original should be consulted for extensive citations and more rigorous discussion of concepts.

At its most general, a learning problem can be thought of as an approach that allows an algorithm to improve its performance on a task based on some training experience. In the case of a classification problem, the algorithm should learn from a set of training examples which have already been classified how to classify unseen instances. The learning algorithm in this case ideally will learn a target function from these training examples. As such we can formalize the learning problem as follows. The data will be a set of instances X. The target function f will map from $X \rightarrow \{a, b, ...n\}$, where $a, b, ...n$ are labels for each instance $x \in X$. That is, the target function can be characterized by the set of ordered pairs, $\langle x, f(x) \rangle$ where x is an instance and $f(x)$ is its true label. The learning algorithm must learn a function h which also maps from $X \rightarrow \{a, b, ...n\}$. In the ideal case, for all x, $h(x) = f(x)$. The input to the learning algorithm, however, is only a subset of X, the set of training examples. The goal then is to learn a function h, which as closely as possible behaves in the same way as the target function f, from only a subset of X. In order to measure the performance of the learning algorithm, a separate subset of X can be reserved as the test data set.

The learning process is guided by the INDUCTIVE LEARNING HYPOTHESIS:

> "Any hypothesis found to approximate the target function well over a sufficiently large set of training examples will also approximate the target function well over other unobserved examples."(Mitchell, 1997, p. 23)

In other words, in forming a hypothesis, the learner assumes that "the best hypothesis regarding unseen instances is the hypothesis that best fits the observed training data." (Mitchell, 1997) This assumption is based on yet another assumption, that the distribution of the training examples is the same as that of the test examples. As Mitchell (1997) points out, "it is important to keep in mind that this assumption must often be violated in practice." For example, when the size of the training set is limited, coincidental regularities in the data may appear, ones that will not be found in the test data. In addition, in practice, the training data is rarely error-free. There may be errors both in the labels of instances, and in

---

[12]Although the use of logistic regression to develop a probabilistic classifier is not unknown.

the features used to represent the instances. When learning from noisy data, the hypothesis learned h may match the target function f well on the training data, but make many errors on the test data. In such a case, the h is said to have OVER-FIT the training data and is thus a poor approximation of f when applied to all instances.

Even when no overfitting has occurred, the learned algorithm h is still only an approximation of the target function f. This is due in part to the problem of representing the problem to be learned. An instance is represented in many cases as a list of attribute-values pairs. The amount of training data needed to learn a good approximation of f will depend on the size and complexity of the representation of the instances. The more expressive the representation used, the better the approximation, and the more training data needed in order learn h.[13] In terms of attribute-value features, the more attributes and the more values of each attribute, the larger the training data set needs to be in order to learn a good approximation to the target function.

In order to decide which hypothesis out of the set of all possible hypotheses is the best, we need a way to evaluate possible hypotheses. One criterion used in Bayesian learning methods is to say that the best hypothesis is the one which is most probable given the training data D and the prior probabilities of each hypothesis. In order to calculate these probabilities, we use Bayes theorem, which can be adapted to machine learning problems in the following way. We want to know the probability that hypothesis h holds given the set of training data D we have to learn from, $P(h|D)$. Bayes theorem is straightforwardly applied here to give equation (111).

$$(111) \quad p(h \mid D) = \frac{p(D \mid h)\, p(h)}{p(D)}$$

The term $P(D|h)$ here means the likelihood of the data under the hypothesis. In other words, given a particular function h, what is the probability that it generated this pattern of data. If we wish to find the maximum likelihood hypothesis, that is the most probable hypothesis, then we compare the right sides of the above equation across all hypotheses. The value for $P(D)$ then is constant across all h. In addition, if we assume that all hypotheses are equally likely, then the $P(h)$ is also constant for any h. In order to determine the most likely hypothesis then, we need only to determine $P(D|h)$ and choose the hypothesis which maximizes the likelihood of the data under itself.

---

[13]As pointed out by Manning (2003) data scarcity is a perpetual problem in corpus linguistics, particularly for studies of syntactic structure. As such, learning from linguistic corpora is particularly affected by limited training data.

4.1.4   Variable rules: statistical models of linguistic variation

One particular type of statistical analysis of linguistic data has grown out of a tradition which has been, on the whole, quite separate from that of the statistical and machine learning techniques used in the computational linguistics community. This is variational analysis. Sankoff (1988) explains the motivation for using the method also known as VARIABLE RULE analysis:

> "Whenever a choice among two (or more) discrete alternatives can be perceived as having been made in the course of linguistic performance, and where this choice may have been influenced by factors such as features in the phonological environment, the syntactic context, discursive function of the utterance, topic, style, interactional situation or personal or sociodemographic characteristics of the speaker or other participants, then it is appropriate to invoke the statistical notions and methods known to students of linguistic variation as *variable rules*."

As a statistical technique, variable rule analysis is especially suited to linguistic analysis because it pertains to the "the probabilistic modeling and the statistical treatment of *discrete* choices and their conditioning."(Sankoff, 1988) Rather than continuous, real-valued variables, the variables of interest in modeling linguistic variation are most often nominal variables, categories that are unordered and discrete (e.g. parts of speech, phones, etc). Sankoff (1988) presents several prerequisites that must be met for a variable rule analysis to be appropriate. First, there should be a perception on part of analyst that there exists a choice the speaker must make when uttering a linguistic form between two or more structures. In addition, the outcome of choice should appear to be (to some degree) unpredictable based on context. In other words, it should not be a categorical or deterministic choice, where in the presence of context C, meaning M must be realized as F; there must be the possibility of variation. The choice of F is stochastic.[14] Finally, the choice between variants must occur often enough to allow for statistical analysis. All of these are characteristics of the current problem, syntactic choice based on discourse context.

Variable rule analysis arose in the context of transformational grammar (Paolillo, 2002). While many transformational, or string-rewrite, rules were thought to apply obligatorily in a linguistic derivation, certain transformations appeared to apply only optionally. Variable rules were conceived as a way of capturing the fact that some variation was conditional on the presence or absence of particular linguistic or social factors (Cedergren and Sankoff, 1974). Variable rules incorporate this conditional dependence on context because formally they are

---

[14]As Sankoff (1988) points out, however, potentially, if enough contextual information were included in the analysis, the possibility exists that one might not need a variable rule analysis any longer.

probabilistic context-sensitive rules (Paolillo, 2002; Sankoff and Labov, 1979). They have the same form as all context-sensitive rules, shown in (112), where A becomes B in the context α_β:

(112) $\alpha A \beta \rightarrow \alpha B \beta$

The probabilistic version of (112) is such that A has two (or more) possible variants B_1 and B_2, and each possible context where the rule may apply α_β_1, α_β_2, etc. has a weight assigned to it, such that that weight is the probability of the rule A being transformed in that context (into the particular variant which is possible in that context). The sum of all the rule weights applying to A should sum to one (Paolillo, 2002).

A crucial part of the insight of Labov (1969) is that the context α_β can be broken down into features (e.g. [+CONSONANT], [+DEFINITE]) and that "the presence of a given feature or subcategory tends to affect rule frequency in a probabilistically uniform way in all the environments containing it."(Cedergren and Sankoff, 1974) That is, any context α_β where α contains some feature [+F] will affect the application of the rule $A \rightarrow B$ the same way. A statistical model of the context-sensitive variable rule then must incorporate this conditional independence. This independence then allows the analyst to make claims about the co-occurrence of a variable form and any particular context feature in which he or she is interested (Bayley and Young, 2002). Another important principle underlying variational analysis that Bayley and Young (2002) point out is that the variable rule can capture the fact that "no single factor is likely to fully explain the variation that we regularly observe in language." This principle makes variable rule analysis particularly relevant to the task at hand, where the choice of a syntactic form is likely to be conditioned by multiple communicative goals.

The particular statistical model that has been most utilized in variable rule analysis, in part because of its implementation in the popular software program Varbrul (Cedergren and Sankoff, 1974), is logistic regression. The logistic regression model, because it is a multiplicative model rather than an additive model, "links Labov's discovery of the independence of feature contribution to the notion of independence in the probabilistic sense."(Cedergren and Sankoff, 1974) In the logistic regression analysis, the variants of A, $B_1, B_2, ..., B_n$ are the dependent variable. One wants to predict the occurrence of the dependent variable given the values of a set of contextual factors, or a context (Sankoff, 1988). The basic case for logistic regression is one where the dependent variable is binomial. In a case where A has only two variants, B_1 and B_2, one can be treated as the case where the rule $A \rightarrow B_1$ applies, and then the other variant then will appear when $A \rightarrow B_1$ does not apply.[15]

The equation used to determine whether a variable rule should apply in a given context appears in (113). Each p_n is the feature weight that factor n con-

---

[15]For discussion of multinomial models see Sankoff (1988); Paolillo (2002).

tributes to the total probability that the rule will apply in any instance where that factor holds. By multiplying together the weight of all the factors holding in a particular instance, the resulting probability is the probability that the rule will apply in a context where each of those factors hold. In this equation, each term is not a single probability, but an odds ratio which contains as subexpressions both the probability that the rule will apply, p, and also the probability that the rule will not apply $1 - p$. This makes the equation symmetric with respect to the two application values. When p is 0.5, the feature weight does not affect the application or non-application of the rule. Weights above 0.5 increase the probability of rule application. Weights below 0.5 increase the probability of rule non-application.

$$(113) \quad \left(\frac{p_{cell}}{1 - p_{cell}} \right) = \left(\frac{\alpha}{1 - \alpha} \right) \times \left(\frac{p_a}{1 - p_a} \right) \times \left(\frac{p_b}{1 - p_b} \right) \times \ldots \times \left(\frac{p_n}{1 - p_n} \right)$$

For ease and speed of computation, the odds multiplicative model shown in (113) is transformed into its log-linear additive equivalent in (114) (Paolillo, 2002).

$$(114) \quad \ln \left(\frac{p_{cell}}{1 - p_{cell}} \right) =$$

$$\ln \left(\frac{\alpha}{1 - \alpha} \right) + \ln \left(\frac{p_a}{1 - p_a} \right) + \ln \left(\frac{p_b}{1 - p_b} \right) + \ldots + \ln \left(\frac{p_n}{1 - p_n} \right)$$

In variational analysis the term *factor group* is used to refer to an attribute. Each *factor* then is one possible value of the attribute.[16] A feature vector with a particular set of attribute-value pairs is referred to as a *cell*. The variable α[17] in (113–114) is roughly the base rate at which the rule applies in the data, also known as the input value or the prior probability. For example, if the two variants of A in the data, B_1 and B_2 are present at 60% and 40%, respectively, then in the absence of any factor weights, for an analysis of the rule of $A \rightarrow B_1$, α will be 0.6.

Ideally, the distribution of variants in the data sample should have the same frequency as found in a naturally-occurring corpus of data. According to Sankoff (1988), however, in the case of syntactic variation especially, sometimes some variants are too rare to be collected systematically in a corpus. They may be still compared to another common variant which has been systematically collected. The resulting statistical model will be identical except that the value of the prior or input probability will be meaningless here. The probabilities of the factor effects, the values for each p_n, however, are not affected by the dual origin of the data and will retain their normal interpretation (Sankoff, 1988).

---

[16]I will continue to use the term *feature* to refer to either a factor (value) or a factor group (attribute) except in cases where the ambiguity seems harmful to understanding.

[17]This use of α is unrelated to the contextual α_β above.

This issue applies directly to the project here. Although the four categories of non-canonical forms have been collected systematically from the SSA oral history corpus, the comparison control class of utterances are only a random sample of canonical utterances. The ratio of control to any particular non-canonical group in this study varies from about 2 to 1 to 1 to 1. In the corpus, the actual ratio of canonical utterances to any given category of non-canonical is about 200 to 1, as was discussed originally in Section 1.4. For the purposes of training and testing the statistical models here, the artificial ratio will mitigate the effects of a highly unbalanced data set. This is because in a highly unbalanced data set, the classification task, i.e. deciding when the rule applies and when it does not, can be done with high accuracy simply by labeling every token as an instance of the more frequent class, i.e. saying the rule always applies.

In performing a Varbrul analysis, the goal is to find the best logistic regression model, that is the one with the highest likelihood of having generated the data. Therefore, we can think of the logistic regression model as a type of machine-learned classification algorithm. In order to determine the feature weights, p_n, of each feature in the model, we use successive approximations to estimate these weights such that they give the best fit to the data, that is the final equation derived from estimating the weights of features is the function h which is most probable given the training data. The measure of best fit used in Varbrul is the log-likelihood, the log of the likelihood of the data, i.e. the probability the model could have generated the observed distribution of the data (Paolillo, 2002).[18]

---

[18] Another measure of of goodness of a model's fit which will be used below is comparison of the model with its fully saturated counterpart. A fully saturated model makes use of every degree of freedom available to the model by calculating a weight for each possible combination of those variables seen in the dataset. The log-likelihood of the fully saturated model is also known as the maximum possible likelihood of the model. Because it assigns a feature weight to each cell, a saturated model perfectly predicts the expected proportion of class labels of each cell. If the likelihood of the unsaturated model is not significantly different from the maximum possible likelihood ($p > 0.05$), then it is a good fitting model for the data. If it achieves significance ($p < 0.05$), then it is a poor fit for the data and to get a better fit, interaction factors (combinations of individual factors) would need to be included. In short, it is an additional measure of how likely it is that the model could have generated the data. In a model with only a single feature (factor group), the model tested is already fully saturated. Therefore, there can be no measure of how well it is fitting in comparison to the maximum likelihood. The test to compare the log-likelihood of the model and the maximum possible likelihood is the same log-likelihood ratio test used to determine feature significance in the stepwise regression analysis. It has a χ^2 distribution from which the p-value can be determined. The comparison of log-likelihood with maximum possible likelihood gives a measure of goodness-of-fit similar but not identical to that of comparing the observed and expected counts per cell. Because an observed vs.

In addition to determining the weights of features, as with many machine-learned classifiers, one also wishes to determine which features should be included in the model at all, so that the final model is the most parsimonious in terms of the feature space it utilizes. Varbrul allows one not only to calculate the log-likelihood of individual models but also to systematically compare the log-likelihood of models which utilize minimally different feature sets in order to select the best and smallest model of the data, and in doing so to determine which features contribute most usefully in a discriminative model of two classes. The model comparison procedure is called a stepwise regression analysis, and it can be performed in two directions. When stepping up, at the completion of each level, the algorithm adds the feature whose presence contributes to the greatest improvement in log-likelihood. In stepping down, the feature compares models and eliminates the feature whose presence has the least significant effect on the worsening of the log-likelihood.

Unfortunately, in selecting features using the stepping-up and stepping-down procedure, the search through the space of all possible models is a not an exhaustive one. That is, the log-likelihoods of every model generated by every possible feature combination are not compared. As such, the addition and removal of features to the model during either stepping-up or stepping-down can result in a non-optimal model being selected. Indications that this has taken place include features which are significant at level 1—the level at which every feature is tested individually for significance—not being selected for inclusion in the optimal model.[19] In addition, if the identical feature sets are not selected during both stepping up and stepping down, this too is an indication of interacting features.

This significance of the change in log-likelihood is a measure of how much explanatory power the independent feature contributes to a model which discriminates between the two classes. In other words, it is a measure of how well the feature differentiates the two classes. As mentioned above, features may be significant at level one, but during a stepwise procedure may be found not to contribute any additional information beyond what is contributed by other features selected or removed earlier in the stepwise procedure. In addition, features may correlate with differences in classes, but not strongly enough to improve the log-likelihood of a model which includes them by an amount significant at the 5% level. The strength of the correlation found depends in part on the total quantity of data.[20]

---

expected count comparison is done on a per cell basis, it also cannot serve as a measure in a model with a single feature.

[19]The zero-level (or null) model is a model without any features which incorporates only the input probability of the classes in order to calculate the expected frequencies of the classes.

[20]This should be kept in mind below where it is certainly a limiting factor in some of the binary comparisons to be performed.

Although it is rarely used as a classifier, the regression model that is learned through performing a Varbrul analysis can be used as such.[21] Given a token, i.e. a feature vector of attribute-value pairs, each feature value is added into the equation and weighted according to its estimated weight. This will result in a probability p that the variable rule will apply, e.g. that the output of the rule is the application value B_1.[22] The probability that the rule will not apply, e.g. output will be B_2, will be $1 - p$. A probability greater than 0.5 can be taken as an indication that that instance should be classified as a case of B_1; less than 0.5, an indication that it should be classified as a case of B_2.

Although variational analyses have played a large role in examining socio-logical and speaker effects in linguistic variation, I will not examine this set of factors here. Presumably, the corpus here might be useful for future research on this topic, because each token could be easily coded for speaker. The relatively small size of the data set, the complexity of the five-way choice, and the fact that not all possible non-canonical forms are examined here make this an unrealistic area to examine with the bounds of the current study. There is quite likely a degree of stylistic and speaker components in the variation examined here. A variable rule analysis would be a good framework in which to pursue such an investigation.

Before we examine the results of performing a Varbrul logistic regression analysis on the data collected for this study, we will look at the corpus and annotation used to create the dataset in more detail.

4.2 Corpus and annotation

This section presents the corpus and annotation which are used as the data for both the statistical model and the probabilistic classifier. A large number of features were annotated on the corpus. Because it was not feasible to incorporate them all into the model and the classifier, only a subset of them—features related to referential connections between utterances and lexical discourse connectives—were used in the end. The last section here, Section 4.2.3, will explain how the final version of the features sets were selected.

The original selection of features were based on two criteria. The first was the ability of the feature to reflect the types of communicative goals related to discourse structure to be examined here, as demonstrated in the literature. In

---

[21]There appear to be no instances in the literature where Varbrul output specifically has been used as a classifier. The use of a logistic regression model as a classifier, however, is well-known. See Rubinstein and Hastie (1997) for a comparison of logistic regression with other types of classifiers and citations.

[22]When using the log-additive model, the resulting value is actually the natural log of the odds ratio of the probability that the rule will apply, and the logistic of this value will give the actual probability of application.

particular, the features annotated here were intended to be low-level indicators of transitions in discourse segments and attentional states. They can be thought of as a way to map roughly from the lexical, syntactic, and semantic content of a set of utterances to the discourse structure, intentional and attentional, these utterances comprise. The second criterion was the relative speed and objectivity with which these features could be annotated. All annotation was completed by a single annotator (the author). As such, the second criterion was essentially the limiting case in the data collection process.

4.2.1   Corpus

As discussed above, the corpus used was from the Social Security Oral History Archives. Included were 58 oral histories with a total of approximately 750,000 words, ranging from about 3500–74,000 words per dialog. The corpus was segmented by sentence using an automatic sentence boundary finder (Reynar and Ratnaparkhi, 1997). Then, all cases of topicalizations, left-dislocations, wh-clefts, and it-clefts were tagged by hand. Topicalizations included all clauses with a leftward-displaced complement of the verb—including noun phrases, that-clauses and wh-clauses—and a corresponding post-verbal gap. In a few cases, the NP was extracted from a prepositional phrase, with the preposition left behind in situ, as in (115).

(115)   **Mr. Corson, again, I can't be objective about** because I had worked with Mr. Corson when he was Assistant Executive Director. (SSA, mullineroral1)

All other clauses with sentence-initial prepositional phrases were not included. Although they were tagged as topicalizations, the 44 focus-preposings like the two in (116) were not included as part of this empirical study. The discourse function of these forms is quite specific (Prince, 1986), as is the discourse structure where they are typically found. Most are parenthetical inside another clause, and therefore cannot affect intersentential discourse structure.

(116)   a.   Those were pre-electronic processing days, you see.
Q: Yes, before IBM.
Altmeyer: Well, no, IBM was in the picture. **The Hollerith cards they called them.** They were in existence, but they required a lot of manual work. (SSA, ajaoral4)

b.   Each one of those had **a program manager, they were called.** (SSA, simermeyer)

There were 111 non-focus preposing topicalizations, 22 with dislocated wh-clauses and 85 with NPs.

For left-dislocations and it-clefts, all tokens were included. Distinguishing between the two functional subtypes of each of these forms was found to be rather difficult in practice. For left-dislocations, deciding whether the left-dislocated NP's referent was inferably related to other NPs in the context rather than a brand-new referent (i.e. not previously evoked and not in a salient inferable relationship) was often quite difficult. In addition, as discussed in Section 2.1.1 there is some evidence to suggest that left-dislocated NPs may also be used in particular centering transition contexts for NPs that are not necessarily new or in a salient poset, but instead occur at a point where the grammatical subject is unexpected, i.e. $C_p(U_{i-1}) \neq C_b(U_i)$ (Manetta, 2001). This corresponds to either a RETAIN or ROUGH-SHIFT transition or to a transition one where U_i has no C_b (Manetta, 2001).

In light of these factors, it seemed better to group all these tokens together as a single class initially. In addition, however, each token was coded for type of left-dislocation, poset or simplifying. This class was later separated into two subclasses each of which could be compared with each other and with the other four classes to give a measure of how distinct they are from each other based on the features we are using here. A clear ability to distinguish one class from the other might be an indication that these two subclasses differ from each other in the types of discourse relation communicative goals they are used to achieve. Below we will discuss to what extent the overall similarities and differences between the two subtypes merely reflect the differences we already know about in the information statuses of the referents of their preposed NPs or alternatively whether the discourse relation goals that the subtypes are used with may in fact be rather similar. It must be noted however, that the confidence with which these conclusions are supported or not is limited by the reliability of the annotation of the two subclasses. Given the difficulty in annotating these tokens as either poset or simplifying left-dislocations, the strength of any conclusions based on this distinction might be rather weak.[23]

For both types of it-clefts, the informative-presupposition it-cleft and the stressed-focus it-cleft, the status of the complement clause is one of semantic presupposition. Once again, determining the pragmatic status, whether the complement clause is entirely new to the hearer or in fact should be inferable, is difficult. Only it-clefts with explicit complement clauses are included, so stressed-focused it-clefts where the complement clause is entirely missing (and therefore presumed recoverable by the hearer from the speaker's perspective) are not part of the corpus. This may mean then that the stressed-focus clauses that are included are ones where the status of the complement clause is somewhat less salient,

---

[23] All cases of unexpected subject-type left-dislocations were grouped with simplifying left-dislocations rather than poset ones. Essentially, these were cases where the referent of the preposed NP was clearly not discourse-new, but where no plausible salient poset to which it belonged presented itself.

and so closer in function to the informative-presupposition type. In addition, the corpus used for this study is entirely spontaneous oral discourse[24] and not in a highly formal register; informative-presupposition it-clefts are primarily a written form. As such, the discourse segmentation effects of the it-clefts here may be more similar than might otherwise be expected even though the information status of the complement clause is variable. This, then, supports the collapsing of the two functional classes. However, the division of it-clefts into two subclasses by discourse function is well-established in the literature (Prince, 1978; Hedberg, 1990; Delin and Oberlander, 1995), and in particular each type of it-cleft is thought to appear with different types of discourse relations. Therefore, as with left-dislocations, each it-cleft was coded for a sub-function, in this case either informative-presupposition or stressed-focus. This distinction was also rather difficult to make for several tokens, and so the same caveat will apply to any conclusions drawn from the statistical analyses based on the division of it-clefts into these two classes.

Wh-clefts are a more uniform class than the other three categories of non-canonical sentence types; no functional split has been established in the literature. However, based on inspection of the data, it does appear that wh-clefts which are not in an ELABORATION relation with another discourse segment are often in a CONTRAST relation. Each wh-cleft was coded for whether or not it was in a CONTRAST relation; this coding can be used as a dependent variable to measure whether or not this distinction is reflected in the other features coded here.

Finally, a control group of 200 utterances with main-clause canonical word order were randomly extracted from the corpus. The selection of control utterances will be discussed in further detail below. The total number of tokens of each type are listed in Table 4.2.

Syntactic Type	No. of Tokens
It-cleft	150
Left-dislocation	258
Topicalization	111
Wh-cleft	280
Control	200
Total	999

Table 4.2: Number of tokens by sentence type

---

[24]With the possible exception of some of the interviewers' questions which may have been written down ahead of time.

4.2.2   Annotation

In order to annotate the properties of each token utterance, the boundaries of an utterance must be defined. Defining what counts as a single utterance unit is not a settled issue. General consensus suggests that the presence of a finite, tensed verb is required. Passonneau and Litman (1997) define as their utterance unit a FUNC-TIONALLY INDEPENDENT CLAUSE (FIC) (Passonneau, 1994). An FIC must be a tensed clause that is neither a verb argument nor a restrictive relative. Along with main clauses, their definition includes question answers, appositive relative clauses, and subordinate clauses. They do not include "formulaic phrases" that serve as interjections, such as *Let's see* and *You know*.

For the most part, the annotation here follows their definition of an FIC. There is substantial evidence to suggest, however, that in English a main clause and its attached subordinates should count as a single utterance for centering purposes (Miltsakaki, 2002). Treating subordinate clauses as comprising a single utterance unit with their main clause results in more coherent set of transitions when measured over a corpus of naturally-occurring discourse. In addition, as mentioned in Section 2.2.1, according to Labov and Waletzky (1967), only main clauses are relevant in establishing the temporal sequence of a narrative. As such, all subordinate clauses are treated as part of a single utterance with the main clause to which they are attached. The exception to this is appositive relative clauses. Functionally, appositive relative clauses appear to be making an assertion separate from that of their main clause. This seems to indicate that they should count as a separate FIC.[25]

In addition, (Passonneau, 1994)'s definition of FICs does not explain how to deal with subjectless main clauses, ones which are not conjoined to another main clause with the conjunction *and*, i.e. a conjoined verb phrase. Corpus studies have shown, however, that in the majority of subject-drop clauses, the missing subject is the sentence's backward-looking center, and so the centering transition would count as a CONTINUE (Sturtevant, 1999). For this reason, clauses of this type were collapsed with the preceding clause for the purposes of defining unit boundaries.[26]

---

[25]After all annotation was completed, however, upon examination nearly every apposi-tive clause appeared to simply be part of either a continue or a smooth shift with respect to its main clause, whether or not that main clause was a non-canonical or a control utterance because, of course, an appositive relative clause shares at least one referential tie with the main clause. As we expect to find some differences in utterances depending on whether the follow a non-canonical or a control utterance, having included these appositive rela-tive clauses may serve to obscure these differences to some extent. For future research, it would be most desirable to control for the effects of appositives.

[26]As such, essentially the opposite choice as made for appositive relative clauses was made here. This was perhaps not the wisest choice; however, instances of subjectless main

Selection of control class

To select a set of canonical utterances as a control class for comparison purposes, lines containing non-canonical utterances were removed from the corpus. Then, the approximately 43,000 remaining lines were rearranged in a random order. Every 213th line was extracted to yield 200 sentences. The first and second of multiple main clauses were chosen alternately when there were multiple main clauses on a single line. Punctuation of the oral histories is somewhat erratic. Hence, the number of main clauses between two periods, the punctuation used to demarcate clause boundaries by the sentence boundary finder, varied. In general, the punctuation follows written standard punctuation. However, in some cases clauses beginning with coordinate conjunctions are separated from the preceding clause by a period. Sometimes full main clauses are only separated by commas, even in the absence of any coordinate conjunction. In some cases, it seems the transcribers were probably using punctuation to indicate degree of closeness of intonational and semantic connections between clauses, but as this was not a linguistic transcription, and the transcribers cannot be consulted with, such an interpretation was not reliable enough to be useful. Decisions about how to determine utterance boundaries based on the concept of an FIC were done in the same way as for the four non-canonical classes.

Features annotated

Extensive annotation of the 999 tokens was undertaken. Here we will describe all of the features and feature values annotated. However, not all of these features were used in the statistical modeling that will be described later in this chapter. The features here were annotated with respect to a three-utterance window around the non-canonical (or control) utterance, U_i. For most feature's the value was annotated for U_{i-1}, U_i, and U_{i+1}. This window was chosen in order to determine the degree of connection between the non-canonical utterance and its preceding and following utterances. It will obviously not allow us to test any claims about how non-canonical utterances may enhance the salience of discourse entities evoked at points further back in the discourse. Instead we will only be investigating what the local context around a non-canonical or a control canonical utterance looks like. As will be discussed below, the closer and more numerous the semantic connections between two utterances, the more likely they are to be part of a single discourse segment; weaker connections indicate that a segment break is more likely, signaling the beginning or end of a discourse segment. The features here were chosen primarily for their ability to potentially indicate the presence and strength of such connections.

---

clauses were rare in the corpus. In addition, the phenomena was treated the same way for all classes, and so should not contribute to enhancing any distinctions between classes falsely.

- EMBEDDEDNESS Embedded clauses include restrictive relatives, complement, and subordinate clauses. Only non-canonical utterances have been annotated for whether or not they were embedded clauses because no embedded clauses were selected as utterances in the control group. In addition, only FIC's could count as utterances, and so the utterances surrounding each token sentence are also only main clauses. The numbers of embedded clauses in each of the non-canonical classes were roughly similar: 38 left-dislocations (14.7%); 40 wh-clefts (14.3%); 10 topicalizations (9%); 25 it-clefts (16.6%). If non-canonical forms can have the same effect from within an utterance as they would have as the main clause in that utterance, then treating these embedded tokens identically to regular tokens should not effect the hypothesis testing. If, however, these non-canonical clauses have no effect on the segmentation boundaries surrounding the larger utterance they belong to when they are embedded, then this will have the effect of lessening any difference between the non-canonical utterances and the control group. In other words, because their main clause order is canonical, by classifying these utterances as non-canonicals, we are in effect "muddying the waters" by putting these canonical-like non-canonicals into the non-canonical classes. However, by removing them altogether we are losing a substantial number of tokens which would also lessen the significance of any feature effects found. For future experiments, the embedded sentences could be removed from the data in order to test their effects although this has not been done to date.[27]

- DISCOURSE MARKERS The presence and type of any discourse markers was annotated for U_{i-1}, U_i, U_{i+1}. All pre-subject constituents were annotated regardless of their status as discourse connectives, including prepositional phrases, non-prepositional phrase time expressions, and non-discourse connective adverbial phrases. For purposes of the statistical analysis, the annotated features could be treated many ways. The presence of any feature on any of the three utterances can be a binary feature with values +/-. In addition, each possible type of discourse marker can be converted into a binary feature also (e.g. CONN(U_i)=*but*). Alternatively, for each utterance one can also simply have a single attribute with multiple values, i.e. CONN(U_i)={none, *but, and, now, then*,...}. In the final feature set, a modified version of the latter was used, which retained the value

---

[27]Parentheticals (e.g. *I think, I suppose, I guess*, and *I mean*) present a problem both for determining embeddedness and for determining whether the subject *I* should count as a referring NP syntactic subject of the sentence for purposes of determining the referential features described below. Deciding whether the parenthetical was not merely a parenthetical was determined on a token-by-token basis. At worst this should merely add some noise to the data but not greatly effect conclusions drawn from it.

NONE, and retained the values for some of the most common markers, but collapsed the remaining markers into a single category of OTHER. This was done primarily because the individual counts for the majority of connectives were too low to contribute to a statistical analysis. Because we lack a complete theory of the semantics of each individual connective and because of the vagueness and polysemy inherent in many discourse connectives, it is difficult to motivate collapsing markers together into subcategories. Both larger quantities of data and more advanced semantic and pragmatics of discourse markers could assist further investigation of this factor in the future.

- COREFERRING ENTITIES IN UTTERANCE PAIRS This feature was annotated for pairs of utterances (U_{i-1}, U_i) and then (U_i, U_{i+1}). If two utterances both have NPs which refer to identical entities (or sets of entities) then the value is positive, otherwise it is negative. The criteria for coreference are essentially those from Passonneau (1994). One case in which my annotation schema differs from that of Passonneau (1994) is the case of discourse deixis. Discourse deictic pronouns can be used to refer to the semantic content of a single utterance, a constituent within a single utterance, or multiple utterances (Webber, 1991). If an utterance U_n has a discourse deictic pronoun that refers to a part or the whole of utterance U_m, then the two utterances will be marked as positive for this feature. However, if the discourse deictic pronoun refers to the semantic content of multiple utterances in addition to U_m, then the relationship of the utterance with the pronoun, U_n, and a single one of those antecedent utterances, U_m, will be classified as having the status of sharing reference to only inferentially-related entities.

- INFERENTIALLY-RELATED ENTITIES IN UTTERANCE PAIRS This feature is also annotated with respect to pairs of utterances, (U_{i-1}, U_i) and (U_i, U_{i+1}). Inferential relations are based on the following criteria. The criteria here are based on two previous discourse annotation schema, Passonneau (1994) and Jordan (2000). Inferential-relatedness is a broader relation than a poset relation because it includes functional dependency (cf. Birner and Ward (1998)).

  - Part and whole (e.g. *pears* and *pear tree*; *bicycle* and *bicycle wheel*).
  - Set and subset or member, including plurals (e.g. *one pear* and *all the pears*).[28]

---

[28]With respect to plurals, a singular noun phrase is annotated as being only inferentially-related to a plural noun phrase whose referent includes the referent of the singular. So for example, a noun phrase N which refers to x alone will only be inferentially related to a plural pronoun *they* which refers to x & y.

- Class and instance (e.g. *any tables* and *a green one*).
- Possessor and possessee.[29]
- Implicit arguments, as in (117), where the utterances in bold would be marked as inferentially-related. Locatives and benefactives are included here as having argument status. The missing argument must be explicit in at least one of the two utterances.

  (117)   I'm not clear just what it does to the Children's Bureau, **but it does something. I'll find out $\emptyset$ tomorrow night.** (SSA, mulliner2)

- Identity, such that +COREF always implies +INFER, but not vice versa.

- CENTERING TRANSITIONS Rather than using a full set of the centering transitions (CONTINUE, RETAIN, SMOOTH SHIFT, and ROUGH SHIFT) which would require an examination of more than the three-utterance window used in this study, an abbreviated set of features that can approximate some of what these transitions encode is used. In particular, the preferred center of U_{i-1} was recorded; the preferred and backward-looking centers of U_i; and the backward-looking center of U_{i+1}. Only the coreference relation (including discourse deixis) as delineated above was used to determine the backward-looking center. That is, an entity can only be the backward-looking center of U_j if it corefers with an utterance in U_{j-1}, i.e. appears on the forward-looking center list of U_{j-1}.[30] When there are no coreferring entities, the C_b was recorded as NONE.[31]

With respect to discourse deixis, a discourse deictic pronoun was taken to corefer with any entities included in the constituents to which the deictic points. So, a discourse deictic pronoun can in fact be the C_b of an utterance if its semantic content includes a reference to the highest-ranked entity on the previous utterance's C_f list. In addition, if a pronoun in U_j refers to

---

[29]However, a possessive pronoun will count as a potentially coreferring NP. For example, if *John* is referred to in one utterance, and *John's father* in the next, these two utterances will be annotated as COREF=YES.

[30]In fact, there has been much debate about whether references to entities in an utterance U_i which are inferentially related to entities on the C_f list of U_{i-1} should be possible candidates for the role of C_b of U_i (Hahn et al., 1996; Kibble and Power, 1999; Walker and Prince, 1996). This project treats inferentially-related entities as substantively different than coreferentially-related entities, for reasons to be discussed in Section 4.3.1.

[31]As such, there is an implicational relationship between the feature $C_b(U_j)$=none and COREF(U_j-1, U_j)=NO, such that one is true iff the other is.

an entity included in a discourse deictic in U_{j-1}, then depending on the realization of each and the other members of the C_f lists in their respective utterances, the referent of the pronoun can potentially count as the C_b of U_j.

In the canonical utterances, the C_f ranking used is based on grammatical role: SUBJECT >> D.O. >> I.O. >> OTHER ARGUMENTS >> OTHER ADJUNCTS. All entities appearing in subordinate clauses are ranked lower than any main clause entities, and ordered by grammatical role with respect to each other. Entities in a complex NP, one with a complement or restrictive relative clause, are ranked at the level of the head, from left to right.

In non-canonical utterances, deciding on C_f ranking is more difficult. In wh-clefts, any entities in the wh-clause are highest ranked; within the wh-clause rankings are based on grammatical role, as given above. Then, the remaining entities that appear in the focus constituent are ranked on the basis of grammatical role ordering. Given that the information status of the wh-clause itself is one where the speaker presumes it is salient, and the basis for using grammatical role as a ranking in English is the presumed relative salience of particular roles over others, such an ordering seems well-justified. In topicalization, ranking is strictly based on grammatical function; this is based on the fact that in almost all topicalizations, the subject NP is realized as a pronominal, while the topicalized NP almost never is. This indicates that the topicalized NP is not as salient. However, it is not as clear what happens after the topicalization is used, i.e. whether the topicalized entity becomes more salient. Using this ordering of the C_f list, the percentage of tokens where the C_p of U_i is the same as C_b of U_{i+1}, does seem quite low for topicalizations, in light of the percentage of tokens where U_i and U_{i+1} share coreferring entities, which is similar to other classes, as shown in Table 4.2.2.

	$C_p(U_i)=C_b(U_{i+1})$	Coref(U_i, U_{i+1})=yes
Wh-clefts	58%	71%
Topicalizations	49.5%	74%
Left-dislocations	55%	74%
It-clefts	59%	75%
Control	57%	72%

Table 4.3: Centering transitions vs. sharing coreferring entities by sentence type

However, for it-clefts and left-dislocations, strictly grammatical role ranking was used also to determine the C_f list in order to identify a C_p. Because grammatical role alone was used for all three of topicalizations, left-dislocations and it-clefts, the difference in percentages listed in the second column in Table 4.2.2 is presumably the result of a difference in usage rather than simply an artifact of annotation decisions.

The remaining features were annotated but not used in the Varbrul analysis for two reasons. The most common reason for this is that they appeared too infrequently. Given that there were only a total of 1000 tokens and five class labels, the discourse markers and referential patterns alone could be converted into anywhere from 32 binary features to a smaller amount of multi-valued features. Even this amount is a rather large amount of features to test in a statistical analysis with such a limited data set, and as such even this feature set was ultimately reduced to include only the features most likely to allow testing of significance and convergence of the parameter estimation algorithm used in calculating the logistic regression model.

An additional reason for not using these features applies in particular to the phrasal cues of segment openings and closings. Coding these features was in fact a more subjective task than for most of the other annotated features. In fact, coding these features is essentially the equivalent of coding the beginning and ending of discourse segments directly, a task which this project was designed to avoid.

- PHRASAL CUES OF SEGMENT OPENINGS AND CLOSINGS In Walker (1993), explicit phrases that are used to indicate the beginning and ending of segments were compared to the use of IRUs. In this project for each of U_{i-1}, U_i, and U_{i+1}, the presence of these cues was marked as +OPEN and +CLOSE. In addition, if an utterance is the first or last in a turn, this was counted as a specific sub-type of opening and closing a segment, respectively.

  Segment opener phrases include: *as far as the Z*; *on the subject of Y*; *getting back to X*; *okay, second/next question*; and *one thing/person/idea+* relative clause. Segment closings include: *yeah I figured*; and *okay, that was my question*. In addition, the last utterance of a multi-utterance sequence of embedded speech was also included as a third subtype of segment closings.

- SYNTACTIC FORM Several syntactic forms were annotated for each of U_{i-1}, U_i, and U_{i+1}. These include: reverse wh-clefts, which have been claimed to be indicators of the end of a discourse segment (Oberlander and Delin, 1996); *there*-constructions, which in English can either be used to introduce hearer-new entities or to list an item in a series of items (Ward, 1998; Ward and Birner, 1995) and so may be indicators of the beginning of a new discourse segment or in a context of parallel discourse segments. If any of the utterances were either yes-no or wh-questions, this was also coded because questions may mark the start of a new discourse segment.

Finally it was recorded if either U_{i-1} or U_{i+1} were non-canonical sentences themselves. The distribution of these features across the classes was in the end too sparse to be of use.

Finally, two additional features which could be used as dependent variables themselves were annotated. Unlike coding for the syntactic form of a token utterance, however, coding these features is more subjective. In addition, unlike the features related to referential patterns, the ambiguities and difficulties inherent in these meaning-related features cannot be minimized simply by specifying the categories in greater detail. Therefore, similar to the functional subcategories coded for left-dislocations and it-clefts, conclusions drawn from data based on these distinctions must be evaluated in light of the ambiguity in the underlying categories used to generate the data.

- CONTRAST Each token utterance U_i was coded roughly on the basis of whether preceding either itself or U_{i+1} with the phrase *in contrast* would yield an acceptable discourse. If so, it was marked as +CONTRAST. Additionally, tokens of U_i, such that P is the denotation of U_i and $\neg P$ is highly salient, were also marked as +CONTRAST.

- POSET Each token utterance was coded for whether there was a relevant salient partially-ordered set relation at the point of utterance of U_i. The identity relation was not included as a possibility here. The best paraphrase that would allow a quasi-linguistic test of this feature was the addition of the phrase *with respect to S*, where S is the potentially relevant poset, to the beginning of U_i. The inherent awkwardness of this test makes evaluating the acceptability of it difficult.

Now that we have seen in detail the entire possible feature set, the next section will describe which of these features were included in the final data set used to test the predictions described above about the correlation of discourse context and non-canonical sentence forms.

4.2.3   Final feature set

The full annotation of all the features discussed in the previous section was first converted into binary features in order to get a clearer picture of which features had a dense enough distribution that they could be of use in a statistical model. This lead to the selection of 32 binary features which incorporated both discourse marker features and referential pattern features. This subset of features was intended to provide a picture of the degree and type of semantic connections between utterances in order to indicate the types of local discourse structure transitions in which the token utterances participated. The details of this are presented in Section 4.3.1 below. Here we will simply explain how the raw annotations discussed above are simplified first into a large set of binary features and then a smaller set of multivalued features. The latter will be used in the comparison of syntactic classes using Varbrul logistic regression analyses.

Across all classes, when summed across all three utterances which comprised the annotation window of each token, the most common discourse markers were the following: *and, but, yes, well, then, of course, now, at any rate, or, no, oh*, time adverbials, other adverbials, prepositional phrases, and subordinate clauses.[32] Of these only the six most frequent were included in the reduced feature set, *and, but, so, sub*, PP, *yes*. In addition, given the relatively clear status of *now* as a marker of beginning a new discourse segment, it was also included in this set. These seven discourse markers are translated into 21 binary features because each one may be present on either U_{i-1}, U_i, or U_{i+1}. The presence or absence of a discourse marker phrase was also included for each of the three utterances. Then, for the pairs of utterances (U_{i-1}, U_i) and (U_i, U_{i+1}) whether the pair shared coreferring entities and/or inferentially-related entities was included. Finally, the existence of $C_b(U_i)$ and $C_b(U_{i+1})$ were annotated as two features, as were whether or not $C_p(U_{i-1}) = C_b(U_i)$ and $C_p(U_i) = C_b(U_{i+1})$.

All of the 32 binary features are presented in Table 4.2.3. The count presented for each feature is the number of times the feature is positive. The data set here is 90% of the full data set. The remaining 10% is reserved as a test set for the classifiers trained on this training set.[33] Each raw count has a percentage following it in parentheses. This is the percentage of the total number of times the feature is positive across the entire training data set. For example, of the 71 instances where *but* appears on the token utterance U_i, nine of those instances or 13% were topicalizations. The features are grouped by type. The first group are all properties of the discourse markers appearing on the utterance preceding the token utterance, U_{i-1}. The second group is the discourse marker properties for U_i; the third is discourse marker properties for U_{i+1}. The last two groups are the referential properties of the pairs (U_{i-1}, U_i) and (U_i, U_{i+1}), respectively.

Even this reduced feature set is too large for inclusion in a statistical model of the data here. Although the total number of tokens in the training data is about 900, the limiting factor here is the size of the smallest two classes to be compared, topicalizations and it-clefts, which together have 235 tokens. In order to perform an accurate and reliable logistic regression analysis, the data set should have several properties. First, features which are either almost always on or almost always off will not be useful as independent variables.[34] A rule of thumb is that a feature should not be on (positive) less than 5% of the time or more than 95%.

---

[32]This list is a union of the top ten discourse markers for each class.

[33]Each class makes up the same proportion of the total in both the training and the test set (e.g. CONTROL's are 20% of the test and 20% of the training data.)

[34]See Guy (1988) for further discussion of this issue and examples, which he refers to as *data overlap with* p_0, that is the input probability.

FEATURE	CONTROL	IT-CLEFT	LEFT-DIS.	TOPIC.	WH-CLEFT	TOTAL
TOTAL COUNTS	180 (20)	135 (15)	232 (26)	100 (11)	252 (28)	899 (100)
+MARKER(U_{i-1})	82 (19)	72 (17)	115 (27)	47 (11)	113 (26)	429 (48)
and	27 (18)	22 (15)	48 (33)	17 (12)	33 (22)	147 (16)
but	12 (16)	15 (20)	11 (15)	10 (13)	27 (36)	75 (8)
yes	5 (36)	1 (7)	4 (29)	2 (14)	2 (14)	14 (2)
now	1 (17)	1 (17)	4 (67)	0 (0)	0 (0)	6(1)
so	7 (16)	4 (9)	13 (30)	5 (11)	15 (34)	44 (5)
PP	10 (20)	7 (14)	13 (26)	6 (12)	14 (28)	50 (6)
SUB. CLAUSE	5 (17)	6 (20)	5 (17)	5 (17)	9(30)	30 (3)
+MARKER(U_i)	73 (19)	65 (16)	105 (27)	37 (9)	114 (29)	394 (44)
and	24 (18)	22 (17)	39 (30)	16 (12)	31 (23)	85 (15)
but	9 (13)	15 (21)	16 (23)	9 (13)	22 (31)	71 (8)
yes	9 (47)	0 (0)	2 (11)	2 (11)	6 (32)	19 (2)
now	2 (11)	1 (5)	8 (42)	2 (11)	6 (32)	19 (2)
so	3 (7)	10 (24)	9 (22)	1 (2)	18 (44)	41 (5)
PP	9 (30)	4 (13)	7 (23)	0 (0)	10 (33)	30 (3)
SUB. CLAUSE	6 (25)	9 (38)	5 (21)	1 (4)	3 (13)	24 (3)
+MARKER(U_{i+1})	82(19)	56 (13)	116 (27)	50 (12)	123 (29)	427 (47)
and	22 (15)	21 (14)	42 (28)	14 (9)	51 (34)	150(17)
but	10 (16)	6 (10)	16 (26)	20 (32)	10 (16)	62 (7)
yes	5 (31)	5 (31)	3 (19)	0 (0)	3 (19)	16 (2)
now	1 (13)	1 (13)	3 (38)	0 (0)	3 (38)	8(1)
so	7 (16)	5 (11)	14 (32)	7 (16)	11 (25)	44(5)
PP	14 (25)	8 (15)	11 (20)	6 (11)	16 (29)	55 (6)
SUB. CLAUSE	5 (19)	3 (11)	9 (33)	6 (22)	4 (15)	27 (3)
$C_p(U_{i-1})$=$C_b(U_i)$	79 (23)	56 (16)	68 (20)	56 (16)	88 (25)	347 (39)
$C_b(U_i)$ EXISTS	120 (22)	85 (15)	124 (22)	73 (13)	151 (27)	553 (62)
COREF(U_{i-1},U_i)	124 (24)	79 (15)	109 (21)	69 (13)	145 (28)	526 (59)
INFER(U_{i-1},U_i)	164 (21)	123 (16)	199 (26)	94 (12)	199 (26)	779 (87)
$C_p(U_i)$=$C_b(U_{i+1})$	79 (20)	53 (14)	102 (27)	48 (12)	109 (28)	391 (43)
$C_b(U_{i+1})$ EXISTS	132 (19)	100 (15)	182 (27)	79 (12)	191 (28)	684 (76)
COREF(U_i,U_{i+1})	132 (20)	101 (15)	169 (26)	75 (11)	180 (27)	657 (73)
INFER(U_i,U_{i+1})	161 (19)	128 (15)	225 (27)	93 (11)	233 (28)	840 (93)

Table 4.4: Reduced binary feature set with raw counts and percentages

Secondly, the less data one has, the fewer features one can reliably include in the model. This is partly due to the fact that with many features, the number of possible feature vectors (or cells) increases rapidly. If there are too many cells and not enough data points, there will be cells with only a few tokens or even no tokens at all. It is impossible to discern whether these low or zero counts are "real" or just the result of a sparse data matrix. In addition, having large numbers of cells where many are empty violates the ideal of having a balanced data set where each cell has roughly the same number of tokens. The parameter estimation algorithm often fails to have converged after its maximum 20 iterations when the number of features and cells is very large, resulting in unreliable parameter estimates.[35]

Finally, a logistic regression analysis assumes that each independent variable (attribute or factor group) is truly independent of all others, which means there should be no interactions between features (factor groups). Sometimes this assumption may be violated in actuality but this cannot be ascertained until after considerable data analysis. Nonetheless, *known* interactions between features should be removed either by regrouping or removing features altogether.

All of these characteristics are problems for the original feature set presented in Table 4.2.3. Using the 32 binary features with the 899 training data points results in only 623 cells. In other words, out of the 2^{32} (or ~ 4.3 billion) cells possible, we only see 623 of them in the data (and at most could only see 899 of them if each of our training tokens was unique.). In addition, within each of the discourse marker groups, at least three features show up in less than five percent of tokens. Known interaction between features is the case for features in each of the five groups in Table 4.2.3. Determining which features to retain when pruning this set of binary features required the combined consideration of all these factors. Ultimately, it lead to a reduction of the 32 binary features to a more reasonable set of two four-valued features and three five-valued features. This feature set yields 10,000 possible feature combinations. While this is an improvement over the 4.3 billion with the unreduced set, it is still a very large number given the quantity of data in any particular binary comparison of classes here.

Among the discourse marker features, both implicational relationships between features and feature sparseness had to be remedied. If an utterance U_n appears with a discourse marker (e.g. *and, but, so*) then it must be +MARKER. In addition, if it appears with a coordinate conjunction, like *but*, then because of the linguistic constraint on the distribution of these conjunctions, the value for the feature MARKER=*and* must be negative. As a result, for each of the three discourse marker feature groups, the eight binary features can b e reduced into a single five-valued feature, as shown in Table 4.2.3.

The conjunctions *and* and *but* were by far the most frequent markers in these groups. They were retained along with the adverbial *so*. Even though they all dis-

---

[35]This maximum number of iterations is unmodifiable in Varbrul.

a	(+MARKER) ∧ (MARKER=*and*)
b	(+MARKER) ∧ (MARKER=*but*)
s	(+MARKER) ∧ (MARKER=*so*)
o	(+MARKER) ∧ (MARKER=OTHER)
n	-MARKER

Table 4.5: Composite feature: Discourse marker type and presence

play ambiguity in their meaning as discourse connectives, they are presumably a more uniform class than the only other group with any frequency, MARKER=PP. The difficulty of interpreting the presence of a sentence-initial PP in the framework to be discussed below motivated its removal from the set as an individual feature. Instead, it was collapsed with all the remaining discourse markers into the category OTHER.

Interpreting the discourse marker feature for U_{i-1} is more difficult than for the other discourse marker features because it is not clear what it would mean for the theoretical model if the tokens in one class have greater than average numbers of discourse markers on the immediately preceding utterance. This will be kept in mind when interpreting the results which use this feature.

Like the discourse marker features, the referential features are related implicationally and so display structural interactions. For example, if two utterances U_n and U_m both contain NPs that refer to the same entity then they will be marked as +COREF. In addition, they will also be marked as +INFER because identity is a subtype of inferential relation.

The following logical relationships between the referential features hold:

(118) $C_p(U_{x-1})=C_b(U_x) \rightarrow C_b(U_x)$ exists

(119) $C_b(U_x)$ exists $\leftrightarrow$ COREFER(U_{x-1},U_x)

(120)   COREFER(U_x,U_y) $\rightarrow$ INFER(U_x,U_y)

Therefore, all of these four features can be collapsed into a single feature with four ordinal values, 0–3. At the top of the scale, 3, the two utterances for which the feature holds have the closest possible connection between the sets of entities to which they refer. At the bottom, 0, the two utterances share no connections between the entities to which they refer. The scale of referential connection and its connection to the features is derived from is shown in Table 4.2.3.

Because the features $C_b(U_x)$ EXISTS and COREFER(U_x,U_{x-1}) should be true in all the same contexts, only one of them needs to be included in the table. In fact, these two features were annotated separately and so in the data there is some disagreement between them—about 75/899 cases for (U_{i-1}, U_i) and 59/899 for (U_i,U_{i+1}). In 24/75 and 16/59 of these cases, respectively, COREFER held, but C_b did not. Disagreement was resolved such that if either feature holds,

	$C_p(U_{x-1})=C_b(U_x)$	COREFER(U_{x-1}, U_x)	INFER(U_{x-1}, U_x)
3	yes	yes	yes
2	no	yes	yes
1	no	no	yes
0	no	no	no

Table 4.6: Composite feature: Degree of referential connection (U_x, U_{x-1})

then COREFER(U_{x-1},U_x) is true. The disagreement illustrates the difficulty of annotating even relatively straightforward features such as these with complete consistency. Disagreement was likely due to subtle changes in categorization of items such as missing arguments during the period of annotation. By collapsing the two categories, however, the noisiness of the data should be minimized.

The feature counts for the modified composite feature set are shown in Table 4.7. Some general trends can be identified simply by examining these raw counts and comparing the percentages of features to the percentages by class. For example for feature 5, REF(U_i,U_{i+1}), the control class has more than its share of cases where there are no connections (0), while the left-dislocation class has much less than its share of the same. With respect to feature 4, REF(U_{i-1}, U_i), topicalizations have very few cases with no connection (0), wh-clefts have inordinately many. For REF(U_{i-1}, U_i)=3, however, topicalizations and controls have disproportionately many; left-dislocations disproportionately few.

For MARK(U_{i-1}), wh-clefts and it-clefts have a larger proportion of the cases of *but*. For MARK(U_i), controls and left-dislocations have relatively few cases of *but*, and wh-clefts and it-clefts have relatively more here too. For MARK(U_{i+1}), topicalizations have an unusually large number of *but*; wh-clefts and left-dislocations have a relatively larger number of cases of *and*. Wh-clefts also have a disproportionate number of cases of *so* both on U_{i-1} and U_i; left-dislocations and topicalizations have relatively more cases of *so* on U_{i+1}.

The interpretation of these trends which are recognizable by inspection alone will be reserved until we look at the features found to be statistically significant in the Varbrul analysis. Table 4.7 is encouraging, however, for the general claim that these features will correlate in interesting ways with the five classes of syntactic form. The explanation of what those correlations might mean for the theory in Chapter 3 will be discussed in the next section.

4.3   A statistical model of the correlations of discourse context and word order

As discussed above, the communicative goals concentrated on in this experimental phase of the project are those related to discourse structure and attentional

		CONTROL	IT-CLEFT	LEFT-DIS.	TOPIC.	WH-CLEFT	TOTAL
TOTALS		180 (20)	135 (15)	232 (26)	100 (11)	252 (28)	899 (100)
1. MARK(U_{i-1})	a	27 (19)	22 (15)	47 (33)	17 (12)	30 (21)	143 (16)
	b	12 (16)	15 (20)	11 (15)	10 (13)	27 (36)	75 (8)
	s	7 (16)	4 (9)	13 (30)	5 (11)	15 (34)	44 (5)
	o	36 (22)	31 (19)	44 (26)	15 (9)	41 (25)	167 (19)
	n	98 (21)	63 (13)	117 (25)	53 (11)	139 (30)	470 (52)
2. MARK(U_i)	a	23 (18)	21 (16)	38 (30)	16 (13)	30 (23)	128 (14)
	b	9 (13)	15 (21)	16 (23)	9 (13)	22 (31)	71 (8)
	s	3 (7)	10 (24)	9 (22)	1 (2)	18 (44)	41 (5)
	o	38 (25)	19 (12)	42 (27)	11 (7)	44 (29)	154 (17)
	n	107 (21)	70 (14)	127 (25)	63 (12)	138 (27)	505 (56)
3. MARK(U_{i+1})	a	20 (14)	20 (14)	42 (29)	13 (9)	50 (34)	145 (16)
	b	10 (16)	6 (10)	16 (26)	19 (31)	10 (16)	61 (7)
	s	7 (16)	5 (11)	14 (32)	7 (16)	11 (25)	44 (5)
	o	45 (25)	25 (14)	44 (25)	11 (6)	52 (29)	177 (20)
	n	98 (21)	79 (17)	116 (25)	50 (11)	129 (27)	472 (53)
4. REF(U_{i-1}, U_i)	3	79 (23)	56 (16)	68 (20)	56 (16)	88 (25)	347 (39)
	2	45 (20)	29 (13)	63 (27)	21 (9)	72 (31)	230 (26)
	1	40 (19)	39 (18)	71 (33)	18 (8)	46 (21)	214 (24)
	0	16 (15)	11 (10)	30 (28)	5 (5)	46 (43)	108 (12)
5. REF(U_i, U_{i+1})	3	79 (20)	53 (14)	102 (26)	48 (12)	109 (28)	391 (43)
	2	55 (18)	54 (17)	83 (27)	32 (10)	85 (28)	309 (34)
	1	27 (18)	22 (15)	42 (29)	13 (9)	42 (29)	146 (16)
	0	19 (36)	6 (11)	5 (9)	7 (13)	16 (30)	53 (6)

Table 4.7: Composite features: counts and percentages by class

structure. In particular, the feature sets utilized here are intended to be low-level indicators of transitions in discourse segments and attentional states. These features are not perfect predictors of where discourse segments begin and end or how two discourse segments are related in meaning. They can, however, be thought of as providing a rough picture of the discourse structure relations, both intentional and attentional, of a set of adjacent utterances by looking at the lexical, syntactic, and semantic content of this set of utterances.

In this section, first the theory of how these features provide a picture of discourse structure will be presented. Then, the predictions about how these correlates of discourse structure correspond with the different non-canonical syntactic forms will be discussed. Finally, the actual results of how well these predictions are borne out in the data as measured by the use of the statistical model will be presented.

4.3.1 A feature-based representation of discourse structure

The approximation of discourse structure used here is constructed primarily through patterns of (1) referential links across sentential boundaries and (2) lexical connectives. As such it can only be an extremely simplified picture of the semantics and syntax of the hierarchical discourse structure constructed and intended by the discourse participants.

With an expectation of how these discourse relations correlate with patterns of reference and lexical connectives, discussed below in this section, we then make predictions of how the non-canonical syntactic forms will also correlate with these same patterns based on the claims in the previous chapter about how non-canonical forms are used to indicate different discourse relations.

Unfortunately, the statistical tools we have to test the predictions we can make will not necessarily allow for a straightforward confirmation or disconfirmation of these predictions. A schematic representation of the problem is shown in figure 4.2. If we want to test whether discourse relation R_1 has a strong correlation with sentence type W, ideally we would test this correlation directly. As discussed extensively above, identifying cases of R_1 directly is too difficult. Instead, because it is far easier to identify referential patterns and discourse markers, we will look for correlations between W and the particular referential pattern x and discourse marker m that we expect to have a strong correlation with R_1.

Unfortunately, multiple discourse relations may influence the use of a single sentence type. For example, we may also want to test whether R_2 is correlated is with W. However, R_2 may correlate with entirely *different* referential patterns and discourse markers than found with R_1. When examining the patterns of correlation between discourse markers and sentence types and between referential patterns and sentence types, we will be aggregating over all possible discourse relations that may have given rise to the markers and patterns. As such, when two different referential patterns are in conflict with each other but both give rise

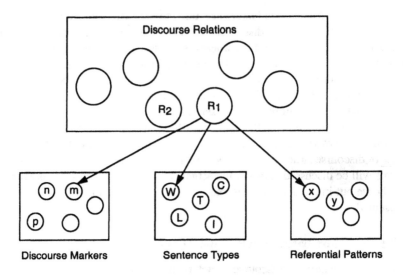

Figure 4.2: Influence of discourse relations on syntactic form, referential patterns, and discourse markers

to increased incidence of a single sentence type, they may cancel out each other's effects in the data. Ideally, one would want a statistical model which would taken into account the discourse markers and referential patterns and from them posit hidden states which correspond to the discourse relations. Then based upon these hidden states, the model would predict which sentence type would best fit the context. Unfortunately, such models require more data and ultimately may be no easier to interpret theoretically. So, instead we will make as many specific predictions as possible about the expected patterns of correlation between referential connections and discourse markers and sentence types, keeping in mind that complex interactions across patterns may make these predictions difficult to test when compared to the actual statistical results.

Overall, the framework here assumes the existence of a hierarchical discourse structure with the following properties, as discussed in Sections 2.2.1–2.2.2 and summarized here. When a new segment node N is attached on the right frontier of a discourse structure, it can be attached to any level of the right frontier. If it is adjoined to the leaf node, it may be the beginning of a new embedded segment, a PUSH, or it may be just a continuation of the previous segment. If it is adjoined higher than a leaf node, then it signals the beginning of a new segment not embedded in the previous segment (and potentially the continuation of a previous larger segment), and simultaneously, the closing-off of an embedded segment, a POP. The semantics of the attachment will be that the new segment will be inferred to be in some relation with the segment to which it is attached.[36] All the features used in the statistical models have been selected because they to some degree reflect how two adjacent utterances are related.

Referential relations and discourse relations

In general, two segments are more likely to be closely related (both semantically and syntactically in the discourse structure), the more semantic content they share. One aspect of sharing semantic content is referring to the same entities. Two adjacent utterances that refer to the same entity are more likely to be part of the same segment than two utterances that refer to entities which are only inferentially related. Two adjacent utterances that refer to entities which are inferentially related are more likely to be part of the same segment than two utterances referring to entirely different sets of entities. Another aspect of shared semantic content is having the same center of attention. So, an utterance U_i that has the same C_b as the preceding utterance U_{i-1}'s C_p should be more closely-related to U_{i-1} than if the C_b of U_i is not the C_p of U_{i-1}.

Different syntactic relations in the discourse structure should display different patterns in these types of shared reference. When one discourse segment is closed off to begin a new (or continue an old, higher) segment, the contents of the closed-off segment and the segment immediately following the POP are less likely to share semantic content. As such we expect that they are also less likely to refer to the same entities or to continue the center of attention. In addition, they will be more likely to have no shared references at all. In contrast, when an utterance U_i is used to begin a new, embedded segment then, it would be unlikely to share no references at all with U_{i-1} and, instead, would most likely refer to some of the same entities as in U_{i-1}, and may have as its C_b, the C_p of U_{i-1}. Two utterances that are adjacent siblings within the same segment will quite likely display a pattern where the C_b of the second is the C_p of the first, i.e. a CONTINUE or SMOOTH SHIFT centering transition. They are unlikely to refer to only inferentially-related entities or to have no references to common entities whatsoever.

These expected correlations between discourse segment syntactic relations and patterns of reference are shown in Table 4.8. The syntactic relation listed in the first column describes a move which takes place between U_{i-1} and U_i.[37]

---

[36] And possibly in a relation to some non-adjacent preceding segment depending on whether a discourse connective with anaphoric properties is used with the segment (Webber et al., 2003).

[37] As is implied by the names of each transition, and discussed in Sections 2.2.2 and 3.3.1, the syntactic relation between segments here can also be regarded as a change in the focus space that takes place when U_i is uttered. Either the focus space is popped off the stack, a new focus space is pushed on, or the same focus space is retained.

The top row in this table should be regarded as an implicational scale, where only one of the four conditions can be appropriate to describe the referential relations between two adjacent utterances, in particular the strongest condition that holds. If the property in a cell holds, no weaker condition in a cell to the right holds between two utterances.[38]

Relation between U_{i-1} and U_i	$C_p(U_{i-1})$ $= C_b(U_i))$	$(C_f(U_{i-1}) \cap$ $C_f(U_i)) \neq \emptyset$	Inferentially-related entities only	No shared reference
POP	unlikely	less likely	possible	likely
PUSH, BEGIN EMBEDDED SEG	possible	likely	possible	unlikely
CONTINUE IN SAME SEG	highly likely	possible	possible	highly unlikely

Table 4.8: Correlations between discourse structure moves and referential relations

The effect of one of these syntactic moves on the discourse structure between U_{i-1} and U_i also has implications for the patterns of reference between U_i and the following utterance, U_{i+1}. When a new segment is started, unless that new segment is a single utterance long, the utterance following the segment-initial utterance is likely to be part of the same segment. Given that U_{i-1} and U_i are not in the same segment (i.e. in the case of either a POP or a PUSH), then the likelihood that U_i and U_{i+1} are in the same segment is increased. The resulting effects are summarized in Table 4.9.

Relation between U_{i-1} and U_i	Relation between U_i and U_{i+1}	$C_p(U_i) =$ $C_b(U_{i+1})$	$C_f(U_i) \cap$ $C_f(U_{i+1}) \neq \emptyset$	Inferentially related entities only	No shared reference
SAME SEGMENT	unknown	possible	possible	possible	possible
DIFFERENT SEGMENT (PUSH, POP)	increased likelihood same segment	likely	likely	unlikely	highly unlikely

Table 4.9: Effects of U_{i-1}–U_i transition on U_i–U_{i+1} referential relations

Patterns of reference can also reflect the rhetorical relation one utterance has with another. For example, when two utterances are in a RESEMBLANCE relation, they may be immediately adjacent segments with a common parent which are interpreted as being coherent, but still have no coreferential links nor common

---

[38] The condition labels in the top row correspond exactly with the feature values 3,2,1, and 0, respectively, for the feature REF(U_{i-1},U_i).

centers of attention between the entities referred to in them, as in the two sample utterances in (121).

(121)   The linebacker bought a canoe. The quarterback rented a dinghy.

These two utterances do not refer to the same entities and do not share centers of attention. They do, however, refer to entities that are inferentially related. *Quarterback* and *linebacker* refer to two types of football players, and *canoe* and *dinghy* refer to types of boats.

Inferential connections without coreferential connections may indicate the presence of a RESEMBLANCE relation. As argued for in Kehler (2002) identity and similarity (e.g. being members of the same poset) of entities play crucial roles in allowing discourse participants to reconstruct (and differentiate) coherence relations. Therefore, if coherence relations are to be distinguished from each other on the basis of referential patterns, these two properties, coreference and inferential-relatedness, must necessarily be kept distinct. The stochastic nature of these patterns allows for exceptions, (e.g. segments in a CONTRAST relation with coreferring entities, segments in a NARRATIVE relation with only inferentially-related entities) without erasing evidence of major trends. The assumption underlying this treatment of inferential entities is that two subsegments may be children of a single common parent, and therefore part of a single coherent discourse segment *without* sharing a C_b. If sharing elements on their C_f lists is not the *sole* way for two utterances to be coherently related, then there is no need to collapse the distinction between coreference and inferentially-related. The significance of features found in this study where this distinction has been maintained support this assumption.

In addition to the connection between resemblance relations and inferentially-related entities, several other patterns of reference and the coherence relations they are predicted to correlate with are listed in Table 4.10.[39]

Relation between U_{i-1} and U_i	$C_p(U_{i-1})$ $= C_b(U_i))$	$C_f(U_{i-1}) \cap$ $C_f(U_i) \neq \emptyset$	Inferentially-related entities only	No shared reference
RESEMBLANCE	unlikely	possible	likely	impossible
ELABORATION	possible	likely	impossible	impossible
NARRATIVE	highly likely	possible	unlikely	impossible

Table 4.10: Correlations between coherence relations and referential relations

It is important to remember that in almost all of these heuristics, the correlations between a reference pattern and a syntactic or semantic discourse relation

---

[39]In this table, RESEMBLANCE includes all resemblance relations except elaboration which is listed separately. The term *possible* refers to cases which are possible but have no greater or lesser likelihood given the presence of the condition in the left column.

are not absolute but only more or less *likely*. By using a probabilistic model, however, we hope to be able to represent these patterns of greater or lesser likelihood found in the data.

From these correlations between reference patterns and syntactic and semantic discourse relations, we can now make predictions about expected correlations between the former and utterances with non-canonical word orders. These predictions are based primarily on how we expect non-canonical utterances to compare with canonical utterances. However, when we test these predictions by running statistical analyses on our data, we will also compare each type of non-canonical utterance with one another.

- Non-canonicals should be more likely than canonicals to appear with a POP. They should have weaker referential ties to the utterance that precedes them. In particular, we should see a greater incidence of having no referential ties to the preceding utterance at all. In addition, we should see a smaller incidence of having no referential ties to the following utterance.

- Non-canonicals should be less likely than canonicals to have a NARRATIVE relation with either the preceding or following utterance. This situation predicts that with respect to both of the utterances surrounding a non-canonical utterance, these utterances will be less likely to share the same center of attention than when the middle utterance is canonical.

- Non-canonicals should be more likely than canonicals to be in RESEMBLANCE relations with preceding or following utterances. The most likely reference pattern here should be one where the utterances refer to inferentially-related entities, but not to identical entities. So we expect to find a greater likelihood of reference to inferentially-related entities in both the preceding and following utterance.

- Wh-clefts should be more likely to appear with patterns which would characterize an ELABORATION relation and/or a discourse PUSH than other non-canonicals or canonicals. This means the most likely pattern for them should be to refer to the same entities as the preceding and following utterances. This may or may not correlate with greater incidence of having a C_b which was U_{i-1}'s C_p, but should correlate with a greater incidence of having a C_p which is U_{i+1}'s C_b.

In general, we will expect canonical utterances will be about equally likely to have referential connections with the utterance that precedes them as the utterance that follows them. That is, the probability that a canonical utterance is in a segment with the utterance that follows it should be about the same as the probability that it is in a segment with the utterance that precedes it. They will probably be slightly more likely to have at least some referential connection with (that is not have *no* referential connection whatsoever) preceding and following utterances because in general, two utterances in the same discourse are on the whole quite likely to be talking about the same or related entities.

For non-canonical utterances, in contrast, the connections with surrounding utterances are predicted to differ as discussed above. The patterns of referential connections should be skewed in some areas (i.e. fewer connections preceding, more connections following.) Because some of the patterns are in conflict with each other, the predictions may not be borne out in as clear a way as one would like. In addition, certain non-canonical forms may be more or less associated with particular discourse relation goals (e.g. wh-clefts and the ELABORATION relation, it-clefts and CONTRAST). This may add complexity to the patterns found across the different non-canonical forms. The non-canonical forms will most likely not behave as a single uniform block. While this will make interpreting the statistical model more complicated, it should help the accuracy of a classifier trained to distinguish between different types of non-canonical utterances.

Discourse connectives and discourse relations

In addition to using patterns of referential relations to infer a picture of the discourse context surrounding non-canonical utterances, as mentioned above, we will also use patterns of utterance-initial discourse connectives. In their study of disambiguating between discourse and sentential uses of cue phrases, Hirschberg and Litman (1994) provide a summary of the discourse-structure-related meanings of lexical cues found in the literature. Most of the cue words, however, are associated with vague meanings, or at best are ambiguous between several (somewhat) specific meanings. This makes making predictions about the correspondence between discourse relations, syntactic or semantic, and discourse connectives rather difficult.

Nonetheless, Passonneau and Litman (1997) did find that simply the presence of a cue word on an utterance was to some extent a useful indicator of a segment boundary in a linear segmentation of a discourse. More useful still was a feature COMPLEX CUE-PROSODY which was partly based on the presence of a cue word other than *and*. Roughly, this feature being on ('+'), corresponded with assignment of a segment boundary.

Based on these findings of Passonneau and Litman (1997) and others, we would expect to find correlations between discourse connectives and non-canonical utterances if non-canonical utterances are more likely than canonical utterances to be found at transitions between discourse segments. In order to test this, in annotating the data set here, all sentence-initial adjuncts were annotated. This includes lexical discourse connectives, prepositional phrases, non-connective adverbs, time adverbials, and subordinate clauses. If these adjuncts are in fact indicators of segment boundaries, we predict that we will find a greater incidence of them on non-canonical utterances than on canonical utterances. Given the diversity of the adjuncts included here though, the heterogeneity of the group may confound the ability of such a feature to be a useful predictor. For one thing, no distinction was made between discourse and sentential uses of these adjuncts. Also, no attempt to include sentence-medial or final adjuncts which have discourse connective meanings was made.

On top of this, it may be that certain syntactic forms, in particular left-dislocations and topicalizations, will have fewer sentence-initial adjuncts for purely syntactic reasons. The presence or absence of sentence-initial adjuncts alone will not necessarily be a helpful feature. Instead, we will make predictions about specific discourse connectives. Because the extent to which these predictions can be tested greatly depends on the availability of data, we are confined to a set of only the most frequent connectives found in the data, as discussed in Section 4.2.3. These happen to be *so, and,* and *but*. The majority of lexical connectives do not appear in the corpus with a great enough frequency to allow claims to be made or tested. In particular, we make the following predictions:

- *And*: Based on findings in the literature, Passonneau and Litman (1997) exclude *and* from the set of connectives that indicate segment boundaries. Hirschberg and Litman (1994) list such meanings for *and* as "parallel," "push," "new dominance," "addition," "continuation," "simple conjunction," and "additive." As such, we expect to find here a decreased incidence of *and* on non-canonical utterances, with the possible exception of ELABORATION uses of wh-clefts.

  In addition, if non-canonical utterances are being used to start segments, then the utterances immediately preceding them and immediately following them should be less likely to be starting segments themselves, i.e. more likely to be at a point of CONTINUE. Hence, there should be a greater incidence of *and* on both U_{i-1} and U_{i+1} when U_i is a non-canonical.

- *But*: For *but*, Hirschberg and Litman provide the following glosses: "contrast," "push," "direct challenge," "adversative," "adversative conjunction," and "interruption". Given these typical meanings of *but*, we expect to find greater incidence of *but* on both U_i and U_{i+1} for non-canonicals because we expect them to be more likely to be used to indicate the RESEMBLANCE relation *contrast* than canonical utterances.

- *So*: Like for *but*, the literature survey in Hirschberg and Litman also gives a meaning of "contrast" for *so*. Additionally, they list "restatement," "conclusion," "development," "response," "resultative," and "causation". It is not entirely clear why *so* should be more likely to appear with non-canonicals than canonicals. However, it is a relatively frequent connective in spoken discourse, and based on preliminary inspection of the data, it does in fact correlate with the incidence of some of the non-canonical sentence types of interest here, so it is included in the study.

The final point above regarding the presence of *so* is in fact illustrative of the role of the discourse markers in this study. Although the meanings and contributions of particular connectives is on the whole poorly understood, everyone agrees that discourse connectives do play some role in allowing speakers to indicate discourse structural relations. In addition, lexical patterns are easy to extract from linguistic data in a form that allows statistical feature-based analysis, and often their idiosyncratic patterns are useful from an engineering point of view if not from a theoretical linguistics perspective. The patterns of correlation between the connectives and the syntactic forms investigated in this study may not provide clear-cut evidence for the correspondence of sentence types with discourse relations but they can lend strength of independent confirmation to the patterns found in the referential connections. They may also be valuable for later use in an NLG system which needs to perform both lexical and syntactic selection because they can provide information about how the two should correspond with each other.

4.3.2   Results: correlations between features and syntactic forms

In the previous section we discussed how the referential and lexical features correlate with discourse structure and how these features were thus predicted to correlate with non-canonical syntactic forms. Now, we will look at the results of the Varbrul logistic regression analyses which measured the strength of correlation between the five features, three lexical and two referential, and the five individual classes of syntactic forms, topicalizations, left-dislocations, wh-clefts, it-clefts, and canonical controls. The patterns we see here will give an indication of the accuracy of the predictions in the previous section about the correlation of these features with non-canonical syntactic forms.

Ten binary comparisons pairing each of the five classes with each other were performed, which lead to ten separate models of the correlation of the features with the forms. For each of the ten comparisons, a stepwise regression analysis was performed to gauge the significance of each individual feature's contribution to the model. Then the most significant features were used together in a model to get a measure of how well that model fit the data. The stepwise regression analysis and goodness of fit tests are those described in detail in Section 4.1.4 above.

Table 4.11 lists the referential and discourse marker features, using the feature numbers from Table 4.7, found to be significant for each of the ten binary comparisons. Each comparison is listed twice to facilitate intraclass comparison. These are features that individually have a significant effect ($p < 0.05$) in improving the likelihood of the model when compared to the likelihood of the model at level zero.[40] For comparisons where multiple features have been found to be sig-

---

[40]In particular, the measure whose significance is tested is the -2*(difference in log-likelihoods of the models), which is χ^2 distributed. The degrees of freedom is the differ-

nificant at the five-percent level, the p-value of the model fit in comparison with a fully saturated model is listed in the fifth column of Table 4.11. Also included in Table 4.11, in column four, is a list of any features found significant at $p < 0.20$ but not $p < 0.05$. These are features which are still indicative of interesting trends in the data set but would require further investigation to confirm or disconfirm.

CLASS 1	CLASS 2	Feat. $(p < .05)$	Feat. $(p < .2)$	Overall Model Fit χ^2 p-value (using $p < .05$ feat.)
CONTROL	IT-CLEFT	**2**	5 (0.097)	n.a.
	LEFT-DIS.	4,5	3 (0.161)	p=0.9289
	TOPIC.	**3**	2 (0.178)	n.a.
	WH-CLEFT	2,4	3 (0.151)	p=0.8696
IT-CLEFT	CONTROL	**2**	5 (0.097)	n.a.
	LEFT-DIS.	–	1 (0.106), 4 (0.086)	–
	TOPIC.	**3**	2 (0.092) , 4 (0.099)	n.a.
	WH-CLEFT	4	1 (0.184)	n.a.
LEFT-DIS.	CONTROL	4,5	3 (0.161)	p=0.9289
	IT-CLEFT	–	1 (0.106), 4 (0.086)	–
	TOPIC.	3, 4	5 (0.129)	p =0.8561
	WH-CLEFT	1,4	5 (0.147)	p=0.7615
TOPIC	CONTROL	**3**	2 (0.178)	n.a.
	LEFT-DIS.	3,4	5 (0.129)	p =.8561
	IT-CLEFT	**3**	2 (0.092), 4 (0.099)	n.a.
	WH-CLEFT	2,**3**, 4	–	p=.6935 (with 3,4)
WHCLEFT	CONTROL	2,4	3 (0.151)	p=0.8696
	IT-CLEFT	4	1 (0.184)	n.a.
	LEFT-DIS.	1,4	5 (0.147)	p=0.7615
	TOPIC.	2,**3**, 4	–	p=.6935 (with 3,4)

Table 4.11: Features significant at $p < 0.05$ and $p < 0.2$ in comparison with zero-level model. Features significant at the $p < 0.01$ level are in **bold**. Features 1, 2, and 3 are discourse marker features on U_{i-1}, U_i, and U_{i+1}, respectively. Features 4 and 5 are referential connection features for the pairs (U_{i-1}, U_i) and (U_i, U_{i+1}), respectively.

Table 4.11 provides information about individual features and entire models.[41] Before we discuss how the individual models bear on the predictions made in the previous section, several general points should be mentioned. First, for nine

ence in the total number of feature values between the two models. The zero-level model is a model which uses no features to predict the distribution of the two classes.

[41] All the features listed in column three in Table 4.11 were found to contribute to the log-likelihood significantly ($p < 0.05$) both in comparison with the zero-level model and

of the 10 comparisons, at least one feature of the five features improves the likelihood of the logistic regression model significantly. The comparison of it-clefts and left-dislocations is the exception here. From the lack of significant features in this comparison we can surmise that the it-clefts and left-dislocations are more similar to each other any of the other forms compared here. In addition, both of these classes are functionally diverse. This may contribute to a non-uniformity within both of them which adds to the difficulty in discriminating between the two. Further tests related to the subtypes within both left-dislocations and it-clefts are the subject of Section 4.3.3.

Another interesting aspect illustrated both in Table 4.11 and more clearly in Table 4.12, is the distribution of significant features across the ten models. While features 3 ($\text{MARKER}(U_{i+1})$) and 4 ($\text{REF}(U_{i-1}, U_i)$), are strong predictors and appear in four and six of the ten comparisons respectively, features 1 ($\text{MARKER}(U_{i-1})$) and 5 ($\text{REF}(U_i, U_{i+1})$) only appear once each.

Now we will look in more detail at the ten models in order to assess whether and how well the predictions presented in Section 4.3.1 are borne out. In order to do this, we need information not just about which features are significant, but what weights were assigned to particular feature values. Table 4.12 lists by model the weights estimated for individual feature values for each of the features that appeared in column three in Table 4.11. These weights are the ones estimated for a model combining all and only the features found significant at the $p < 0.05$.[42] Although ideally the estimated weights will not vary from model to model, these features are likely not entirely independent. Therefore, their weights do vary by a small amount from level to level in the stepwise analysis. However, given that these features were all selected because they were expected to have some correlation with the dependent variable, syntactic type, it is not surprising to find that there is some correlation with each other. If it is the underlying semantic content of an utterance and its relation to the content of the surrounding utterances that determines *both* the referential connections it has with another utterance *and* the discourse connectives that appear on it and surrounding utterances, then we can expect that these two things are connected.

We will now discuss how the predictions in Section 4.3.1 relate to the statistical model for each of the non-canonical classes in turn although discussion of each class necessarily overlaps with the others.

---

when added to previously selected features. The single exception to this is feature 2 for the comparison of topicalizations and wh-clefts. Although significant by itself, when added to a model which already included features 3 and 4, feature 2 did not significantly improve the log-likelihood. This is evidence of interaction between feature 2 and the other features; it will be discussed further below.

[42] Feature 2 in the comparison of topicalizations and wh-clefts is also exceptional here. Its weights are taken from the level-1 model where it is the sole feature.

		CONTROL IT-CLEFT	CONTROL LEFT-DIS.	CONTROL TOPIC.	CONTROL WH-CLEFT	IT-CLEFT LEFT-DIS.	IT-CLEFT TOPIC.	IT-CLEFT WH-CLEFT	LEFT-DIS. TOPIC.	LEFT-DIS. WH-CLEFT	TOPIC. WH-CLEFT
MARK (U_{i-1})	a	0.548								0.655	
	b	0.399								0.326	
	s	0.249								0.500	
	o	0.689								0.542	
	n	0.628								0.481	
MARK (U_i)	a				0.600						0.665
	b				0.444						0.604
	s				0.246						0.172
	o				0.628						0.483
	n				0.602						0.630
MARK (U_{i+1})	a			0.514			0.595		0.603		0.343
	b			0.266			0.232		0.268		0.804
	s			0.408			0.406		0.470		0.579
	o			0.738			0.685		0.641		0.311
	n			0.574			0.602		0.533		0.429
REF (U_{i-1}, U_i)	0		0.418		0.352			0.334	0.662	0.420	0.279
	1		0.443		0.575			0.639	0.566	0.634	0.574
	2		0.511		0.493			0.458	0.501	0.493	0.467
	3		0.627		0.583			0.571	0.280	0.450	0.686
REF (U_i, U_{i+1})	0		0.785								
	1		0.401								
	2		0.370								
	3		0.409								

Table 4.12: Individual feature weights in best model

Topicalizations

From the significant features and feature weights found when comparing topicalizations with the other four classes, it seems that in general, topicalizations are more likely to be in the same segment as the utterance that immediately precedes them than any of the other classes based on both the referential and lexical feature correlations. In addition, they also seem more likely to be in a CONTRAST relation with either the preceding or the following utterance. The patterns that allow us to draw these conclusions, however, are quite complex and must be examined in detail.

First, in comparing topicalizations with all of the other four classes, feature 3, the discourse marker on utterance U_{i+1}, was significant for all. In all cases, the presence of *but* on U_{i+1} is more likely when U_i is a topicalization, the presence of *and* on U_{i+1} correlates negatively with topicalizations in comparison with all of the other four classes. The greater incidence of topicalizations when there is a *but* on the utterance following the token is probably due in large part to the constructions where the preposed constituent is a wh-clause, as in (122). This construction appears to be a particularly likely to have a *but* at position U_{i+1}. Although topicalizations with a displaced wh-clause make up only 27 of the 111 topicalizations (24%), they make up 10 of the 22 (45%) cases of MARKER(U_{i+1})=*but* within the class.

(122)   Well, we developed rules on guardianship. We insisted on guardianship. **How enforced that ever was I don't know.** But we would insist that the payment was made to the guardian on behalf of so and so. (SSA, hboral)

In comparison with wh-clefts, topicalizations are more likely to have both *and* and *but* on U_i itself and much less likely to have *so*. These same tendencies appear in the comparisons of topicalizations with the control class and with it-clefts also, although in the case of these two, the feature is only significant at $p < 0.20$.

With respect to the referential features, 4 and 5, in comparison with both left-dislocations and wh-clefts, topicalizations are considerably less likely to be found when there are no referential connections with the previous utterance (U_{i-1}) and much more likely to occur when their C_b is the C_p of U_{i-1}. This same pattern is found for it-clefts vs. topicalizations also although the feature is not as significant when added to this model. In comparison with control utterances, the referential patterns surrounding topicalizations do not differ significantly. However, the feature value weights estimated at level one for REFER(U_{i-1}), although significant only at $p=0.235$, display a pattern similar to that found with the non-canonical classes, where no connections favors the control class and $C_p(Ui-1)=C_b(U_i)$ favors topicalizations.

From these referential and discourse marker patterns characteristic of topicalizations, we can tentatively conclude that in comparison with all the other classes, topicalizations are more likely to be in the same segment as the utterance that immediately precedes them. This is based on the fact that they are more likely to continue the same center of attention as the previous utterance and much less likely to refer to a completely different set of referents. In addition, they are more likely than controls, wh-clefts, and it-clefts to appear with *and*, which can also be taken as an indication of segment continuation. Topicalizations also seem more likely to be involved in some type of contrast relation, with either the preceding or the following utterance, as the distribution of the connective *but* on both U_i and U_{i+1} supports. However, because *but* is ambiguous between the various ways propositions can be "in contrast" with each other, a better understanding of this claim requires further investigation of the lexical properties of *but*.

With respect to the predictions set out in Section 4.3.1, topicalizations do not easily fit into these schema. Although in terms of syntactic discourse structure they appear to definitely be a case of CONTINUE with the segment of U_{i-1}, this conflicts with their use of *but* and the numerous cases of topicalizations used in RESEMBLANCE relations seen in Chapter 3 because one would expect in this framework for there to be little coreferential and center of attention continuity in the case of RESEMBLANCE relations. The representation in the tables in Section 4.3.1 of how patterns of reference change from utterance to utterance is actually far too simple. For example, it cannot represent as distinct an utterance with an old and a new entity and an utterance with only old entities. Both will be coded as either $C_b(U_i)=C_p(U_{i+1})$ or +COREF. Finer distinctions such as this one would be necessary to distinguish more nuances of intrasegmental transitions.

From this we suggest that the framework needs to be modified in such a way that it can incorporate the function of topicalizations which appear to combine center continuity with resemblance relations. The highly simplified model of discourse context that we are using in these statistical models is too crude to capture this because the only semantic relation compatible with CONTINUE is NARRATIVE. As shown in the literature (Prince, 1998), topicalizations are almost always cases of CONTINUE. As demonstrated in the previous chapter, however, they do not stand in a NARRATIVE relation with the surrounding utterances. The statistical study provides additional evidence to support both of these claims.

In order to reconcile this conflict, it seems that we should allow for a discourse relation that combines both aspects of the discourse role of topicalizations, a resemblance relation that holds intra-segmentally. Intrasegmental resemblance relations will have the same attentional structure as CONTINUE. The focus space stack will neither PUSH nor POP a space. However, an utterance in this relation with the previous utterance will not be a narrative clause in the sense of Labov (1997), and there will be no temporal juncture between it and the previous clause. An intrasegmental resemblance relation can be thought of as alternative way of organizing content within a single segment. Instead of organizing the content with respect to time, it organizes the content with respect to entities, in particular the members of the poset to which the referent of the preposed NP belongs, whether these members are propositions, questions, or entities. As the data here clearly show, however, this organization occurs within a single discourse segment, one where the local center-of-attention is maintained. The following two examples illustrate this intrasegmental organizational pattern. The continuity of the center-of-attention here is shown through the use of italics.

(123)   So in my capacity as Acting Chief Actuary, *I* had to testify before the Senate and the House committees. **Some questions asked of me *I* was prepared to answer,** such as how much would this national health insurance proposal cost in the first year, what would be the incremental increase to the national health expenditure, what tax rate would be required. But then the senators may ask *me* how this proposed legislation would impact on inflation, employment and foreign trade. (SSA, hsiao)

(124)   It seems to *me* that there are three key functions of the Commissioner as I have defined the Commissioner. **One, *I* had a ton of experience in, one *I* had a fair amount of experience in, and one *I* had no experience in.** (SSA, apfeloral)

Wh-clefts

Overall, it appears that wh-clefts are favored in contexts where the speaker is starting a new segment, where the utterance with a wh-cleft has weak connections with the preceding utterance and strong connections with the following utterance.

In particular, in terms of the referential connections with the preceding utterance, as reflected in feature 4, $\text{REF}(U_{i-1},U_i)$, wh-clefts are essentially the mirror image of topicalizations. They are much more likely to share no connections at all, and less likely to share only inferential connections. This same tendency holds for wh-clefts in comparison with controls, it-clefts, and left-dislocations. In addition, compared with everything but left-dislocations, wh-clefts are less likely to share their center of attention with the preceding utterance. Feature 4 is significant in the comparison of wh-clefts with all other classes.

In terms of discourse markers, feature 2 and 3 are significant when comparing topicalizations and controls with wh-clefts (although feature 3 is only weakly significant in comparing wh-clefts and controls.) For feature 2, $\text{MARKER}(U_i)$, wh-clefts are less likely than either of the other two to appear with *and* and more likely to appear with *so*. For feature 3, however, the presence of *and* on U_{i+1} favors wh-clefts over topicalizations and controls.

The most likely context in which to find wh-clefts then is one with no referential connections to the previous utterance and marked with the discourse adverbial, *so*. When the utterance following the token begins with *and*, which we assume is some type of continuation of the previous content, wh-clefts are also favored.

This pattern resembles most closely the description of a discourse POP given in Table 4.8 but does not correspond to any of the coherence relation referential patterns in Table 4.10. However, we know that wh-clefts are used in two different types of RESEMBLANCE relations, CONTRAST and ELABORATION. These resemblance relations will likely coincide with different discourse marker and referential patterns which will be obscured in an examination of all wh-clefts together. This will be investigated below when we compare contrast and non-contrastive uses of wh-clefts.

Here again we can see the inherent limitations of the model we are using. As discussed with respect to Figure 4.2, when diverse patterns appear within a single class, they may be conflated and lose significance when compared with other classes, obscuring the actual behavior of the class in question. Furthermore, the only indicators we have in this statistical model of starting a new segment are lack of referential connection, presence of a connective like *so*, and absence of *and*. This is a very crude measure given the fact that we know some new segments will continue discussion of previously mentioned entities, in particular when that segment begins with a utterance in an ELABORATION relation with the previous content.

Finally, one additional interesting pattern found with wh-clefts is the significance of feature 1. In particular, the presence of *so* favors wh-clefts when compared with it-clefts; *but* favors wh-clefts when compared with left-dislocations. From a theoretical point of view, it is hard to know what the presence of discourse markers on the utterance preceding the token utterance might mean for the present model of discourse. Nonetheless, from an engineering perspective, this information could still be useful in generating multi-utterance texts; for instance it could be used to make segments surrounding a wh-cleft sound more natural.

Left-dislocations

Similar to wh-clefts, the context that most favors left-dislocations over any of the other constructions appears to be one where there are few or no connections with the previous utterance and close connections with the following. In particular, a context where there is no connection with U_{i-1} favors left-dislocations in comparison with controls, topicalizations and it-clefts. This tendency is the strongest for comparison with topicalizations and somewhat weaker for it-clefts. In contrast, a context where the C_b of U_i is the same as the C_p of U_{i-1} shows a decreased incidence of left-dislocations in comparison with everything but wh-clefts. This tendency is the weakest in comparison with it-clefts, for which feature 4 achieves significance only at the 20 percent level.

A context with no connections to U_{i-1} favors wh-clefts slightly in comparison with left-dislocations whereas a context with reference to inferentially-related entities only favors left-dislocations over wh-clefts. Inferential-only connections with the preceding utterance also slightly favors left-dislocations in comparison with controls and topicalizations.

A very different pattern emerges when the utterance following the token utterance U_i is examined. In comparison with controls, topicalizations, and wh-clefts, a context where there are no referential connections at all, i.e. REF(U_i,U_{i+1})=0, is very unlikely to have a left-dislocation. All other degrees of referential connectedness favor left-dislocations here in comparison with the other three classes.

The patterns found for left-dislocations with respect to discourse markers are less distinct. In comparison with topicalizations, *and* on U_{i+1} favors left-dislocations. This is also seen—though somewhat less strongly—in comparison with controls. The connective on the left-dislocation itself, feature 2, does not achieve significance in any of the models. In other words, none of the U_i connectives examined here appear to correlate with the incidence of left-dislocations.

The discourse marker on U_{i-1} does have a significant distribution which distinguishes left-dislocations from wh-clefts and it-clefts. In particularly, *but* disfavors left-dislocations but favors the cleft constructions. *And* favors left-dislocations compared to wh-clefts; *so* favors left-dislocations compared to it-clefts.

The most favorable context for left-dislocations appears to be one where there are no or inferential-only connections with the previous utterance, and very close connections with the following utterance. Like wh-clefts, it appears that left-dislocations are favored when starting a new segment. Although feature 5 is not significant in a comparison of wh-clefts and left-dislocations, by examining the comparison of each of these non-canonicals with the control class, we can make a further claim about the differences between the two. Feature 5 does achieve significance when comparing controls and left-dislocations, but not when comparing wh-clefts and controls. We can infer from this that wh-clefts and controls are somewhat more alike in terms of the referential connections between U_i and U_{i+1}. This is possibly because left-dislocations are actually more uniform for this feature than wh-clefts. We can interpret this evidence as a preference for left-dislocations as the form to use when starting a new segment which has weak coherence with the immediately preceding local context. Wh-clefts may instead be useful both for starting a new segment which may or may not have coherence with the immediately preceding local context but will have coherence with the following context, i.e. ELABORATIONS, but also for CONTRAST relations between U_i and U_{i+1} where the two utterances will not necessarily share their centers of attention.

There is some evidence for left-dislocations being in RESEMBLANCE relations with the preceding utterance, U_{i-1}. The positive evidence is a context with inferential-only connections with U_{i-1} favoring left-dislocations. The negative evidence is the *dis*favoring of left-dislocations in contexts where U_i shares its center of attention with U_{i-1}. Such a context is unlikely to be one where U_{i-1} and U_i are in a NARRATIVE relation.

Because we know that a subset of left-dislocations, simplifying left-dislocations, have a discourse function such that they allow reference to a discourse-new entity in subject position, it is plausible to claim that the differences we see between contexts that favor left-dislocations and the contexts that favor the other classes of utterances here result solely from the behavior of this subclass of simplifying left-dislocations. That is, utterances where a new entity is in subject position are likely to be utterances with fewer referential connections to the previous utterance. They are also more likely to have stronger connections to the following utterance because once a new entity is introduced in subject position, as the highest ranked entity on the C_f list it will be likely to continue to be the center of attention. In other words, the analysis here might only be revealing patterns we already had evidence for before. In order to test this, the left-dislocations have been sub-classified as poset and simplifying left-dislocations. The results of comparing the subclasses are discussed in Section 4.3.3. In general, they indicate that the trends found here for all left-dislocations together hold for each of the subclasses of left-dislocation also.

It-clefts

It-clefts appear to be a more diverse class than the other three classes of non-canonicals in terms of the distribution of the feature values examined here. In comparison with controls, the presence of *but* or *so* on U_i favors it-clefts. In comparison with topicalizations, as mentioned previously, the presence of *so* also favors it-clefts. *But* weakly favors topicalizations. The discourse marker feature MARKER(U_i) is not as significant in the comparison of it-clefts and topicalizations, however.

In terms of referential features, it-clefts, like topicalizations, are less likely than wh-clefts and left-dislocations to have no referential connections with U_{i-1}. They are more likely to share their center of attention with U_{i-1}. These tendencies for it-clefts are not as strong as those of topicalization because in comparison with the latter, it-clefts are still more likely to have no referential connections and not have the same center of attention as U_{i-1}. In comparison with both wh-clefts and topicalizations, however, shared reference to inferentially-related entities between U_{i-1} and U_i favors it-clefts.

The feature for referential connections with the following utterance is weakly significant in the comparison of it-clefts and controls. Here having no connections favors the control class. Referring to the same entities, but not sharing the same center of attention favors it-clefts.

The diversity of the significant feature distribution makes it difficult to have a single unified characterization of the it-cleft class. In general, it-clefts do not

Sentence type	Most Favorable Discourse Contexts
Topicalizations	CONTINUE with U_{i-1}; CONTRAST with U_{i-1} or U_{i+1}
Wh-clefts	POP after U_{i-1}; CONTRAST or CONTINUE with U_{i+1}
Left-dislocations	POP after U_{i-1} or RESEMBLANCE with U_{i-1}; CONTINUE with U_{i+1}
It-clefts	No strong tendencies for begin/end of segments; possible CONTRAST relations with U_{i-1}, U_{i+1}

Table 4.13: Summary of most favorable contexts by type of non-canonical

appear to be favored in contexts where they either end or begin entirely new segments. Because the presence of *but* on U_i does favor it-clefts over controls, this does support the general idea that it-clefts are used for CONTRAST relations. The connective *so* on U_i also favors it-clefts over controls and topicalizations.

Although these patterns do not offer much for a coherent theory of the discourse contexts that favor it-clefts, nonetheless, in models comparing it-clefts with wh-clefts, topicalizations, and canonical controls, a subset of the features examined here can contribute to distinguishing between contexts which favor one over the other. Even the weakest model, one comparing left-dislocations with it-clefts using two weakly significant features, still shows improvement over a null-model which is significant at $p < 0.20$. Hence, even if the experimental results have not furthered the understanding of it-clefts in particular, it is suggestive of ways this non-canonical class can be distinguished from other non-canonicals and from canonicals in terms of discourse contextual features that merit further investigation. Table 4.13 very briefly summarizes the most probable contexts in which each of the four types of non-canonicals are found. We now turn to a closer look at three of the non-canonical classes to measure the correlations of the discourse structure features used here with these classes' functional subtypes.

4.3.3 Discriminating between functional subtypes

As mentioned previously, three of the non-canonical classes have functional subtypes, left-dislocations, it-clefts and wh-clefts. Further experimental analysis of these subtypes was undertaken for two reasons. First, we wanted to find out if the functional subtypes differed with respect to the two types of features investigated here, referential connections with surrounding utterances and discourse connective patterns. In addition, in the case of it-clefts and left-dislocations, we wanted to know if separating these two classes and comparing them individually with controls could lead to better models of the how the subtypes differ from canonical utterances. We will look at each of three classes here in turn. For all of the experiments in this section, the full set of data, training plus test, were utilized in running the regression analyses. This portion of experiments were performed after the training and test classifier experiments were complete, and because no test classifications of the categories examined here were to be run, it seemed best to forego the information lost through excluding ten percent of the data. This was especially important for the three classes to be partitioned. The data set is further limited when attempting to create statistical models within a single class, and so even small amounts of data missing further hinders the ability to draw conclusions from these models.

Left-dislocations

As outlined above, left-dislocations (LDs) have two functional subtypes which differ with respect to the discourse status of the referent of the preposed noun phrase. In simplifying LDs, the NP's referent is discourse-new and would normally be a very unlikely candidate for the syntactic position, subject or possessive, it appears in. In poset LDs, the NP is a member of a poset salient at that point in the discourse. The two other subtypes found in the literature, unexpected subject LDs and island-violation amnestying LDs, were collapsed with simplifying and poset LDs, respectively. This resulted in a dataset with 195 tokens of poset LDs and 63 simplifying LDs. As simplifying LDs are more likely to be associated with less formal, non-standard registers, it is perhaps not surprising to find fewer of them in this corpus. Although it is comprised of spontaneous oral discourse in a setting which is not highly formal, a one-on-one interview, the speakers are for the most part highly-educated, middle-class retired government administrators speaking about their work history.

In order to allow comparisons with the simplifying LDs, the values for feature 5, $\mathrm{REF}(U_i, U_{i+1})$ had to be altered because of knockouts, or zero instances of particular feature values for a class. Here there were no cases for the simplifying LDs where there were no referential connections at all between U_i and the following utterance. The five tokens of poset LDs where $\mathrm{REF}(U_i, U_{i+1})=0$ (no connections) were collapsed with instances of $\mathrm{REF}(U_i, U_{i+1})=1$ (inferential-only connections).

The comparison of poset LDs and simplifying LDs did reveal some significant features in the stepwise regression analysis. In particular, feature 4, $\mathrm{REF}(U_{i-1}, U_i)$ is significant ($p = 0.013$), features 1 and 5 are less so ($p = 0.077$ and $p = 0.053$ respectively). The presence of *and* on U_{i-1} favors simplifying LDs, *so* favors poset LDs. With respect to the referential features, not surprisingly, having no connections with U_{i-1} favors simplifying LDs, and having inferential connections with U_{i-1} favors poset LDs. For connections with U_{i+1}, the value which combines no or inferential-only connections favors posets over simplifying LDs; sharing center of attention or at least referring to coreferring entities favors simplifying LDs. Certainly then, as speculated above, simplifying LDs do contribute to the increased incidence of LDs as a whole in contexts where U_i has weak connections with U_{i-1} and strong connections with U_{i+1}.

In order to see whether poset LDs alone have these same characteristics, they were compared with the control set of 200 canonical utterances, using the same feature set used in the original experiments. Here features 3, 4, and 5 were significant when compared as level-1 models with the null-model, with $p = 0.031$, $p = 0.024$, and $p = 0.008$, respectively. For feature 3, the marker on U_{i+1}, the values *and*, *so*, and *but* all favored the poset LDs. With respect to referential connections with U_{i-1}, when the token utterance continued the same center of attention as U_{i-1}, this context favored controls. When the two utterances referred only to inferentially-related entities, it favored poset LDs. With respect to referential connections with U_{i+1}, reference only to inferentially-related entities also favored poset LDs. In addition, having no connections whatsoever here, strongly favored controls over poset LDs.

These three features are the same ones found significant in the comparison of controls with all left-dislocations in the training set. When the feature weights estimated for the individual values are compared for features 4 and 5, we can see that these two are relatively unchanged, as in shown in Table 4.14.[43]

		3	2	1	0
POSET LDS VS CONTROL	REF(U_{i-1},U_i)	0.616	0.490	0.426	0.466
	REF(U_i,U_{i+1})	0.417	0.387	0.403	0.766
ALL LDS VS CONTROL	REF(U_{i-1},U_i)	0.627	0.511	0.443	0.418
	REF(U_i,U_{i+1})	0.409	0.370	0.401	0.785

Table 4.14: Referential connection feature weights for model with only poset left-dislocations vs. model with all left-dislocations in comparison to control class. Application value in both models is CONTROL. Weights >.5 favor CONTROL; less than <.5 favor left-dislocations.

To some extent, the results here are rather unremarkable because the comparison is still using about 75% of the original data used to compare left-dislocations and controls. However, these feature distributions are still significant even having removed a subclass of tokens which are known to be the greatest source of the patterns we have seen. Nonetheless, those patterns are still evident. Even among poset LDs alone, we still find a pattern where left-dislocations are disfavored when U_{i-1} and U_i share their center of attention and when U_i and U_{i+1} have no referential connections.

We can conclude from these findings that with respect to their correlations with discourse structure, left-dislocations are in some ways a more uniform class

---

[43]These are the weights as estimated in a model which uses both of the features. Both in the original comparison and the second one undertaken here feature three was not found to add significant discriminative power to the model beyond that provided by features 4 and 5.

than one might have expected. The previously known discourse conditions can be seen to play a role within the class because poset LDs are favored when there are inferential-only connections with preceding and following utterances, and simplifying LDs are favored when there are no referential connections with U_{i-1}. But, the two subclasses are highly similar when compared to canonical utterances because all left-dislocations, poset and simplifying, are favored in contexts where a new segment is beginning.[44]

It-clefts

We will now look at a comparison of subtypes of it-clefts. The it-clefts were classified as either informative-presupposition (IP) or stressed-focus (SF) type it-clefts. IP it-clefts should have a discourse-old focus constituent, often a pronominal subject or time or place adverbial phrase. The sentence final complement clause is semantically presupposed but hearer-new and should bear the primary pitch accent of the sentence. In stressed-focus it-clefts, the focus constituent should bear the pitch accent and should be an instantiation of the (discourse or hearer) old complement clause, which is deaccented. This classification resulted in 29 tokens of IP it-clefts and 121 SF it-clefts.

Annotation of this distinction was rather difficult. In particular, for cases where the focus constituent was the syntactic subject, it was difficult to reconstruct where the most likely location for the sentential stress was, and it was simultaneously difficult to gauge how familiar the speaker expected the hearer to be with the content of the complement clause. Example (125) typifies such a difficult-to-categorize construction, where the primary pitch accent could fall either on *Nixon* or *along*. The proposition MILLS WAS GOING ALONG WITH SOMEONE'S PROPOSAL has not been previously made salient.

(125)   Fullerton: The biggest one [=health issue] when I came on Ways and Means was welfare reform. [...]
Santangelo: Around when would this have been?
Fullerton: This went from 1970 to '71 to '72, all three years, and even into '73 a little bit. It was a situation where we passed the thing twice in the House but it was never bought in the Senate. **Of course it was the Nixon administration's proposal which Mills was going along with.** (SSA, fullert)

Despite these coding difficulties, however, the two classes were separated. In order to run a regression model using the feature set used previously, knockout feature values had to be recoded. Here feature 4, REF(U_{i-1}, U_i) , never appeared

---

[44] In independent research, Gregory and Michaelis (2001) have drawn quite similar conclusions about left-dislocations based on a somewhat different set of features annotated on left-dislocations from the Switchboard corpus.

with value 0 for the IP class, and so 0 (no connections) was collapsed with 1 (inferential-only connections). In running the regression model comparing the two classes, no features were found to be significant, even at the $p < 0.20$ level.

The stressed-focus tokens were also compared with the control training data. This did not result in any features being found significant, compared with feature 2, found significant at $p < 0.05$, and 5 at $p < 0.2$ in the model comparing all it-clefts with the control set.

The comparisons here are rather inconclusive. They are certainly hampered by small number of tokens. The difficulty in coding for the distinction might also have contributed to the lack of significant differences in comparing the two subclasses. It-clefts as a whole were not characterized particularly clearly using the features found to be significant in any of the previously created models in any case, and so it is perhaps not surprising that this experiment did not yield conclusive results either.

Wh-clefts

The final subclass comparison attempted was within wh-clefts. Some wh-clefts appear to be used in a context where they are in a CONTRAST relation, and others are clearly not. The separation of the class into these two categories used the +CONTRAST feature that was coded for all the tokens in the corpus but not included in any other models. It was intended to correspond roughly with whether the use of the phrase *in contrast* would be acceptable on either the token utterance itself or the utterance immediately following it. This distinction split the class into two groups, 64 (23%) contrastive wh-clefts and 216 (77%) non-contrastive.

Using the stepwise regression model, features 2, 4, and 5 were found to contribute significantly ($p < 0.05$) to a model using the +CONTRAST feature as the dependent variable.

Non-contrastive wh-clefts were much more likely to appear with the marker *so* (feature weight 0.816) and much less likely to appear with *but* (0.183). Non-contrastive wh-clefts were much more likely to have a $C_b = C_p(U_{i-1})$ (0.680) and less likely to have either no connections at all with the previous utterance (0.370) or inferential-connections only (0.363).

The referential patterns found between the wh-clefts and the following utterance were somewhat less transparent. Contrastive wh-clefts have very few cases where there are inferential-only connections with the following utterance. This feature is weighted heavily in favor of non-contrastive uses (0.761). However, contexts where there are no connections with U_{i+1} disfavor non-contrastives (0.345). Contexts where the $C_p(U_1) = C_b(U_{i+1})$ also disfavor non-contrastives.

Feature 3, MARKER(U_{i+1}) is significant at $p = 0.126$. Here too *but* favors contrastive wh-clefts, and *so* favors the non-contrastive type.

In the comparison of all wh-clefts with the four other sentence type classes, the results for wh-clefts matched up rather poorly with the tables in Section 4.3.1.

There appeared to be no particular evidence for an ELABORATION type of wh-cleft versus a CONTRAST. Although the presence of *so* on U_i favored wh-clefts, in general contexts where there were no referential connections with U_{i-1}, which should not be ideal contexts for ELABORATION relations, did too.

By separating the wh-clefts into two functions, we have evidence for the claim that two different underlying patterns give rise to the single set of features which favor wh-clefts. In one, the token utterance has either no or inferential-only connections with the preceding utterance. It is marked with *but*, or the utterance following it may be marked with *but*. This is the context that favors contrastive wh-clefts. In the other, the utterance has a C_b which is the previous utterance's C_p. It is marked with *so*, or the utterance following it may also be marked with *so*. This context favors non-contrastive uses of wh-clefts, and it appears to be a good match with what we expected an utterance in an ELABORATION relation with the previous utterance to be like. The corpus example in (126) exemplifies a non-contrastive wh-cleft use; (127), a contrastive use.

(126)   Santangelo: After nine months you managed to find something?
Fullerton: **What happened was that I wasn't really looking for anything else.** I was thinking about looking, about where I would go. Then I got a call from the Library of Congress asking whether I would like to come and work over there in the Legislative Research Service, and I did. I went to work on January 1st or 2nd, 1967. (SSA, fullert)

(127)   How was HCFA's relationship with Congress in the early days?
Derzon: I think it was quite satisfactory with the Senate Finance Committee and with the Ways and Means Committee.[...] I think we did all right with Congress. Bill Fullerton helped a lot with that. **I think that where the relationships may have been a little bit unsatisfactory was between HEW and the President.** The President wanted stronger support from Joe Califano. (SSA, derzon)

Of all the models examined so far, this one appears to be the clearest in terms of what it can tells us about the discourse context that favors one utterance type over another. However, this is because it is a very different type of model. In the all the other models considered here, the sentence form was the dependent variable. The goal was to find interesting correlations between this dependent variable and the independent variables, lexical and semantic characteristics of the local context. In this model, the dependent variable was an explicit coding of the presence of a coherence relation, and the goal was to find out whether the linguistic features of the local context correlated with it. Perhaps not surprisingly, the latter model is easier to interpret and draw conclusions from.

4.3.4   Conclusions

Many of the features used to train statistical models of the comparisons between the five classes here were significant discriminators between two or more classes, and in some cases functional subtypes of these classes. As the model discussed in the previous section of contrastive and non-contrastive wh-clefts quite clearly illustrates though, the structure of the models trained here distinctly limits their ability to tell us about the discourse structure context which favors one class over another. The more diverse the set of contexts which favors a single form, the more difficult it is to use a single system which assumes fully independent features to model those contexts and makes no explicit reference to discourse relations. To refer again to Figure 4.2, if both R_1 and R_2 are correlated with a single form W, then to the extent that R_1 and R_2 give rise to conflicting patterns of reference and discourse markers, creating a model which is both easily interpretable theoretically but which can predict accurately the form from these patterns without reference to the discourse relations is necessarily a very difficult task. Even so, from the correlations found, we have tried to *indirectly* draw some conclusions about the relationships between sentence types and discourse relations.

This task has met with some small success here, but the features and techniques would certainly need to be revised in further extensions of this research. They would greatly benefit from application to a larger dataset which would allow more detailed analysis, in particular of the lexical patterns which were the most hampered by data scarcity. The methods used here would also be greatly enhanced by using more sophisticated features that could give a better and more detailed approximation of the semantic and syntactic discourse relations that utterances enter into. Using this type of feature set would require far more data, however, and possibly a more complex statistical model that could take into account so-called hidden states in order to have some representation of these discourse relations. The present project has managed to show that even an extremely simple featural representation of the context when combined with a relatively simple and well-understood statistical model of linguistic variation can yield interesting insights into the contexts that favor the use of particular non-canonical forms.

In the next section we will try to further apply this model, this time not simply to see what it can tell us about the distribution of non-canonical and canonical forms, but instead to see whether it can be used as classifier to choose word orders given a context.

4.4   A probabilistic classifier for selecting clausal word order

The statistical models discussed in the last section can not only be used as a way to investigate which features correlate most strongly with particular classes, but also as probabilistic classification algorithms. Given a feature vector, a classifier returns a label and a probability of that label applying to the vector. In terms of the task examined here this procedure can be framed in the following way: given a particular discourse context formulated as a set of properties of that context, the probabilistic classifier can label that context with the sentence form that is most probable. Ultimately, this classifier could potentially be used as a module in an NLG system to select clausal word order. This application will be discussed at the end of this section.

First, we report results of using the statistical models from Section 4.3 as classification algorithms applied to the training data consisting of 899 tokens and to a separate test set of 100 tokens. This is a very small test set, and so it does not provide a particularly good measure of how the classifier will perform on unseen data. It must be kept in mind that the classifiers trained here are utilizing only a very small subset of the properties that we know actually play a role in the selection of word order. We are ignoring two of the three major areas which appear to affect speaker's choice of form which were presented in Chapter 3: 1) the basic discourse conditions which motivate a speaker's use of non-canonical word order to mark attentional structure and 2) the phonological and prosodic structure of the utterance which motivates a speaker to choose a form in order to disambiguate an utterance's partition into focus and ground. By only providing our classifiers with information from an approximation of the local discourse structure, they are in a sense handicapped from the start in their ability to discriminate between different syntactic forms. A more realistic classification algorithm would utilize far more than this limited information.

The output of a Varbrul logistic regression analysis can very easily be transformed into a probabilistic classifier. The feature weights estimated during the regression can be used directly in Equation (114) in order to calculate a probability which is the expected proportion of rule application for each cell. Because Varbrul also outputs the expected and observed counts for each cell in the training data, this information can be used to calculate the probability of application even more straightforwardly.

The calculated probability is then transformed quite directly into the following simple labeling algorithm in (128).

(128)   Given a rule $A \rightarrow B$, with application value B_1
         and non-application value B_2,
         for each token t in cell c,
         If $P(c) > 0.5$, then label t as B_1.

```
If P(c) < 0.5, then label t as B₂.
Else output 'either.'
```

So, even though we know that for most cells (feature vectors), there will be instances where the rule applies and instances where it does not, the labeling algorithm simply outputs a single most probable class label.

When the feature set used in the classifier characterizes the two classes with little overlap, classification error rates will be quite low because for any particular cell there will be many instances of one label and very few of the other. If the two classes are not that different based on the feature set, error rates will be much greater. As we have already seen from the statistical model, although some features do improve the (log-)likelihood of the discriminative models trained here, in general, the differences between classes are not dramatic ones. Hence, we do not expect amazingly low error rates.

Nonetheless, it is interesting to see how well a model trained to predict counts or proportions of application can do when asked to label individual instances. In nine of the comparisons tested in Section 4.3, significant features were found, and in five of those models, multiple features were selected. For each of those five models, the expected counts for the possible cells were an acceptable match in comparison with the observed counts, as measured by the summed χ^2 of the error between the two, as shown in Table 4.15. After using these same models to do a classification of each individual instance in the data we will be able to see if the per-cell error rate corresponds to classification error.

	Summed Error	df	χ^2/cell	p-value
WH-CLEFT VS TOPIC.	14.0674	7df	0.7034	p=.0500
LEFT-DIS. VS WH-CLEFT	13.4126	7df	0.6706	p=.0627
LEFT-DIS. VS CONTROL	11.0436	7df	0.4901	p=.1367
LEFT-DIS. VS TOPIC.	10.9811	7df	0.5491	p=.1394
WH-CLEFT VS. CONTROL	7.8421	6df	0.5522	p=.2499

Table 4.15: Summed differences between per-cell observed vs. expected errors for models with multiple features. The p-value here should be ≥ 0.05 for the model to have acceptable goodness of fit.

For all of the nine models where some feature or features were found significant at the $p < 0.05$ level, those will be the models used in the classification algorithm. In the case of the comparison between it-clefts and left-dislocations, no features were significant at the five percent level, and so our "best" model will only perform at baseline. A second round of training classification was also done adding features to the model that improved the log-likelihood over a model without them at the 20 percent significance level. The more features that are added, the better the classification accuracy should be because the overall likelihood of the model necessarily increases. However, as additional features are added in and weights estimated for them, the model may simply be modeling noise in the data rather than actual trends that will transfer well to unseen data. Varbrul's stepwise analysis provides a way to decide which features are the most useful, so although in some ways selecting features based on particular degree of improvement is rather arbitrary, in light of the limited data we have to work with, it is arguably a sensible way to proceed. If a larger data set were available, the training data could be partitioned into a training set and a validation set, so the model could be repeatedly trained, increasing the number of features used each time, and then tested on the validation set. Once the error rate on the validation set begins to increase, no more features should be added. There was not enough data in this project to allow the use of a validation set, however.

For each comparison performed on the training set, we will get a classification error rate. In order to gauge how well the classifier has done we need to compare it with how well we might expect to do using a naive model which outputs labels either only by chance or based on the proportion of labels in the training set. If the proportion is not 1:1, the proportional classifier will label every instance with the label of the more frequent class. The error rate of the naive classifier will then be the same as the frequency of the smaller class. For each of the nine classifiers, Table 4.16 shows the error rate of the logistic regression classifier and that of baseline.

	CONTROL (%)	IT-CLEFT (%)	LEFT-DIS. (%)	TOPIC. (%)
WH-CLEFT	175/432 (40.5)	135/387 (34.9)	194/484 (40.1)	92/352 (26.1)
BASELINE	180/432 (41.6)	135/387 (34.9)	232/484 (47.9)	100/352 (28.4)
TOPIC	91/280 (32.5)	85/235 (36.2)	98/332 (29.5)	
BASELINE	100/280 (35.7)	100/235 (42.6)	100/332 (30.1)	
LEFT-DIS.	164/412 (39.8)	*135/367 (36.8)*		
BASELINE	180/412 (43.7)	135/367 (36.8)		
IT-CLEFT	122/315 (38.7)			
BASELINE	135/315 (42.9)			

Table 4.16: Training error: Classifiers using features significant at $p < 0.05$

Out of the nine classifiers using features from the model, one is performing at no better than baseline, IT-CLEFT VS. WH-CLEFT. The other seven out-perform baseline by varying degrees, from about 1 to 8 percentage points. Although these may not appear to be dramatic numbers, from an engineering point-of-view, performance improvements across different algorithms are often only matters of a few percentage points. Hence, a classifier trained with the features used here could then be used on top of another syntactic choice algorithm which uses attentional marking and focus disambiguation-type features to boost its performance.

In all the classifiers, the bulk of the error rate is due to items from the less frequent class being classified as an item from the larger class. In other words, recall is high on the larger class and precision is low; for the smaller class, recall is low and precision is high.

Comparing the values in Table 4.15 to the results in Table 4.16 we can see that the errors in predicted counts by cell do not correspond well to the error rates in classification. For example, of the models in Table 4.15 one of the worst is LEFT-DIS. VS WH-CLEFT, and the best model is WH-CLEFT VS CONTROL. With respect to the error rates in Table 4.16, the classification error rate of WH-CLEFT VS CONTROL is about 1% better than baseline. The LEFT-DIS. VS WH-CLEFT classifier is about 8% better.

For some of the comparisons performed in Section 4.3, features were found to improve the models which were significant only at the 20% level. Models using these features in addition to those found more strongly significant were run in order to gauge the training error using these more complex models. Only models where the additional features improved the log-likelihood of the original "best" model by a quantity significant at the $p < 0.20$ level were used for this purpose.[45] The effect of the use of these more complex models on the training error is shown in Table 4.17. In three of the five models, training error did improve in comparison with the simpler classification algorithm. As discussed above, without a validation set, it is difficult to tell whether the addition of features leads to overfitting. In any case, the evidence for useful improvement here is not stunning, and for purposes of determining test error, we will use the simpler models.

The classifiers were applied to the unseen data using the same method used on the test data. For each cell, the proportion of rule-applications expected was converted to a probability of application, and this was used to select the label for each cell. There were no cells in the test data that were not seen in the training data, and so there was no need to calculate any application probabilities by hand. The test data were 100 tokens, and the number of any particular class made up the same proportion of the total here as it did in the training set. The results for each of the ten classifiers are presented in Table 4.18.

Overall, the results on the unseen data are rather poor, with most of the classifiers performing at (or in some cases below) baseline. Hence the models learned on the training data do not generalize well to this small set of unseen data. The reliability of test error is, like everything, dependent on how much data one has. A very small test set can be quite unrepresentative of the data. More likely though, because the size of the effects we are seeing in the training data were on the order of less than 10% of a difference with respect to the baseline, these effects will

---

[45]That is, some features were significant at a $p < 0.20$-level when compared with a zero-level model, but did not contribute the same degree of improvement when added to a model which already incorporated significant features, and so these less-significant features were not included in the models used for the second round of training error determination.

	CONTROL (%)	IT-CLEFT (%)	LEFT-DIS. (%)	TOPIC.(%)
WH-CLEFT				87/352 (24.7) **2,3,4**
	175/432 (40.5)	135/387 (34.9)	194/484 (40.1)	92/352 (26.1)
BASELINE	180/432 (41.6)	135/387 (34.9)	232/484 (47.9)	100/352 (28.4)
TOPIC		85/352 (36.2) **3,4**	99/332 (29.8) **3,4,5**	
	91/280 (32.5)	85/235 (36.2)	98/332 (29.5)	
BASELINE	100/280 (35.7)	100/235 (42.6)	100/332 (30.1)	
LEFT-DIS.		131/367 (35.7) **1,4**		
	164/412 (39.8)	135/367 (36.8)		
BASELINE	180/412 (43.7)	135/367 (36.8)		
IT-CLEFT	118/315 (37.5) **2,5**			
	122/315 (38.7)			
BASELINE	135/315 (42.9)			

Table 4.17: Training Error: Models augmented with features sig at $p < 0.20$. Features in bold were not included in the previous model. The counts and percentages listed first are for the more complex model.

	CONTROL (%)	IT-CLEFT (%)	LEFT-DIS. (%)	TOPIC. (%)
WH-CLEFT	20/48 (41.7)	15/43 (34.9)	27/54 (50)	12/39 (30.8)
BASELINE	(41.6)	(34.9)	(47.9)	(28.4)
TOPIC	10/31 (32.3)	11/26 (42.3)	12/37 (32.4)	
BASELINE	(35.7)	(42.6)	(30.1)	
LEFT-DIS.	17/46 (37.0)	*15/41 (36.6)*		
BASELINE	(43.7)	(36.8)		
IT-CLEFT	15/35 (42.9)			
BASELINE	(42.9)			

Table 4.18: Test Error. The top row is the raw counts and percentages of incorrect classifications. The bottom row is the baseline error rate of a naive model. It-cleft vs. left-dislocation uses a zero-level model as classifier.

be nearly invisible when we are only looking at a tenth of as many tokens. At the very most there was a difference in classification of about 40 tokens between the training classifier error rate and the baseline error rate. When translated into the test set, that is a difference of less than five tokens. Improvements over the baseline by only a couple tokens in the training set may be overwhelmed in the test set simply by the presence of one or two outliers.

To conclude this section, we will briefly discuss how these individual binary classifiers could be extended to a multinomial classification algorithm.

Although we only looked at binary distinctions here, in actuality, the classification needs to select one label from a set of several possible labels. There are several possible solutions to this problem. First, a multinomial regression model could be trained on the data. This was not performed here because a basic goal of this very exploratory research was one where the distinctions between each possible pair of classes was of interest. Varbrul does support multinomial logistic regression analysis but only for one-level analyses making the stepwise regression analysis a much more labor intensive process. As such, this analysis remains for future work. There are numerous other multi-class classification methods besides multinomial logistic regression that could also be tried.

Secondly, the combination of binary classifiers is the subject of a great deal of investigation both in the statistical machine learning literature and in the area of variational linguistics. In the case of the latter, it is usually discussed as an issue of rule ordering (Sankoff, 1988). Instead of learning rules to distinguish between two single classes, a variable rule is learned that subdivides the data into one vs. many or many vs. many classes. In order to classify a single instance, all the rules are applied until a single most-probable class label is generated.

Rather than having the decision making process be the result of many binary decisions in turn, a multiclass algorithm can also combine the results of several purely binomial classifiers in a type of voting schema in order to determine a single most likely label. For the present project this might entail a process like the following. First, each of the ten classifiers would output a label and a probability for an instance. Then a five by five matrix would be filled in with these probabilities or their inverse such that the contents of the cell i, j would be the probability p of rule application for the token according to the Class i–Class-j classifier. If there is no Class i–Class j classifier, then there must be a Class j–Class i classifier which gives a label of j with probability p. In such a case the cell i, j is filled in with $1 - p$. All cells except those on the diagonal will be filled in. Each row can be summed, and the label of the row with the greatest sum will be the label selected. In addition, if the individual classifiers used to fill in the matrix are known to have better or worse discriminative ability, then their contribution to the row sum can be weighted to reflect this.

4.4.1   Use of a probabilistic classifier as a NLG module

Although the accuracy of the classifier trained here limits its usefulness in its present form, with a modified feature set and larger data set, a probabilistic classifier could be trained and then used as one step in a NLG system. Such a classifier would use as its input the values of the referential and discourse marker features to select the best syntactic form in which to realize the semantic content. The values for the features would have to be predetermined along with or as part of the semantic content to be realized.

The feature set as used here is in line with such an approach. With respect to the referential connection features this is certainly the case. If a multi-utterance text is planned, then the entities referred to in each utterance must also be planned out, and the syntactic role of each entity chosen. With this information, the values for features like $REF(U_{i-1}, U_i)$ and $REF(U_i, U_{i+1})$ could easily be calculated and used as input into a probabilistic classifier. For the lexical connectives, the situation might be more complex because such a procedure would require lexical choice before syntactic choice, an unusual ordering for most generation architectures. In a system like SPUD where syntactic and lexical choice proceed as a single process, this would essentially be impossible. In order to resolve this, a semantics of discourse connectives is required so that having learned from purely lexical data, this information could be mapped back to semantic content that underlies the use of those lexical items. As steps in this direction have already been taken, this may in fact be possible at some point (Forbes, 2003; Creswell et al., 2002).

For whatever set of features were selected in the end, the role of the classifier in the generation procedure would be roughly as follows. First, given a set of discourse conditions and a communicative goal, all *possible* constructions would have some base probability of being selected.[46] This probability would then be used as the input probability in a statistical model which would modify it using the appropriate weights applied to the values of the features used in the model. Then either the most probable form could be always chosen, or the output probability itself could be used as a sort of "weighted coin flip" to determine which form is chosen. To illustrate, if, given a particular input feature vector, the output of the classifier is that the probability of form X is .85, and the probability of form Y is .15, then the form selected would be X in 85 of 100 instances with this particular input context and Y in 15 of 100 instances. Given the relative rarity of the forms examined here, the input probability could be set to generate fewer non-canonicals.

As part of a fully-implemented generation system, the effects of the probabilistic classifier for syntactic choice could then be evaluated by human speakers

---

[46]If the necessary conditions for the use of a construction do not hold, the base probability will be 0.

for how natural and understandable the output is. The benefit of using a statistical algorithm trained on a corpus of naturally-occurring data, however, means that simply by evaluating the algorithm on a test set one has some basis of comparison with human performance even without additional evaluation. As argued for above, however, it must be kept in mind that matching a corpus of human speech simply by generating output that matches the frequency of the trees and strings in the original can guarantee only the grammaticality of those strings, not the acceptability of them in any particular context or their usefulness for communicating a particular meaning in that context. The approach suggested here is an attempt to utilize more than just frequency as a basis for syntactic form selection and instead incorporate aspects of the semantic content of the surrounding discourse as a basis for using a particular form.

4.5   Conclusions and implications for further work

At the start of this chapter, two goals were set out. The first was to develop a featural representation of discourse structure and then use this representation in a statistical model of the differences among different non-canonical word orders and a control class of canonical tokens. The second was to develop a probabilistic classifier which could be used as part of a natural language generation system to select the clausal word order most appropriate for a discourse context and communicative goal. Here we will just briefly summarize the results and suggest some possible additional avenues of research to extend what was done.

The statistical model here used a combination of referential and lexical features annotated for a small window surrounding the target utterance to represent the local discourse context of the utterance. This annotation window was intended to give an approximation of the context such that conclusions about the syntactic and semantic discourse relations of the target utterance could be drawn from it. The ultimate goal was to be able to model the correlation between communicative goals related to discourse structure and non-canonical syntactic forms. Due to the difficulties inherent in annotating either these goals or the discourse structure itself directly, the featural approximation was devised as the best practical alternative that could still give some picture of the patterns we were interested in.

Logistic regression models using this feature set were then run for all pairings of the five classes of syntactic forms, topicalizations, wh-clefts, left-dislocations, it-clefts, and a control class of utterances with canonical word order. For nine of the ten pairings of classes, at least one of the five features used was found to give a highly significant improvement to the likelihood of the model discriminating between the two classes. In addition, when examined in detail, the feature weights did lend support for some of the predictions about how the non-canonical classes were expected to correlate with various patterns of reference and discourse connective usage. In general, the patterns for each class of non-canonical were quite complex, indicating that no class could be characterized as exhibiting a pattern of features which would correspond to only a single syntactic or semantic discourse relation.

Overall, the methods used here led to some interesting results and certainly support the idea that some aspects of discourse relations can be inferred from combinations of lower-level linguistic features. The complexity of this approach does make it difficult to draw simple conclusions about the relationship between discourse relations and non-canonical syntactic forms. However, the strength of some of the correlations found here are an indication that further investigation is merited.

The key factor in improving upon the approach and results of the current project is an increased amount of data. The significance of any particular feature is greatly affected by the quantity of data. Particularly for the lexical features used, this was a severe limitation on the inclusion of several of the less frequent connectives with better understood discourse structuring properties, like *well* and *now*. Although the distribution of the referential features was less sparse, here too additional data points would certainly have helped.

The ultimate cause of data scarcity here was the size of the original corpus of token utterances. A fairly unusual coincidence of properties was needed to give rise to a corpus with large numbers of the non-canonical utterances of interest here. Unfortunately, there are currently no corpora like this one to which automatic parsers can be applied with reasonably error free results such that the resulting parsed corpus could be automatically searched for the forms of interest. Instead, the 800 non-canonical tokens had to be collected by hand. The features used here were also all annotated by hand. Although the lexical features could be extracted automatically, automatic coding of the referential features is still nearly impossible at this point. Ideally, however, if there were a larger corpus coded for referential features and with a rich variety of syntactic forms, we could more fairly evaluate the feature set used here.

Somewhat unfortunately, it would also be desirable to broaden this feature set, augmenting it with more lexical features, other properties related to the changes in reference surrounding the target utterance, and prosodic information. As was discussed with respect to the logistic regression model above, the number of features which can be included in any model is limited by the quantity of data used, and so there is essentially no limit to the amount of data that might be useful in such a project.

With respect to the classifiers trained and tested here, clearly they too would benefit from both more features and more data. More data would allow the use of a validation set as a way to determine how many features could be usefully included. It would also allow a fairer evaluation on a more reasonably-sized test set. More data would also allow for the use of more features. As stated above, two of the three types of communicative goals that play a role in speaker's choice of form, disambiguation of focus structure and manipulation of attentional structure, were not addressed in the present model at all. To actually be able to use a statistical generation algorithm for clausal word order selection successfully, both of these would need to be included. Given the current size of the data set, however, the addition of more features would not have allowed the creation of reasonable models because it would be too difficult to get reliable estimates of the feature weights.

Because in reality there is not an unlimited supply of data annotated with the necessary information at this point, decisions must be made about what features to include or not include in future investigations of non-canonical word order selection. The best guide to these decisions is what practical use is to be made of the classifiers later. If they are to be used in an actual generation system, then it would be best to include features which are part of the conceptual representations already used in the input to the generation algorithm. In this way, the selection of a main clause word order could be improved without making any additional demands on the conceptual representations needed.

CHAPTER 5

Conclusions and future directions

The purpose of this project was to provide a solution to the problem set out in the introduction, namely how can we better model when speakers choose to use non-canonical syntactic forms. Previous literature provided only necessary conditions which must be fulfilled if the use of the non-canonicals are to be felicitous. This simple model of condition-form pairing, where there is a one-to-one mapping from conditions to form, is unable to account for a variety of problematic cases: (1) cases where the discourse conditions are present but the form is absent, (2) cases where the discourse conditions are present, but the form is still infelicitous, and (3) cases where the discourse conditions hold, and the non-canonical is not merely acceptable, but in fact crucial to the meaning and coherence of the discourse in that particular context. In addition, this simple model is of little use in an NLG system because of its inherent capacity for overgeneration, such that the non-canonical form is generated whenever the necessary conditions hold.

In order to remedy these problems a more complete model was presented of when human speakers choose to generate different syntactic encodings of propositions. Rather than a simple function from a discourse condition to a form, choice of syntactic form depends on the speaker's intention to communicate information beyond just the truth-conditional content of a proposition. The model laid out here explicitly tied this choice of form to the additional communicative goals which could be achieved by using it.

In particular, the types of communicative goals that were claimed to play a role in motivating the use of the four non-canonical sentence types examined here are (1) attention marking, (2) discourse relation marking, and (3) disambiguation of information structural focus. Attention-marking goals are those where the speaker intends to communicate information about the attentional status of individuals (propositions, entities, and relations) in the discourse model. For each form, this attentional goal was closely tied to the necessary conditions of its use posited in the literature. The other two types of goals are derived inferentially from the attentional goals. With respect to discourse relations, the attentional-marking goals allow the speaker to communicate additional information about how the utterance relates syntactically and semantically to other discourse segments. For focus disambiguation, the fact that attentional-marking goals structure the propositions communicated in particular ways means they also allow speakers to communicate unambiguously the information structure of the proposition in a way that prosody alone cannot. Each of the three types of goals were described and supported with evidence from both naturally-occurring and constructed data.

In order to support this theory of the interaction of communicative goals and syntactic form, additional evidence beyond native speaker intuitions on the appropriateness of particular forms in particular contexts was required. Additionally, the theory as it stood could not be readily implemented in an NLG system. In order to solve both of these problems, it was desirable to create a statistical model of communicative goal-form pairings. Such an empirical model could confirm the theoretical model and serve as a probabilistic classifier that could take goals as its input and yield syntactic forms as its output.

As discussed in Chapter 4, however, annotating communicative goals is not a viable task. The approach taken here was designed to circumvent this difficulty but still allow a measure of the correlation between communicative goals related to discourse structure and particular non-canonical syntactic forms. In order to do this, a set of easily and objectively annotated features were selected which could give a low-level approximation of the discourse context surrounding each token used in the study. Then, a logistic regression statistical analysis of the correlations between these contextual features and the non-canonical sentence types was performed. This statistical model gave a detailed and complex picture of how each of the classes of non-canonicals correlated with referential and lexical features of their surrounding context.

This same model was then used as a classifier trained to choose, based on context, which form was the most appropriate in that context. Although the classifier performed poorly on unseen test data, it was intended primarily as an illustration of how to approach the problem of utilizing a very abstract mapping from communicative goals to syntactic form in a statistical NLG system. The classifier used here is a first attempt at creating an algorithm which given a context (i.e. a set of features and their values) can select the form that best fits that context, based on what it has learned from the corpus of training data about context-form correlations.

Overall, this project has made several contributions to the understanding of the selection by humans (or generation by non-human agents) of non-canonical syntactic forms. First, it has shed some new light on what is actually motivating speakers to use certain forms in certain contexts, supporting these new claims with evidence from a large corpus of naturally-occurring tokens. In addition, it has provided an innovative approach to analyzing discourse structure as a set of more easily annotated features in order to measure the correlations between discourse structure and syntactic form. This approach overcomes the need to annotate communicative goals and discourse structure directly. Finally, it has suggested a first step to incorporating meaning and discourse context into statistical, corpus-trained generation algorithms for syntactic realization.

Clearly, in all of these areas there is much room for improvement on the current project and additional completely new work to be done. If such work is to succeed in covering new ground, however, several practical and theoretical needs must be addressed. The first of these is the existence of a larger corpus of non-canonical tokens, preferably automatically selected and annotated for the features examined here and other features. As discussed at the end of the previous chapter, in order to have a clearer statistical picture of the correlation of discourse context and syntactic form, more data is crucial.

Beyond this practical need, a detailed theory of the contribution of individual lexical connectives to the inferring of particular discourse relations is also needed if one wanted to in fact use the information about the correlation between lexical discourse markers and syntactic forms in an NLG system. Additionally, a more general theory of how communicative goals, those related to discourse relations and others, are inferred from linguistic form, lexical, syntactic, and prosodic, is necessary to make theoretical and practical headway in the area of selection of syntactic form. In lieu of a general theory of how goals are inferred, it is quite difficult to be specific about the actual mechanisms which connect a speaker's use of a non-canonical word order (or any linguistic form) to a hearer's understanding of the speaker's goal in using that word order (or other form). Although the communicative goals associated with specific linguistic forms can be investigated and modeled without such a theory, its existence would certainly enrich and improve these endeavors.

Bibliography

Abney, A. 1996. Statistical methods and linguistics. In *The balancing act: combining symbolic and statistical approaches to language*, ed. J. Klavans and P. Resnik. Cambridge MA: MIT Press.

Allen, J., L. Schubert, G. Ferguson, P. Heeman, C. Hwang, T. Kato, M. Light, N. Martin, B. Miller, M. Poesio, and D. Traum. 1995. The TRAINS project: a case study in building a conversational planning agent. *Journal of Experimental and Theoretical Artificial Intelligence* 7:7–48.

Anderson, A., M. Bader, E. Bard, E. Boyle, G. Doherty, S. Garrod, S. Isard, J. Kowtko, J. McAllister, J. Miller, C. Sotillo, H. Thompson, and R. Weinert. 1991. The HCRC Map Task Corpus. *Language and Speech* 34:315–366.

Ball, C. 1994. The origins of the informative-presupposition it-cleft. *Journal of Pragmatics* 22:603–628.

Bangalore, S., and O. Rambow. 2000. Exploiting a probabilistic hierarchical model for generation. In *Proceedings of the 18th Conference on Computational Linguistics (COLING 2000), July 31 - August 4 2000*. Universität des Saarlandes, Saarbrücken, Germany.

Bangalore, S., O. Rambow, and S. Whittaker. 2000. Evaluation metrics for generation. In *Proceedings of the 1st International Conference on Natural Language Generation*. Mitzpe Ramon, Israel.

Bayley, R., and R. Young. 2002. VARBRUL: a special case of logistic regression. Manuscript.

Biber, D. 1986a. On the investigation of spoken/written differences. *Studia Linguistica* 40(1):1–21.

———. 1986b. Spoken and written textual dimensions in English: resolving the contradictory findings. *Language* 62(2):384–414.

———. 1989. A typology of English texts. *Linguistics* 27:3–43.

Biber, D., S. Johansson, G. Leech, S. Conrad, and E. Finegan. 1999. *Longman grammar of spoken and written English.* London: Longman.

Birner, B. 1992. The discourse function of inversion in English. Ph.D. thesis, Northwestern University.

———. 1994. Information status and word order: an analysis of English inversion. *Language* 70(2):233–259.

———. 1996. *The discourse function of inversion in English.* Outstanding dissertations in linguistics, New York: Garland.

Birner, B., and G. Ward. 1998. *Information status and noncanonical word order in English.* Amsterdam/Philadelphia: John Benjamins.

Brennan, S.E., M.W. Friedman, and C.J. Pollard. 1987. A centering approach to pronouns. In *Proceedings of the 25th Meeting of the Association for Computational Linguistics,* 155–162. Stanford, CA.

Cedergren, H.J., and D. Sankoff. 1974. Variable rules: performance as a statistical reflection of competence. *Language* 50:333–335.

Chomsky, N. 1972. Deep structure, surface structure, and semantic interpretation. In *Studies on semantics in generative grammar,* ed. N. Chomsky. The Hague: Mouton.

Creswell, C., K. Forbes, E. Miltsakaki, R. Prasad, A. Joshi, and B. Webber. 2002. The discourse anaphoric properties of connectives. In *Proceedings of the 4th Discourse Anaphora and Anaphor Resolution Colloquium (DAARC 2002),* 45–50. Lisbon, Portugal: Edicoes Colibri.

Delin, J. 1992. Properties of it-cleft presupposition. *Journal of Semantics* 9(4):289–306.

———. 1995. Presupposition and shared knowledge in it-clefts. *Language and Cognitive Processes* 10(2):97–120.

Delin, J., and J. Oberlander. 1995. Syntactic constraints on discourse structure. *Linguistics* 33:465–500.

Dryer, M. 1996. Focus, pragmatic presupposition and activated propositions. *Journal of Pragmatics* 26:475–523.

di Eugenio, B., P. Jordan, and L. Pylkkänen. 1998. The COCONUT project: dialogue annotation manual. Tech. Rep. 98-1, Intelligent Systems Program, University of Pittsburgh.

Forbes, K. 2003. Discourse semantics of S-modifying adverbials. Ph.D. thesis, University of Pennsylvania.

Geldof, S. 2000. From context to sentence form. In *Proceedings of the 1st International Natural Language Generation Conference*. Mitzpe Ramon, Israel.

Green, G. 1980. Some wherefores of English inversions. *Language* 56:582–601.

Gregory, M., and L. Michaelis. 2001. Topicalization and left-dislocation: a functional opposition revisited. *Journal of Pragmatics* 33:1665–1706.

Grice, H. P. 1975. Logic and conversation. In *Speech Acts*, ed. P. Cole and J. L. Morgan, vol. 3 of *Syntax and Semantics*. New York: Academic Press.

Grosz, B. J., A. K. Joshi, and S. Weinstein. 1995. Centering: a framework for modeling the local coherence of discourse. *Computational Linguistics* 21(2):203–25.

Grosz, B. J., and C. L. Sidner. 1986. Attention, intentions, and the structure of discourse. *Computational Linguistics* 12(3):175–204.

Gundel, J. 1974. The role of topic and comment in linguistic theory. Ph.D. thesis, University of Texas at Austin.

———. 1999. On different kinds of focus. In *Focus*, ed. P. Bosch and R. van der Sandt. Cambridge University Press.

Gundel, J., N. Hedberg, and R. Zacharski. 1993. Cognitive status and the form of referring expressions. *Language* 69:274–307.

Gussenhoven, C. 1984. *On the grammar and semantics of sentence accents*. Dordrecht: Foris.

Guy, G. 1988. Advanced varbrul analysis. In *Linguistic change and contact (Proceedings of NWAVE 16)*, ed. K. Ferrara, B. Brown, K. Walters, and J. Baugh, 124–136. University of Texas, Department of Linguistics.

Hahn, U., K. Markert, and M. Strube. 1996. A conceptual reasoning approach to textual ellipsis. In *Proceedings of the 12th European Conference on Artificial Intelligence*, 572–576.

Hajičová, E., and P. Sgall. 2001. Topic-focus and salience. In *Proceedings of the 39th Annual Meeting of the Association for Computational Linguistics*, 268–273.

Halliday, M. A. K. 1985. *An introduction to functional grammar.* Baltimore: Edward Arnold Press.

Hedberg, N. 1990. The discourse function of cleft sentences in English. Ph.D. thesis, University of Minnesota.

Heim, I. 1983. File change semantics and the theory of definiteness. In *Meaning, use, and the interpretation of language,* ed. R. Bauerle, C. Schwarze, and A. von Stechow. Berlin: Walter de Gruyter.

Heycock, C., and A. Kroch. 1999. Pseudocleft connectedness: implications for the LF interface level. *Linguistic Inquiry* 30(3):365–397.

Hirschberg, J. 1985. A theory of scalar implicature. Ph.D. thesis, University of Pennsylvania.

Hirschberg, J., and D. J. Litman. 1994. Empirical studies on the disambiguation of cue phrases. *Computational Linguistics* 19(3):501–530.

Hirschberg, J., and G. Ward. 1995. The interpretation of the high-rise question contour in English. *Journal of Pragmatics* 24:407–412.

Hobbs, J., M. Stickel, D. Appelt, and P. Martin. 1990. Interpretation as abduction. Tech. Rep. Technical Report 499, AI Center, SRI International, Menlo Park, California.

Hobbs, J. R. 1990. *Literature and cognition.* CSLI lecture notes 21, Stanford, CA: CSLI.

Hockey, B. A. 1998. The interpretation and realization of focus: an experimental investigation of focus in English and Hungarian. Ph.D. thesis, University of Pennsylvania.

Horn, L. 1986. Presupposition, theme and variations. In *Papers from the 22nd Regional Meeting of the Chicago Linguistics Society,* vol. 22.

Hovy, E. H. 1988. Planning coherent multisentential text. In *Proceedings of the 26th ACL conference,* 163–169. Buffalo, NY.

———. 1990. Approaches to the planning of coherent text. In *Natural language in artificial intelligence and computational linguistics,* ed. C. Paris, W. Swartout, and W. Mann, 83–102. Boston: Kluwer.

———. 1993. Automated discourse generation using discourse structure relations. *Artificial Intelligence* 63(1-2):341–385.

Humphreys, K. 1995. Formalising pragmatic information for natural language generation. Ph.D. thesis, University of Edinburgh.

Jackendoff, R. 1972. *Semantic interpretation in generative grammar.* Cambridge, MA: MIT Press.

Jordan, P. 2000. Intentional influences on object redescriptions in dialogue: evidence from an empirical study. Ph.D. thesis, University of Pittsburgh.

Joshi, A. 1987. Word-order variation in natural language generation. In *Proceedings of AAAI-87*, 550–555.

Joshi, A., L. Levy, and M. Takahashi. 1975. Tree adjunct grammars. *Journal of the Computer and System Sciences* 10:136–163.

Joshi, A., and S. Weinstein. 1981. Control of inference: role of some aspects of discourse structure-centering. In *Proceedings of International Joint Conference on Artificial Intelligence*, 385–387. Vancouver.

Jurafsky, D., E. Shriberg, and D. Biasca. 1997. Switchboard SWBD-DAMSL shallow-discourse-function annotation coders manual. Tech. Rep. 97-02, Institute of Cognitive Science, University of Colorado, Boulder. Draft 13.

Kallmeyer, L., and A. Joshi. 1999. Factoring predicate argument and scope semantics: underspecified semantics with LTAG. In *Proceedings of the Twelfth Amsterdam Colloquium*, ed. Paul Dekker, 169–174. Amsterdam: ILLC/Department of Philosophy, University of Amsterdam.

Kallmeyer, L., A. Joshi, and M. Romero. 2003. Flexible composition in LTAG: quantifier scope and inverse linking. In *Proceedings of the Fifth International Workshop on Computational Semantics IWCS-5*, 179–194. Tilburg.

Kameyama, M. 1996. Indefeasible semantics and defeasible pragmatics. In *Quantifiers, deduction, and context*, ed. M. Kanazawa, C. Pinon, and H. de Swart, 111–138. CSLI Publishers.

Kartunnen, L. 1977. Syntax and semantics of questions. *Linguistics and Philosophy* 1: 3–44.

Kehler, A. 1997. Current theories of centering for pronoun interpretation: a critical evaluation. *Computational Linguistics* 23(3):467–475.

———. 2002. *Coherence, reference, and the theory of grammar*. CSLI Publishers.

Kibble, R., and R. Power. 1999. Using centering theory to plan coherent texts. In *Proceedings of the Twelfth Amsterdam Colloquium*, ed. Paul Dekker, 187–192. Amsterdam: ILLC/Department of Philosophy, University of Amsterdam.

Kingsbury, P., and M. Palmer. 2002. From Treebank to Propbank. In *Third International Conference on Language Resources and Evaluation (LREC-02)*. Las Palmas, Canary Islands, Spain.

Klabunde, R., and M. Jansche. 1998. Abductive reasoning for syntactic realization. In *Proceedings of 9th International Workshop on Natural Language Generation*, ed. E. Hovy, 108–117. Niagara-on-the-Lake, Ontario, Canada.

Kozima, H. 1993. Text segmentation based on similarity between words. In *Meeting of the Association for Computational Linguistics*, 286–288.

Kroch, A., and D. Hindle. 1982. A quantitative study of the syntax of speech and writing. Tech. Rep., University of Pennsylvania. Final report to the National Institute of Education.

Kruijff-Korbayová, I., G. J. Kruijff, and J. Bateman. 2002. Generation of contextually appropriate word order. In *Information sharing*, vol. K. van Deemter and R. Kibble, 193–222. CSLI Publishers.

van Kuppevelt, J. 1995. Discourse structure, topicality, and questioning. *Journal of Linguistics* 31:109–147.

Labov, W. 1969. Contraction, deletion, and inherent variablity of the English copula. *Language* 45.

———. 1997. Some further steps in narrative analysis. *Journal of Narrative and Life History* .

Labov, W., and J. Waletzky. 1967. Narrative analysis. In *Essays on the verbal and visual arts*, ed. J. Helm, 12–44. Seattle: University of Washington Press.

Ladd, D. R. 1996. *Intonational phonology*. Cambridge: Cambridge University Press.

Lambrecht, K. 1996. *Information structure and sentence form*. Cambridge Studies in Linguistics 71, Cambridge: Cambridge University Press.

Langkilde, I., and K. Knight. 1998a. Generation that exploits corpus-based statistical knowledge. In *COLING-ACL*, 704–710.

———. 1998b. The practical value of n-grams in derivation. In *Proceedings of the Ninth International Workshop on Natural Language Generation*, ed. Eduard Hovy, 248–255. New Brunswick, New Jersey: Association for Computational Linguistics.

Levin, N., and E. Prince. 1986. Gapping and clausal implicature. *Papers in Linguistics* 19(3):351–364.

Lewis, D. 1979. Scorekeeping in a language game. *Journal of Philosophical Language* 8: 339–359.

Liberman, M., and A. Prince. 1977. On stress and linguistic rhythm. *Linguistic Inquiry* 8: 249–336.

Manetta, E. 2001. Unexpected left dislocation. Pragmatics 591 Colloquium, Department of Linguistics, University of Pennsylvania.

Mann, W. C., and S. A. Thompson. 1987. Rhetorical Structure Theory: description and construction of text structures. In *Natural language generation: new results in artificial intelligence, psychology, and linguistics*, ed. G. Kempen. Dordrecht: Martinus Nijhoff Publishers.

————. 1988. Rhetorical Structure Theory: towards a functional theory of text organization. *Text* 8(3):243–281.

Manning, C., and H. Schütze. 1999. *Foundations of statistical natural language processing*. Cambridge MA: MIT Press.

Manning, C. D. 2003. Probabilistic syntax. In *Probabilistic linguistics*, ed. R. Bod, J. Hay, and S. Jannedy. Cambridge, MA: MIT Press.

Marcu, D. 1997. Rhetorical parsing, summarization, and generation of natural language texts. Ph.D. thesis, University of Toronto.

Marcu, D., E. Amorrortu, and M. Romera. 1999. Experiments in constructing a corpus of discourse trees. In *Towards standards and tools for discourse tagging: proceedings of the workshop*, ed. Marilyn Walker, 48–57. Somerset, New Jersey: Association for Computational Linguistics.

McKeown, K. R. 1985. *Text generation*. Cambridge University Press.

McNally, L. 1998. On the linguistic encoding of information packaging instructions. In *The limits of syntax*, ed. P. Culicover and L. McNally, vol. 29 of *Syntax and Semantics*. New York: Academic Press.

Miltsakaki, E. 2002. Towards an aposynthesis of topic continuity and intrasentential anaphora. *Computational Linguistics* 28(3).

Mitchell, T. M. 1997. *Machine learning*. New York: McGraw-Hill.

Moore, J., and M. Pollack. 1992. A problem for RST: the need for multi-level discourse analysis. *Computational Linguistics* 18(4):537–544.

Morgan, J. L. 1978. Two types of convention in indirect speech acts. In *Pragmatics*, ed. P. Cole, vol. 9 of *Syntax and Semantics*. New York: Academic Press.

Nunberg, G. 1978. The pragmatics of reference. Ph.D. thesis, City University of New York.

Oberlander, J., and J. Delin. 1996. The function and interpretation of reverse wh-clefts in spoken discourse. *Language and Speech* 39:183–225.

Paolillo, J. 2002. *Analyzing linguistic variation.* Stanford, CA: CSLI Publications.

Passonneau, R. 1994. Protocol for coding discourse referential noun phrases. Tech. Rep., Columbia University.

———. 1996. Using centering to relax Gricean informational constraints on discourse anaphoric noun phrases. *Language and speech* 39(2–3):229–264.

Passonneau, R., and D. Litman. 1997. Discourse segmentation by human and automated means. *Computational Linguistics* 23(1):103–139.

Pierrehumbert, J., and J. Hirschberg. 1990. The meaning of intonational contours in discourse. In *Intentions in communication*, ed. P. R. Cohen, J. Morgan, and M. E. Pollack. Cambridge MA: MIT Press.

Prevost, S. 1995. A semantics of contrast and information structure for specifying intonation in spoken language generation. Ph.D. thesis, University of Pennsylvania.

Prince, E. F. 1978. A comparison of wh-clefts and it-clefts in discourse. *Language* 54(4): 883–906.

———. 1981. Towards a taxonomy of given/new information. In *Radical pragmatics*, ed. P. Cole, 223–256. New York: Academic Press.

———. 1986. On the syntactic marking of presupposed open propositions. In *Papers from the Parasession on Pragmatics and Grammatical Theory*, ed. A. Farley, P. Farley, and K. E. McCullough, vol. 22nd Regional Meeting. Chicago Linguistic Society.

———. 1992. The ZPG letter: subjects, definiteness, and information-status. In *Discourse description: diverse analyses of a fund raising text*, ed. S. Thompson and W. Mann. Philadelphia/Amsterdam: John Benjamins.

———. 1996. Constructions and the syntax-discourse interface. Manuscript.

———. 1997. On the functions of left-dislocation in English discourse. In *Directions in functional linguistics*, ed. A. Kamio, 117–144. Philadelphia/Amsterdam: John Benjamins.

———. 1998. On the limits of syntax, with reference to topicalization and left-dislocation. In *The limits of syntax*, ed. P. Culicover, , and L. McNally, vol. 29 of *Syntax and Semantics*. New York: Academic Press.

———. 1999. How not to mark topics: 'topicalization' in English and Yiddish. Manuscript.

Ratnaparkhi, A. 2000. Trainable methods for surface natural language generation. In *Proceedings of the 6th Applied Natural Language Processing Conference and the 1st Meeting of the North American Chapter of the Association of Computational Linguistics*, 194–201. Seattle, WA.

Reinhart, T. 1981. Pragmatics and linguistics: an analysis of sentence topics. *Philosophica* 27:53–94.

Reynar, J.C., and A. Ratnaparkhi. 1997. A maximum entropy approach to identifying sentence boundaries. In *Proceedings of the Fifth Conference on Applied Natural Language Processing*, 16–19. Washington DC.

Rich, C., and C. Sidner. 1997. COLLAGEN: when agents collaborate with people. In *Proceedings of the First International Conference on Autonomous Agents (Agents'97)*, ed. W. Lewis Johnson and Barbara Hayes-Roth, 284–291. New York: ACM Press.

Roberts, C. 1998. Focus, information flow, and universal grammar. In *The limits of syntax*, ed. P. Culicover and L. McNally, vol. 29. New York: Academic Press.

Rochemont, M. S. 1986. *Focus in generative grammar*. Amsterdam: John Benjamins.

Rooth, M. 1985. Association with focus. Ph.D. thesis, University of Massachusetts, Amherst.

———. 1992. A theory of focus interpretation. *Natural Language Semantics* 1.

Rubinstein, Y., and T. Hastie. 1997. Discriminative versus informative learning. In *Proceedings of the Third International Conference on Knowledge Discovery and Data Mining*, 49–53.

Sadock, J. 1978. On testing for conversational implicature. In *Pragmatics*, ed. P. Cole, vol. 9 of *Syntax and Semantics*, 281–298. New York: Academic Press.

Sankoff, D. 1988. Variable rules. In *Sociolinguistics. An international handbook of the science of language and society*, ed. U. Ammon, N. Dittmar, and K.J. Mattheier, 984–997. Berlin: Walter de Gruyter.

Sankoff, D., and W. Labov. 1979. On the uses of variable rules. *Language in Society* 8(3): 189–222.

Schabes, Y. 1990. Mathematical and computational aspects of lexicalized grammars. Ph.D. thesis, University of Pennsylvania.

Scharzschild, R. 1998. GIVENness, AvoidF and other constraints on the placement of accent. *Natural Language Semantics* 7:141–177.

Selkirk, E. 1995. Sentence prosody: intonation, stress and phrasing. In *The handbook of phonological theory*, ed. J. Goldsmith. Oxford: Blackwell.

Sgall, P., E. Hajičová, and J. Panevová. 1986. *The meaning of the sentence in its semantic and pragmatic aspects*. Dordrecht, The Netherlands: Reidel.

Snyder, K. 2000. Reconfiguring syntax, or some good reasons why we shouldn't. In *Conference on the Interaction Between Syntax and Pragmatics*. University College London.

——. 2003. On ditransitives. Ph.D. thesis, University of Pennsylvania.

Sperber, D., and D. Wilson. 1986. *Relevance, communication and cognition*. Oxford: Blackwell.

Steedman, M. 1991. Structure and intonation. *Language* (67):260–296.

——. 2000. Information structure and the syntax-phonology interface. *Linguistic Inquiry* 31(4).

Stone, M., and C. Doran. 1997. Sentence planning as description using tree adjoining grammar. In *Proceedings of the 35th Annual Meeting of the Association for Computational Linguistics*, ed. P. R. Cohen and W. Wahlster, 198–205. Somerset, New Jersey: Association for Computational Linguistics.

Stone, M., C. Doran, B. Webber, T. Bleam, and M. Palmer. 2001. Communicative-intent-based microplanning: the Sentence Planning Using Description system. Rutgers University.

Sturtevant, S. 1999. Centering constraints on English null subjects in narrative. Master's thesis, University of Pennsylvania.

Theune, M. 2000. From data to speech: language generation in context. Ph.D. thesis, IPO, Center for User-System Interaction, Eindhoven.

Vallduví, E. 1990a. The informational component. Ph.D. thesis, University of Pennsylvania.

——. 1990b. The role of plasticity in the association of focus and prominence. In *Eastern States Conference on Linguistics '90*, 295–306.

Vallduví, E., and M. Vilkuna. 1998. On rheme and kontrast. In *The limits of syntax*, ed. P. Culicover and L. McNally, vol. 29 of *Syntax and Semantics*. New York: Academic Press.

Walker, M. 1993. Informational redundancy and resource bounds in dialogue. Ph.D. thesis, University of Pennsylvania.

——. 1996. Limited attention and discourse structure. *Computational Linguistics* 22(2): 255–264.

Walker, M., A. K. Joshi, and E. F. Prince, eds. 1998. *Centering theory in discourse*. Oxford: Oxford University Press.

Walker, M., and E.F. Prince. 1996. A bilateral approach to givenness: a hearer-status algorithm and a centering algorithm. In *Reference and referent accessibility*, ed. J. Gundel and R. Fretheim, 291–306. Philadelphia/Amsterdam: John Benjamins.

Ward, G. 1985. The semantics and pragmatics of preposing. Ph.D. thesis, University of Pennsylvania.

———. 1988. *The semantics and pragmatics of preposing*. Outstanding dissertations in linguistics, New York: Garland.

———. 1998. A comparison of postposed subjects in English and Italian. In *Functions and structure*, ed. A. Kamio and K. Takami, 3–21. Philadelphia/Amsterdam: John Benjamins.

Ward, G., and B. Birner. 1995. Definiteness and the English existential. *Language* 71: 722–742.

Ward, G., and J. Hirschberg. 1985. Implicating uncertainty: the pragmatics of fall-rise intonation. *Language* 61:747–776.

Ward, G., and E. Prince. 1991. On the topicalization of indefinite NPs. *Journal of Pragmatics* 16.

Webber, B. 1988. Tense as discourse anaphor. *Computational Linguistics* 14.2:61–73.

———. 1991. Structure and ostension in the interpretation of discourse deixis. *Language and Cognitive Processes* 6(2):107–135.

Webber, B., and A. Joshi. 1998. Anchoring a lexicalized tree-adjoining grammar for discourse. In *Discourse relations and discourse markers: proceedings of the conference*, ed. M. Stede, L. Wanner, and E. Hovy, 86–92. Somerset, New Jersey: Association for Computational Linguistics.

Webber, B., A. Knott, M. Stone, and A. Joshi. 1999. Discourse relations: a structural and presuppositional account using lexicalised TAG. In *37th Annual Meeting of the Association for Computational Linguistics*, 41–48. College Park, MD.

Webber, B., M. Stone, A. Joshi, and A. Knott. 2003. Anaphora and discourse semantics. *Computational Linguistics* .

Whitton, L. 2004. The relationship between the pragmatics of preposed objects and the decline in topicalization in the history of English. *Penn Working Papers in Linguistics* 10(1).

Index